I had one thought, to push on, to start the long haul on foot from Attica to Mount Olympos on the fringe of Macedonia – I had been thinking about it for years

LEFT Katie's Sanctuary: half a mile beyond the city limit of Thebes I found that I had carried off the huge brass key to our hotel bedroom and, worse, I'd forgotten to pick up our passports. Leaving Katie with a book by this mosque-like church, I strode back ...

RIGHT Graffitology: beneath the more recent political slogans, in letters cut so incisively that the rock retained a ghost of the original paint, we read: *Those not Royalist are Communist, Down with Bevin* and, in English, *Welkom to our Callant Allies*, a touching salutation

RIGHT Wayside shrine

BELOW Broken homes: how
they managed to survive in
their shacks through the blast
of winter is something we
could scarcely imagine

LEFT Family Kyllini: we were
overwhelmed by irrepressible
hospitality

RIGHT Megdova bridge: approached through avenues of acacias, planes and pink-flowered Cercis and spanning the Tavropos

BELOW Ideal camp-site: with a carrier bag of cold meat, bread, tomatoes and wine bought in Kastania, we strolled round the ins and outs of the lake's shore looking for the perfect spot …

RIGHT Nimble tortoise: here in their native environment, these heat-loving animals scuttled away on the tips of their claws at our approach

Classical landscape: late in the afternoon we reached one of the innumerable tributaries of the Pinios, and fell upon what could have been a line-and-wash sketch for a picture of Arcadia by Edward Lear or Claude

LEFT Olympian glimpse: almost immediately above us we could make out a line of battlements partly obscured by the Gatherer of Clouds. We were within sight of our destination

RIGHT Prionia: a small hamlet where the Black pines looked fit for Christmas cards. Except for those in the restaurant, everyone seemed to be getting out in a hurry ...

On Mount Olympos: the Black pines and Greek firs had been twisted and gnarled into weird shapes by the winds and snow of many winters

wind or lithe warships with rams lustily rowed by one, two, or occasionally three banks of oarsmen, according to whether they were biremes of triremes. Some were oared by up to 170 men, to the rhythm of two huge goatskin drums. Unless the ships were known or carried their home country's device, coastguards had to decide whether they were deep-laden with gold for the treasuries at Delphi. Or with armed men.

Pausanias says: 'It seems that from the beginning there had been innumerable plans to invade and sack Delphi. There was this Euboean bandit and the Phlegya people some years later. Then Pyrrhus, son of Achilles attempted it; then a detachment from the forces of Xerxes, then the rulers of Phokis who made the longest and strongest attack on the wealth of the god, and then the Gaulish army.'*

Throughout Greece 'Phokian desperation' connoted ruthless fighting down to the last man on his feet. They were artful fighters, too. Expecting a Thessalian raid into their country they buried water jars up to their necks and covered them over with a thin layer of soil. Not knowing this, the enemy galloped over the jars; horses broke their legs and riders were thrown and promptly slaughtered. Retribution followed, but after another foray when camp faced camp at a pass into Phokis, 500 picked Phokians watched for the full moon and attacked the Thessalians at night, covered in white-washed armour. If what Pausanias was told is true, they carried out a terrible massacre against adversaries who thought 'what was happening had something more of the gods about it than a night attack'.

From the bone-white bed of the Pleistos we clambered up steps that led us, conveniently, to the last tavern and the last hotel on the down-slope from the village of Delphi

---

* Peter Levi's translation of *Pausanias' Guide to Greece*, Penguin Classics, 1971.

to that riot of columns and treasuries around the inner Sanctuary.

We rested on the rails and looked across at that deep gorge bounded on the one side by the cliffs of the Phaedriades, an outlier of Mount Parnassus and on the other by Mount Kirphis, and reckoned that few if any notable sites of antiquity could be more easily defended; indeed that gorge between a clamp of defiles had been used in the sixth century as a novel means of attack, that of chemical warfare when the uppity inhabitants of Kirra on the Gulf were physically purged by the torrent.

They became covetous over the wealth bound for Delphi, unshipped within sight of their sea-facing balconies. To the extreme dissatisfaction of the League of Neighbours, the Amphictionies, it was alleged that they had committed sacrilege against the Delphic deity, Apollo, and had stolen land from the god. War was declared against them. Commanders were appointed who in 580 BC or thereabouts brought in Solon, the celebrated Athenian legislator, as Strategic Consultant.

The top brass consulted the Oracle who, as it usually did, gave them enigmatic but, on this occasion, rather subtle advice: they wouldn't win, they were told, until the sea broke over Apollo's enclosure. So they consecrated Kirra to the god and diverted the waters of the Pleistos which ran through their city into a large reservoir. But the Kirrans still held out against the siege, drinking from shallow wells and what water the god rained on them. Whereupon Solon ordered that cart-loads of roots of hellebore, a powerful vermifuge for domestic animals, should be thrown into the reservoir, and when the water was heavily toxified he turned it back into its channel. The delighted Kirrans glutted themselves on what they had incautiously prayed for, 'and the men on the walls had to abandon their positions through never-ending diarrhoea'.

Over and above some badly needed rest we had much to do in Delphi. There were clothes to be laundered, repaired or replaced; to lighten our loads everything that could be dispensed with was left with friends; we needed local information about a cross-country track to the township of Amphissa, the last place of any size before we tackled the formidable Pindos; and, most important of all, Kàtie had blisters which urgently needed attention.

The first chemist we came to sold us four grams of Terramycin with a polymyxin additive for the equivalent of about a pound sterling: in Greece powerful antibiotics can be bought over the counter like wine and cheese. The pros and cons of a possible path caused a deal of argument in an underground retreat near the bus station much resorted to by a self-appointed council of knowledgeable locals. Two taxi-drivers, a wholesaler of wine and a fish merchant couldn't understand, predictably, why we didn't take to the road which we knew snaked down to Krissa before losing its identity in the busy highway north-west to Lamia. We smiled bleakly. A man we knew, Carlo the Cop, said he thought, wrongly as it turned out, that we could reach Amphissa by following some eight or nine miles of the local irrigation canal. We said we'd try it, and they drank to our success.

It is twenty years since I first began to visit Delphi at fairly regular intervals. It follows that I'm familiar with the labyrinth of small squares, back lanes and narrow streets, one above the other, joined by flights of steep steps. We sat over a supper table in the gathering dark, looked at our maps and wondered whether we could rely on Carlo's advice. Who knew where the canal led to? No Greek would admit to ignorance about his immediate neighbourhood.

Apart from the murmur of voices, the sound of laughter and the scream of swifts the town grew strangely quiet for a popular tourist resort. As for the swifts, those most aerial of birds which actually copulate in mid-air, they whirled over our heads as they swooped to and from their nests under the roofs of the buildings around us. Nobody, I suggest, has bettered Gilbert White in his description of what they are up to. In one memorable passage he says: 'They get together in the evening and dash round the steeples and churches, squeaking as they go in a very clamorous manner; these by nice observers are supposed to be the males, serenading their sitting hens; and not without reason since they seldom squeak till they come close to the walls or eaves and then those within utter at the same time a little inward note of complacency.'

We took to our bed, early, and were up and about again before the two main streets which converge on the short slope down to the Sanctuary were jam-packed with what my Great-aunt Clarissa called in her most disapproving voice 'those sharybangs', those mobile easy-chairs for tourists the length and breadth of Europe. As we'd been in each other's company since the walk began, we were content to go our own ways until nightfall.

By climbing up by way of the wine merchant's own vineyard ('Tears of Eurydice') I outflanked the convergence and reached the stadium on the hillside some two hundred metres above the busyness of the Sanctuary. There amidst a protective screen of conifers the only sound you are likely to hear is the pleasant thrush-like song of Orphean warblers in sombre capes and jet-black masks through which can be seen, with the help of binoculars, their staring white eyes. Altogether a handsome bird with a commanding voice. In company with hoopoes they tend to haunt cemeteries and parkland.

The Sanctuary – what a splendid word! Man in the presence of what he feels obliged to venerate. Over a period of perhaps a quarter of a million years it has meant different things, even to some of the earliest relatives of the human race. Neanderthal man, that slightly bow-legged, chinless fellow with prominent brow-ridges and a receding forehead, had a brain in size and possibly weight as large as our own. Careful burials with funerary offerings and hand-prints on the walls of their tombs provide the earliest surviving evidence for religious beliefs.

Their successors, the Magdalenians, the art-inspired cave-painters of south-western France and elsewhere, were adept in the use of pigments and carvings on bone and ivory. Among the Greeks and early Europeans, certain springs and groves were set apart from the profane world. Complex rituals followed. In the Christian church, the Sanctuary is the most sacred part of the building.

At Delphi in classical times, I learnt from Peter Levi, musical festivals were partly replaced by athletic competitions, the Pythian Games. Pausanias claims that some otherwise unidentifiable man called Eleuther won a Pythian victory simply by his sweet loud voice, since the song he sang was not his own. He also mentions that Hesiod was disqualified for not knowing how to play the harp as he sang; and that Homer came to question the Oracle 'but even if he knew how to play the harp it would have been useless because of the tragedy of his eyes'. The League added flute-playing to the list of events, but took it out because it was an unlucky sound when Echembrotos, winner of a bronze tripod dedicated it to Herakles 'singer of music and the poetry of death'. Funeral songs were accompanied by flautists.

The Council of Judges debated the matter at some length and substituted horse-racing for the melancholic sound of reeds. Since this is being written on Derby Day there is a case to be made out for its continuous success through the centuries. Less can be said on ethical and aesthetic grounds for replacing the flute with all-in fighting with whatever weapons the combatants agreed to, also a race for men in armour which must have sounded rather like a folk-dance for Daleks.

Mentally blocking my ears against the siren call of yet another warbler, the Sardinian species (*Sylvia melanocephalus*) which dances in the air, singing like our British whitethroat, I mooched down through the huge theatre to where everybody seemed to be bored by what the guides were telling them. The crowds were thickest in the vicinity of the great temple of Apollo where, in the manner of the ancient processions, they obediently queued up as far back as the circular area, the *halos*, notable for a handsome Ionic capital and a curved seat, the *exedra* for the priests.

Only the podium and peristyle of the temple are complete although several columns have been replaced in their original position. The building runs along the mountainside, supported by a magnificent wall of polygonal masonry. Deep below in its foundations used to lie the sacred chasm where the priestess was said to have been turned on by drinking the waters of Cassotis, composition unknown, and inhaling stupor-inducing fumes from the Underworld.

To the Oracle all the various cities and states looked for guidance in war and matters of foreign policy, especially colonial expansion; not uncommonly, the lovelorn turned up with questions about affairs of the heart. Before the Pythia got down to the job of answering them, mostly in ambivalent *aenigmata*, the priests inspected the proffered booty and, if adequate, interpreted the priestesses' shrieks and wails which have been likened to those of women in sexual transports. Were they, to put it plainly, being screwed in the manner of temple *hetaerae*? Unlikely. They were usually far from young and Euripides in the *Ion* says that at one period at least, the prophetesses were guarded by continent priests to ward off the profane. As a writer with a smattering of geology I find it difficult to believe that what the Victorians called 'mephitic vapour' could have emerged from pink and brown rock largely composed of inert metamorphic limestones and dolomites. Drugs may have induced the Oracle's condition. Theophrastus wrote about opium in the third century BC and also Scythian pot.

A long succession of oracles did well out of the local industry from about 750 BC, the questionable date of the founding of both Rome and Athens, until Theodosius shut down the licensed prophecy shops in AD 381, that is shortly after the Legions were recalled from Britain and not long before Alaric and his lively lads struck south through the Balkans.

What at least we may be certain about is that the decline and fall of the prophetesses marked the transition of the Homeric world of inscrutable self-interest – aided by the intervention of the gods – to the beginnings of solid moral principles with the new learning, the so-called 'Greek miracle', somewhere in between. The vaults below the temple are now empty but had the Oracle been at home that morning and could I have asked her but one question – and were there unambiguous truth in her oracular heart – she might well have answered that the change was brought about by the swing from symbolic to conceptual thought.

Voluble guides were at work inside the Sanctuary and outside the turnstiles near the Agora remodelled by the Romans; they stood on the wall above the Castalian Spring where motorists are enjoined not to wash their cars in water used in ancient times for ritual purification. They talked in front of the blinding white and wholly inappropriate façade of the modern museum which, although it houses priceless treasure, much resembles a maternity hospital in Abu Dhabi.

I mingled, quietly, with outsiders in groups of Elks,

Shriners and Daughters of Freedom engaged in a three-week crash course on European culture from the luxurious confines of a coach complete with bar, toilets and showers. They were getting the classical run-down from Reb Meyer, a strident New Yorker. As one of his flock put it, they 'had picked him up in Thessaloniki just for the Greek stretch'. Reb certainly knew his stuff and put it across in the corrosive Yinglish of the Lower East Side. He had been talking about the gods and the Homeric heroes, Perseus, Theseus, Odysseus and Herakles. 'Jeez!' he said, 'some guy that Herakles was. Excuse the expression, a real *gontzer macher*. David would have been glad to have him around.

'But d'ya suppose that sophisticated spielers like old Homer really believed that Zeus – who was known as the Gatherer of Clouds – knocked off just about everybody, from Danaë who was fooled when he appeared in a shower of gold? That he sometimes disguised himself as a bull or a swan when he felt randy? Who was he fooling? I ask you? Next to nobody! They was listening to a top-of-the-bill entertainer putting it across that it's a wise man who knows who his own father is and God help those who go around knocking off members of their own families.' I began to warm to Reb.

'*Muthologica* means "talking about things, the retelling of old tales". An egg becomes harder the more you boil it: that's why we Jewish boys put *bielers*, hard-boiled eggs, among the other goodies on the table at Passover. They are symbols of immortality.

'Ya don't think those tales hurt anyone, do ya? Well apart from one disaster ya couldn't be more on the ball. After we've had a bite and maybe a beer or two we're gonna drive about ten minutes to Arachova. And not far from that village we'll take a quick look at a place known to every dollar-grabbing shrink as the Crossroads. And what happened there, you ask me? I'll tell ya. Homer says that once upon a time the real old city of Thebes was ruled by King Laius who for wife had a *shayner*, a beautiful girl called Jocasta. So pretty she was that this *shmuck* Laius asked the Oracle up there what he could do to protect her. It didn't really matter, he was told, because his number was up. He had been doomed to die anyhow and at the hands of his own son. And who was that? Surely you've heard of a guy called Oedipus?

'One night, not long after Oedipus was born, his dad stuck a knife through his feet. He bound them together and left the baby to the wolves and eagles on Mount Kithairon. *Oy veh!* Happily for him he was found by shepherds who took him to their king, a feller called Polybus of Corinth, who liked the look of the little chap and brought him up as his own son. He called him Oedipus which is Greek for Swollen Foot.

'Now we come to a bit of the story which is hard to swallow. Oedipus grew up to be a tough guy, good at games and apt to throw his weight around. Moody, too. Something bothered him. There were things that the folks at home wouldn't talk about. So what does this *shlemiel* do? He also goes and has a costly session with that Oracle. It didn't improve things when he was told it was his fate to kill his dad and have an incestuous affair with his momma.

'Thinking that Polybus was his dad he decided not to return to Corinth. Unhappy for him, on the way back from where you're standing right now he arrived at those Crossroads I was telling you about and met a chariot coming the other way. How was he to know it was driven by his *real* father, King Laius? There were arguments about who had the right of way. It ended in a scuffle. Oedipus flung his javelin at Laius and knocked him cold. That might have ended the matter if Freud hadn't come to the fool conclusion that many if not most of us want to continue sleeping with our mothers and end up by hating our father. That's what Oedipus-Schmoedipus is all about. D'ya wanna sleep with your mamma and keep up the row with your papa? Don't let the head-shrinkers think they've got even half the answers. Over the last seventy years more people have been taken for a ride by Freud and his hangers-on than by Standard Oil.'

Prologue to the Pindos

Because we hoped to see the emerging sun strike the eastern face of the Phaedriades, the cleft pillar of rock above the Castalian Spring, we set off early, far too early. Only the topmost turrets justified their name of the Shining Ones. In their shadows lay a jumble of monuments as untidy as a builder's yard: the Sphinx of the Naxians, the Stoa of the Athenians, the ruined treasuries of the Boeotians, the Thebans, Megarians and I forget what else. Yet that early hour carried its compensations: the light and the colours changed from minute to minute and, again right on cue, two immense birds of prey pitched off the topmost pinnacles and began to circle, slowly, in concert with a breeze which, heard from ground level, had about it the whispering rip of a scythe through grass.

There are two distinctly different opinions about the identity of those birds. There is first the classical one, which is that in a god-like gesture to determine the centre of the world known to his Olympian companions, Zeus – who considered the earth to be flat like a disc – released two eagles, one at the point of the sun's rising and the other at the point of the sun's setting. The birds met at Delphi over what became the *omphalos*, the huge stone navel of the earth. Below lay the sacred cave of Mother Earth's oracle, guarded by the monster, Python.

Even today the site is both overlaid and surrounded by enormous beauty which ignores rather than defies exploitation since pilgrims, nowadays called tourists, have been tramping up to the shrine of Apollo and his successors for about 3,000 years. To anybody with a shred of imagination – if not spirituality – godhead seems inherent in the landscape.

The previous day I had heard – not for the first time – the story of the eagles from Reb Meyer who gave it a touch of authenticity by adding, 'Folks around here will tell you the birds are the descendants of the original pair who pecked to pieces what was left of Aesop, author of the famous fables, who had been thrown off the cliff for poking fun at the local administration. They didn't realize he was just as much of a *meshuggener* as they was.'

Madame Anastasia, our guide for the IUCN trip to Delphi which followed the Athens Conference*, had told us the same story. Already irritated by the fact that her audience was clearly more interested in purple-flowered campanulas, wild tulips, the Giant orchid (*Barlia*) and half a dozen other smaller rarities among the blocks of marble, than the history of the lovely Doric *tholos*, she incautiously mentioned the eagles.

Jan Dorst, one of the best ornithologists in Europe, glanced up at the birds without even raising his field-glasses. 'Black vultures,' he murmured quietly. She heard him. 'Eagles!' she insisted, angrily. At this several professional biologists rallied to the support of their distinguished colleague. The delegate from the West German Republic muttered, '*Mönchsgeier*'; the director of the Paris Medical School called them *Vautours moine* whilst Harold J. Coolidge of the U.S. Academy of Sciences, a pedantic fellow, gave their scientific name, *Aegypius monarchus*.

* *See page 39.*

Outclassed by such a spread of expertise, our guide smiled wanly at the Mayor of Athens and his friend the Secretary-General for Tourism, and went on to speak rapidly, first in English, then in French, followed by German, about how between 1892 and 1904 the French parliament voted nearly a million francs to demolish the village on top of the site, rebuilt it further up the road and for years dug like moles into what became one of the greatest treasures of Greece.

Even from below Katie and I could see that the birds were unquestionably Black vultures: almost wholly sooty-coloured creatures with massive bills, stumpy necks, short tails and extremely broad and elongated wings, longer than any other vulture in Europe, over nine feet from tip to tip in some specimens.

With an occasional glance over our shoulders we watched them as we scrambled down into the gorge, searching for that elusive canal. They were circling, slowly, like an immense mobile. In the air they are impressive but at close quarters, as I had seen them on the carcases of sheep in the Pyrenees, they look morose if not downright ugly. They half-flap their wings, squeak, and stamp their feet in a grotesque dance to scare off rivals. In company with birds of prey throughout the whole world, their numbers are declining. The last we saw of Anastasia's eagles that morning was over Mount Kirphis up which is scribbled the zigzag of a mule track leading to places where you could well believe only the gods, the local shepherds and vultures feel at home.

It had taken us ten days of abundant sweat to get from Athens to Delphi via Thebes and Kirra on the Gulf of Corinth. That morning we paused on the rim of the gorge between the Phaedriades and Mount Kirphis not at all sure about how to reach the biggest olive market and capital of the region, the town of Amphissa, without bruising our feet on the first busy twelve-mile length of the mountain road to Lamia.

At Amphissa we hoped to be rid of roads for at least a week. All maps we'd consulted, all enquiries we had made indicated that Amphissa stood not too far above a network of tracks through two more impressive ranges, the Giona and Vardoussia, the prologue to the Pindos, the range that reared northwards to the Vlach highlands of Albania. We were following a route plotted by Lord Hunt in charge of a company of lively lads. Meanwhile, a minor setback: where in the name of all the marvellous, the multitudinous water gods of central Greece was that damned canal?

Water is the life-blood of the upland regions and the natives dispose of it as stingily as widows with meagre but regular pensions. To judge from the lie of the land on the steep slopes below Amphissa, the vast groves of olives are dependent on the up-welling of springs, and the water has to be shared out from communal aqueducts. On the face of it an admirable arrangement, but in that underground retreat near the bus station, Carlo the Cop had hinted darkly at a local Mafia run by the chieftains of two or three cooperatives who controlled wholesale prices and, if nothing worse, threatened to divert the water supplies of those incautious enough even to think of stepping out of line.

From our uneasy track which showed every sign of disintegrating into a riot of scrub we stared down an undulatory slope looking for a mere glimpse of that canal, a task made doubly difficult by localized irrigation ditches and shallow pools which winked like watery eyes under the unrelenting light. Because we were both thirsty and tired we made for a ramshackle farmstead surrounded by an impressive palisade of cactus, a place bigger than it looked at first glance.

Behind the back door were terraces of fruit trees: plums,

apricots, quinces, almonds, and carobs or locust beans used mainly for fodder on stony ground. Perched up in the trees, cheerfully shouting at each other, were a dozen or more long-skirted women, young and old, spraying, pruning or maybe gathering fruit.

Could we come in? They laughed, screeched a welcome and waved their arms.

Inching through a wood-block gap in the cactus we were set upon by several mongrels who, by bounding about or lying on their backs, clearly wanted nothing more than to be scratched.

Apart from the cheerful dilapidation of the propped-up front door the place might have been a small villa on the Costa Brava with a vine-sheltered veranda and a tremendous view down to the sea. Two middle-aged men and an oldster fondling his worry-beads waved us to their benches in the shade. When they learnt we came from *Megali Brettania* a bushy-haired man with bright red eyebrows somewhere between Squirrel Nutkin and an Arctic lynx asked us in a nice mixture of Greek, simple English and sign-language if we'd care to take a little wine, or perhaps *soom milch*. He called out to his wife.

During the few minutes it took that cheerful soul to walk over with wine, barley bread and olives, we exchanged glances with our old feeling of bewilderment. Katie had asked how far it was to the canal. 'Two hundred metres,' said our host. 'It is near the bridge, just below that tree over there; you can't see it from here.'

'And does the canal lead to Amphissa?'

He answered her by closing his eyes and tilting his head backwards, slowly.

'How do we get to Amphissa?'

He pointed to a ribbon of road far up the hill, the one we had left two hours ago.

'Where does the canal lead to?'

He pointed to a road below us, the one up from Itea,
then with a digging motion of his hand he made it clear
that it disappeared underground.

'How far from there to Amphissa?' asked Katie.

He pursed his lips, shrugged and said about seven kilometres. He turned to me and smiled.

'No matter,' she said. 'We'll walk through the olives as
we did on the way up.'

After warm goodbyes all round our host said, 'May
good fortune be with you this day.' And it turned out like
that.

Hospitality shrinks mileage. The water of the canal – fit
to drink – was thickly populated by small minnows which
scattered in a flurry as if a handful of gravel had been thrown
in when arrowing kingfishers stopped dead in mid-air and
hovered. We counted near a dozen before we struck the
torment of the highway.

Nose-to-tailers indulged in promiscuous tootology when
held up by small donkey-drawn carts. Holding her reins in
one hand a dark-eyed girl with provocative breasts stood
bare-footed on a hillock of small onions. With her left hand
she finger-gestured the noisiest of her tormentors. Her black
headscarf, we noticed, had been wrapped over her nose. A
Muslim? Or was it to dampen the smell of bruised onions
and dung? The donkey's backside had been draped in a
bulging diaper to catch the valuable droppings. We endured,
in fact rather enjoyed the spectacle, not least because in
various places we could slip down maintenance tracks into
the silence of the yards on both sides of the road.

We chose an archway of willows over a ditch the better
to wander down that natural herbaceous border of purple
and yellow irises, flowering rush, Love-in-a-mist and that
most memorable of Mediterranean flowers, the Crown
anemone, thought by some to be the lily of the field which
surpassed Solomon in all his glory.

When Linnaeus visited England for the first time in 1735 he is said to have dropped down on his knees and lifted up his arms at the sight of acres and acres of gorse on the cliffs of Dover. In his day the plant was an absolute rarity in Sweden. We felt much the same when more Camberwell Beauties swooped over us.

This purple-brown butterfly with a yellowish fringe to its wings is known as the Half Mourner in its native Scandinavia. Very few reach Britain but as a youth I saw one on the cliffs at Scarborough and duly reported it to the local natural history society, where I don't think the resident lepidopterists altogether believed a lad of twelve. When three or four were captured the following week and traced back to timber boats from Stockholm in the harbour, the *Yorkshire Post* picked up the story and misspelt my name, so that some people still think the butterfly was first seen there by the man who got to the top of Everest.

What with the Half Mourners and other locally common butterflies, including one with black blotches and red spots on its hind wings, the Eastern Festoon (*Zerynthia*), and a true mourner in almost black, the Great Sooty Satyr, I put down my sack, pranced after them and felt young again.

Olive yards are inhabited by a group of warblers which have no common name except the scientific one, *Hippolais*, and the habit of singing as if they were canaries crossed with nightingales. Plato's most famous pupil, Aristotle noticed this and said they were much beset by cuckoos. In this he was wrong, but the tutor of Alexander the Great could well be excused for slipping up on a small point of ornithological ethology. Those olive-green skulkers soar up and down the avian scale like prima donnas.

All in all it took us nearly six hours of pleasurable dawdling to reach the handsome township of Amphissa, known to the Turks as Salona and as late as the seventeenth century believed to be the site of ancient Delphi.

Sunday afternoon in the town square. Next to nobody about. Nothing open, not even a tavern. So we dozed leaning back on our rucksacks in the shade of a plane tree outside the locked-up temptations of an extremely well-stocked pastry shop.

Sleepy mutterings about what to do next were noisily interrupted by two truckloads of soldiers driven fast with police on motorbikes ahead and behind them, their sirens *ee-awing* incessantly.

To stretch my legs I stood up and sauntered into the next street to see if the tavern was still locked up. It was. On the way back to Katie a cop stepped out of a doorway and with no affability asked to see my passport.

That vague uneasiness at a policeman's direct questions is like being asked unexpectedly to drop your pants in front of a doctor. I smiled bleakly, wished him good-day, said *Engländer*, pointed towards the square and went through the motions of pulling on a pack.

He flicked through the pages. He seemed satisfied, said thank you in English, and touched his cap. Katie came along and took over.

Was there a camping-site in Amphissa?

He shook his head. 'Closed,' he said. 'Where you go next?'

Thinking it better to name a big town rather than a venture into the outback, I said, 'Lamia, perhaps tomorrow.' Saying that there would be a bus going there in an hour, he gave us a full salute and a smile.

Although 'wild camping' is officially forbidden in Greece we settled for an out-of-the-way patch with a water tap, near the town limits. With only the outer fly up and beds down, Katie was reading Pausanias. I mooched about among the olive trees, champing at the bit, yearning for company.

At seven o'clock I walked back to the square, promising to bring something fresher than dehydrated chicken risotto for supper.

Somnolent Amphissa had woken up. People were talking and laughing in groups; chairs and tables had sprung up close to shuttered places which we'd never suspected were cafés and small restaurants. Couples hand in hand were beginning to stroll round the square for that endearing Greek custom, the evening perambulation, the *volta*.

Several cars were parked against the sidewalk. Among them was a misty-blue Mercedes. Surprised, delighted, I peered into it. Empty.

Disappointed, I strolled towards the well-stocked pastry shop now bright with lights and busy. M. Théophane, that trim bearded fellow who had reminded me of Svengali, was sitting outside over a coffee and looking at me.

He sighed. 'Kyr' Ioanni,' he began. 'I have been sitting here for nearly an hour and beginning to get a little cold. *Allons-y*, let us go upstairs.'

He steered me through the cascades of sugared fruits, *baklava*, those things that look like sticky Shredded Wheat, *mille feuilles, petits fours*, small fingers of almond cake, and *louhoumis* which we call Turkish Delight.

Upstairs in a small but finely appointed room he motioned me towards a cushion on an ornamental chair of cedarwood. Except where niches sheltered a wealth of antique vases almost the whole room, that is the walls and the parquet floor, were covered with Turkish rugs embellished with diamond shapes, zigzags and quasi-botanical forms in a harmony of colours. '*Quinzième siècle*, from Ushak near Smyrna in Asia Minor,' he murmured.

'Comfortable, *n'est-ce pas*? Before I left for Ascona and she came here, for many years Madame Konstania and I were neighbours in Famagusta – a woman of taste, eh?'

'How on earth did you know we should be here today?'

Théophane smiled. 'I had business in Thessaloniki but drove down to Delphi today. I went to *la gendarmerie* to ask if you had arrived, and your friend M. Carlo Akhilleas told me you had just left.'

'Was your business at Vergina?'

His smile faded. For a moment I saw irritation, a touch of hostility in his eyes.

'*Moi, je ne suis pas un vautour, une goule, m'sieur.* The site, I know is perhaps the finest discovery of the century. Who could have imagined that Philippe of Macedon was buried in the northern shadow of Mount Olympos except my good friend Professor Manolis Andronicus? Him I have known for many years. And now he has struck – how you call it? The jackpot. The one-eyed skull, the shattered bones, *les couronnes d'or*, the jewellery! Believe me, Kyr' Ioanni, I had no commerce, no contact with Manolis nor anybody associated with him. Some of them are *moins honnêtes* than others. I trade among traders. It is my ability to distinguish between them. Also the provenance of what they have to sell and whether or not *les objets* are what they say they are.'

Perhaps to ease the tension he lifted up a decanter of Metaxas and raised his eyebrows. I nodded. 'Now tell me, *m'sieur*, how long had you in Thebes?'

'Two days,' I said.

He affected to look indignant. '*Eh bien*, if I had come to your country, to one of your famous cities, say York or Edinburgher and admitted I was there *deux jours* only, what would you have said?'

'But we intend to walk over 500 miles. How can we stay anywhere for more than a day or two? For people of our age there are limits to exertion.'

'A wise man will not dispute with a man in a hurry,' he said.

'Your proposition is disputed. The person who relies on

proverbs doesn't realize there are two sides to a question, he knows only the roundness of answers.'

'*Pardon, m'sieur*, but you have been *piégé* by your own aphorism. *D'après* Montaigne, a proverb is the literate child of common experience – *mais* it is good to play with words; I have few opportunities in this country. *En France* it is different. We have many disputants, and all our writers are important. I know little about the situation in your own country, but I have discovered myself that in Australia one is obliged to explain what a writer is. But to serious matters. Where do you go now?'

'Have you a map?' I asked.

He zipped open his briefcase and spread our a *carte routière*, 1:400,000 on the table.

'I haven't seen the sheet before,' I told him. Ours were about half that scale and they were wildly inaccurate – purposively, in our opinion. Who did the Greeks think they were deceiving? What nation did they fear the most? Théophane repeated what he had told me before: '*Tout le monde.*'

With my finger I traced our line of march. It seemed we must walk some eight or nine miles up the main road towards Lamia and then fork to the north-west along a faintly dotted track, first to Kaloscopi then to Pira.

He shook his head. He had never heard of the place. '*Pays sauvage*,' he said. My turn to sigh.

'After that, Mavrolithari,' I said.

At that he beamed expansively. 'The place of black stones the size of golf balls. Volcanic. *Pas loin*, there is a famous temple to *Hercule*.' He and an archaeologist had looked for it without success. 'Did Pausanius mention it?'

'I don't know, but if it is so wild how did you get there?'

'In the Giona mountains, about twenty kilometres to the west from here, there is a direct road to it. It comes up from

165

Evritani on the Gulf. Where will you go after the place of the black stones?'

'All we know is what's on the dotted line: Daphni, Anatoli, Marmara and Platanos, up to Timfristos.'

'Have you any idea of what you will find there?'

I shook my head.

'One of the highest ranges in Central Greece, about 2,500 metres, I think. *Écoutez*, there is a road over the lower slopes and', he added mischievously, '*un autobus* about once a day. But no doubt you will walk. *Pour moi*, the only exercise I indulge in nowadays is backgammon. *Et après le* Timfristos?'

'To Trikala from Karpenissi by way of the Agrapha.'

'Agrapha!' He bowed his head and put his hands over his eyes in mock horror. 'Do you know what the word means? *La place sans nom*. No roads. They say one still finds wolves and bears in those deep ravines. During the German Occupation people fled there in their thousands. At the time of the Civil War it was dominated by ELAS. Trikala, now, *ça c'est autre chose*. Highly civilized. The Paris of Thessaly. *Dites-moi*, will Madame accompany you in this masochistic exercise?'

I nodded.

'Tell her with my compliments that she defies Nietzsche, who said marriage is a bribe to make a housekeeper think she is a householder. *Comme institution*, he thought it belonged more to the *domaine de la comédie* than philosophy. *Cela ne fait rien*. With the worries you are obliged to endure *en route*, perhaps it is that *amor vincit insomnia*.'

He glanced at his watch. '*Mon dieu!* I have a rendezvous in Delphi in almost half one hour. *Dites-moi*, how long do you think you will want to reach Trikala?'

'With any luck about two weeks, perhaps a little more.'

'*Bon!* We must have another talk together. I recommend the Hotel Divani. About the time of your arrival I will leave a note there in your name, with my telephone number.

Perhaps you will take another drink? *Non? Donc*, I must go. *Bonne chance.* As Gide always concluded his farewells: "I give you my hand." '

He squeezed mine, lightly stroking my palm with his forefinger as he said goodbye. We went downstairs and he drove off. A first-rate male impersonator.

I got back over an hour late. Katie is uncommonly patient but I'm pretty sure if it hadn't been for two or three pestiferous curs I should have been in the doghouse myself. I heard the clamour within 200 yards of where we'd put the tent up. Not the deep-throated barking and baying of guard dogs, but the yap and yelp of lesser breeds within the law.

With the exception of the outer fly, literally her last refuge, Katie had packed up. She said she'd been sitting on our rucksacks since soon after I'd set off for the square.

'I tried to shout to you,' she said, 'but you had gone and as for that damned fudge of yours, the dogs loved it and came back for more.'

'But why didn't you chuck something at them?'

'You try,' she said.

I turned round. The dogs were invisible in the dusk, but seemed to be closer, from the noise they made, to small mongrels than mastiffs. Two came quite near, growling peevishly. They looked like terriers. I slung a substantial piece of rock in their direction and they promptly bolted. Hero returned to beleaguered spouse and wasn't over-encouraged by her reaction. 'They'll be back in five minutes,' she said. 'Do you want to put up with this all night? What's for supper?'

I told her that thanks to the intervention of the mayor, the chief of police and the neighbour of an old friend of mine I had arranged for a meal for two in the best restaurant in town. We occasionally go in for this sort of thing; it masks the platitudes of domesticity.

'What you really mean', she said, 'is that for the last two hours you've been knocking back ouzo in that awful-looking tavern.'

I kept up the mild deception until we'd nearly finished the aubergine purée followed by *barbounia*, which is grilled red mullet, before I told her whom I'd really met.

'What! That old poofter from Thebes?'

'You are referring,' I said, 'to Monsieur Théophane, a distinguished antiquarian, who not only sends you his compliments but has given us some valuable information about what we're in for. I have arranged to meet him again in Trikala.'

'That's fine, but where are we going to spend the night?'

In fact on the second or maybe the third loop of the steep highway out of Amphissa on the way to Lamia, we encountered deserted roadworks. By torchlight we inspected and without qualification settled for a deserted workmen's hut where we slept like curled up dormice from near midnight until six in the morning.

Within minutes of stifling yawns and breaking wind in our uninhibited way – though not, of course, without a muttered, 'I beg your pardon' – we had but one thought and that was to put on jackets and nether garments before the road gang turned up. We needn't have hurried. Nobody arrived and we had the best of reasons for lingering outside the hut for nearly an hour.

In nearly half a century of cross-country walking I have on many occasions cursed roads, but at the very start of that brief but uphill bout with the Lamia highway we were presented with shelter and a wholly unexpected free breakfast within sight of artwork which, had it been carried off to the Thames embankment, the trustees of the Tate Gallery might well have been tempted to buy.

We had spent the night on that rare thing in the Greek countryside, an area of soft, flat and stone-free ground, the product of road-making on a steep hillside. For many yards both above and below an acute bend in a series of loops, engineers had blasted out hundreds of tons of hard rock, leaving untouched – except for in-filling – an almost vertical face opposite the workmen's hut.

This had provided political slogan-daubers with almost limitless opportunities for graffiti, another palimpsest of forty years of Greek history in blue and red lettering. The latest, the brightest ones reflected the political war-cries of the Communists, KKE and PASOK, the followers of Mr Papandreou, but below them in diminishing shades of colour and intelligibility we decoded and laboriously translated *Shit to the Bulgarians, Demokratia* and *Coalition*. Below them all, in letters so high and so incisive that the rock must have been cut to retain the ghost of the original paint, we read: *Those not Royalist are Communist, Down with Bevin* and, in English, *Welkom to our Callant Allies*, a touching salutation.

To enjoy the last few feet of that political masterpiece we stood on the very lip of the loop. To our mild consternation an open truck, driven as fast as Greek truckers drive, raced up the hill towards us. It contained brimful baskets of fish. We flattened ourselves against the rock face. It swung round the bend with no apparent diminution in speed and, centrifugal force being what it is, flung a handful or two of sardines at our very feet.

Poseidon be praised! If not manna from heaven, we felt thrice blessed with a sea-fresh breakfast from Itea.

A small problem: we had left all our expendable gear, including a rather bulky aluminium frying-pan, with friends in Delphi. Usurping Katie's role as *maîtresse de cuisine* I insisted that *Sardina pilchardus*, one of the smallest and most toothsome relatives of the noble herring, should be treated

169

as native custom demanded, that is to be grilled quickly, barbecue-fashion.

We needed a coarse sieve. There were several *in situ*. We borrowed one. We needed a small but reasonably air-tight oven. The Swiss family Hillaby manufactured one from flat rocks lined with slates and bits of corrugated iron. Then screwing up a few pages of the *Herald Trib*, we pushed them into the base of our little stove and set fire to them. As soon as the sardines on the sieve caught the flames they dripped oil, which would have kept that fire alight for quite a long time. They were done to a turn in a matter of minutes.

When we got unutterably fed up with dehydrated foods we put that fortuitous trick to good use on several occasions. The difficulty was to find a sieve; otherwise Greece abounds in the elements of oven-making especially among the carboniferous shales.

Days that begin well often carry a sort of talisman of sustained good fortune, and it went that way with us. After establishing our country of origin, destination, names and ages, cheerful gangs of workmen further up the highway showed uncommon interest in the health of Bobby Charlton, Madame T'atcher and Kyr' Scargill.

How much did our boots cost? Could they try on our rucksacks? Had we friends in Lamia? 'By God, no!' said I and got a reproachful look from Katie. At one point they cheered so loudly at our approach that their mates on the loop above echoed the salutation although they couldn't have had an inkling about who we were. Our helpful friends introduced us to wayside springs whose water tingled our palates.

They pointed out distant peaks with incomprehensible and somewhat awesome names, since from compass bearings it looked as if we should be obliged to breach that wall; yet all this was done simply to make us feel at home. We liked those good-natured fellows and wished only that we understood more of what they were doing their best to explain.

Twice during that morning police cars hurtled past us with lights flashing and sirens screaming, and it wasn't until we met a couple of Irishmen, lads from County Fermanagh who'd jumped their ship in the Piraeus, that we heard about what was going on. Translated through accents as thick as their arms, it seemed that a Greek political prisoner, an ex-ELAS Communist bottled up on the infamous island of Makronisos, had escaped for no better reason than to shoot his brother who had brought about a family feud by joining what one of them called 'the other side'. Presumably he meant the politically mixed-up Security Battalions who were no less guilty of atrocities than the worst elements of ELAS. The story was that in a wood near his brother's home the fugitive had hidden himself for two days before shooting him through the coat, so he could tell him 'a t'ing or two' before finishing him off. Without a trace of emotion, the Irishman said: 'The police t'ink the murtherous bastard is still there, waiting to take a potshot at other members of the family who were on his brother's side.'

'Where is this village?'

He didn't know. They were strangers. At night the trucks came to take them back to Lamia. Nor did they know where Makronisos was. His other gangers had been children at the time of the Civil War. We learnt later that the Greek Alcatraz lay off the south-eastern tip of Attica.

On the precipice below yet another loop we looked down on a vast quarry with men at work with cranes, bulldozers and other mechanical gear shovelling clay-like material into a procession of trucks. We had seen several of these operations since that day when we said goodbye to the hospitable Lieutenant Perouse on the dockside at Paralia. Most of them were under the control of the Société Anonyme des Mines Bauxites de Parnasse.

171

In Greece enormous deposits of hydrated oxide of aluminium known as bauxite have a low grade aluminium content and, lacking cheap electric power, Greece has next to no aluminium industry. Poor-quality bauxite is used in the manufacture of cement and refractories. M. Perouse had told us that SAMBP held proved resources of about fifty million tons.

The predecessor of the Lamia highway and its extension north was originally built by Britain in 1916 to avoid using sea transport to Macedonia when shipping was subject to enemy submarine attack, and there above that quarry we came to a full stop for a mildly dramatic quarter of an hour.

In large red letters a board propped up by trestles proclaimed: ΚΙΝΔΥΝΟΣ. Katie spelt it out, slowly: *Kappa Iota Ni Delta Epsilon Ni Omicron Sigma!* 'Danger,' she said. 'Perhaps a landslide. Maybe this is where we start some real climbing.'

The drivers of two trucks and a private car ahead of us were waiting impatiently. A cheerful little fellow in fluorescent orange-coloured overalls spoke to them one after another in an explanatory torrent of Greek. He came up to us. Katie heard him out politely before she wished him good day and regretted that, alas, she didn't understand a word.

Then began another fine example of Greek sign-language. The fellow was a born mime. In far less time than it takes to describe his act he began by closing his eyes, lowering his head and putting his right hand over his heart. We were receiving the profound regrets of *M. le Président* of Société Anonyme et cetera for the delay. Then he stood straight up and stabbed the air with his forefinger. A small crisis had arisen. Slow downward jabs with his finger in the direction of the quarry made it quite clear that that's where the danger lay. To underline his point he screwed his face up like a man who had incautiously bitten into an unripe plum. He put his hands over his ears and said '*Boom!*'

'The damn fool means they're going to fire a shot,' I said, crossly. 'Ask him how long we're going to hang about and tell him to get on with it.'

After a brief question, Katie said: 'Ten minutes, he hopes.'

To the consternation of the little chap we leaned over the railings, the better to enjoy the spectacle. It happens that because of a day spent in the archetypal marble quarries of Europe, the Carrara series in Tuscany, during an ill-fated walk from Nice to Florence, I know a fair amount about what in a melodious Italian phrase means ripple-blasting. Six minutes to go.

A skilful quarry man who wants to detach a relatively small piece of rock from its massive matrix takes his hammer and chisel and makes a fine incision into the grain of the face. Five minutes to go.

This done, he picks up his mallet and drives a big wet wedge into the parent rock just below the point where he knows that, if he is successful, it will drop on to cushions of sand and then he hits it hard. Four minutes to go.

Much can be done on the grand scale with explosives. Small pockets of dynamite are fused and coupled up along the equivalent of that chisel-cut line. The important thing is not to blast out what might injure the face and the immediate product. Three minutes to go.

In Carrara this is enormously important. Marble is extremely valuable stuff. There are about 600 quarries throughout the Apuan Alps, worked in the times of classical Rome but abandoned after the fall of the Western Empire. Next to nothing more was heard about them until the growth of Pisan architecture and sculpture during the twelfth and thirteenth centuries. Today, once the huge blocks of marble are detached by ripple-blasting they are snared by a web of moving wires on wheels which put you in mind of Gulliver bound down with ropes by swarms of Lilliputians.

173

The moving wires provide power for the hand drills and chisels of the master masons. Two minutes to go.

For bauxite delicacy doesn't matter. The object is to blast out as much as possible with a line of shots to determine the dimensions of the downfall and ensure that it drops near the waiting trucks. One minute to go.

The engineers scrambled into the back of one big truck which was promptly driven off. A hooter howled. Spurts of grey smoke sprang from the vertical face at intervals of about twenty yards, to the accompaniment of thumps no louder than from rolled-up carpets thrown from the roof of a house. And then an almighty explosion as from a battery of twenty-five pounders fired simultaneously, as the super-charge tore into the guts of the Jurassic limestone. We felt it underfoot but apart from the noise and a cloud of dust a prodigious quantity of rock fell to the floor of the quarry gently, like a coat that had slipped off a coat-hanger. As we trailed after the traffic ahead we saw that a police car had joined the queue behind us and it drove past howling.

For eight miles beyond the signpost to Kaloscopi we ran the dusty gauntlet of trucks carrying bauxite on a narrow dirt road from another quarry to the north-west. We did our best to scramble out of the way. We tied vests round our necks so that at the approach of yet another vehicle they could be pulled over our sweaty hair and sore eyes, but it didn't do much except increase our discomfort from the heat.

We had no difficulty whatever in finding the quarry which was even bigger than the one we had left. The problem was how to get out of it. The dirt road, the trucks' escape route, emerged from a death-white arena some two or three hundred yards in diameter, ringed by Cyclopean terraces too high to be climbed. It was curiously white-striped-with-reddish rock. Perhaps bauxite may be fairly compared with Joseph's coat. We never found out what it was. Clearly the immediate workings had been abandoned.

Nobody about. No industrial gear. We felt like two ants on an enormous soup plate.

Ahead of us we heard a curious clinking noise punctuated by intervals of silence. It might have been a bird, perhaps a Greek Nuthatch. To avoid the ferocious light we clung to the shadow below the north wall of the quarry. We rounded a corner to find a bare-chested fellow on a terrace some fifty feet from the ground chipping away at what looked like a stone coffin. He waved to us and I waved back and bawled: '*Parakalo, pou ine Kaloscopi?*'

He made a downward chopping motion gesture with his right hand. We were bidden to keep straight on. His hand then jerked to the left and then pointed upwards. '*Efharisto!*' I shouted and the echo shouted it back.

It all came out that way. Around the corner the terraces had been sliced to cut a series of steps, hundreds of them. Halfway up we were obliged to rest for a few minutes and then more up and up, until we came out into a wood on the very edge of the quarry where a knee-high signpost pointed to Kaloscopi, the place with the good view. Eight kilometres.

> *O blessed shade and green'ry,*
> *Not e'en i' the courts of Shiraz Khan*
> *Could there be more gladness-granting,*
> *More enchanting blithesome place.**

In the classical Greece of long ago there was – and in my mental list of spiritual friends there still is – a great goddess, leader of the nymphs who usually accompany her. She is called Artemis, 'Lady of the Wild Things'. She haunts the mountains, the forests and even small woodlands where there are tree-cults with springs and rivers. She protects

---

*   Christopher Tower, *Oultre Jourdain*, Weidenfeld & Nicolson, 1980.

women in childbirth and she watches over little children, especially curious strays. Girls used to bring offerings to her before marriage. The homage is different in different parts of Greece but essentially it always goes back to those characteristics mentioned.

Her habitual appearance has been sung about by Homer and in the great literature of Attica. She is the virgin twin sister of Apollo. Of course the supreme goddess who haunts wild places must be a hunting goddess. Artemis was much more than that but the Homeric knights had no relationship to the free life of nature except in the sport of hunting, so she is usually portrayed with a bow and arrows.

Conservationists say we must save forests because people enjoy them. St Francis, God's jester, thought we should save them for squirrels, not for men. Surely St Francis worshipped a God who was the God of both squirrels *and* men? The unknown author of the Benedicite, that canticle or song of praise put into the mouths of Shadrach, Meshach and Abednego as they stood in that fiery hell at the command of King Nebuchadnezzar, was much of the same opinion. The Benedicite may have more of a future than a past.

After being hounded on the roads by trucks we felt under the spell of Artemis in that superb woodland. We both heard and saw one of her familiars, a squirrel, the red species with its long bushy tail curled so far over its back, like a question mark, that the tip extended above its whiskery ears. It saw us and scampered up an Aleppo pine, making a reproachful chattering noise. From the safety of an upper branch it turned round and stared at us and I could have sworn that the handsome little creature winked.

We heard orioles, the warble of unseen warblers, the laughter of the Great green woodpecker and, more ominously, within minutes of taking to a meagre road within sight of Kaloscopi, a hamlet on a small hill, we heard yet again the unmistakable bark of a high-speed rifle.

High Noon at Kaloscopi

An undistinguished place midway between mediocrity and downright seediness. A police car and what looked like an armoured van were parked in the shade of a plane between two taverns facing each other. A sergeant of police, his constable and a Civil Guard were talking to groups of locals and making notes. The sergeant looked up; he acknowledged my somewhat contrived salute and went on talking. Nobody else spoke to us.

Without ignoring the tremendous view, the privilege of the rather better-looking house on the far side of the square, we settled for its neighbour on the grounds that it didn't face the midday sun and we could see what was going on.

'Get the beer, enquire about food, but *don't* order anything until we've seen what they've got over there,' said the ever-practical Katie.

I came back with the man of the house bearing two bottles on a battered tin tray. What with the dusk and the heat of the morning it went down singing hymns. 'He doesn't speak much English; the food's pretty trad, but he's got a fresh-looking moussaka and plenty of salad,' I said. 'I wonder what's going on?'

I finished the first two glasses, ordered some more and strolled over to the house opposite, glancing into the police car on the way. A rifle lay across the two front seats.

On the veranda, facing the vista, a short red-faced man in a naval jacket was talking to a chubby dark-haired woman in Italian, rapidly. A bull terrier at their feet half stood up and growled. '*Basta!* Georgio,' he said to the dog, and greeted me in German. '*Buongiorno,*' I replied somewhat coldly.

I walked through the tavern. The food looked a bit dried up. Not much liking the look of Georgio, I returned to Katie via the back door shortly before the sergeant with a cigarette dangling from the corner of his mouth sauntered over.

'There might be some awkward questions about how we got here,' I whispered. 'Don't forget that we don't know much Greek. He'll probably speak to me. If I don't know what he's talking about I'll turn to you.'

'Yes, but give me time – first try to find out how much English he knows,' Katie replied.

Surreptitiously, perhaps *philotomo* in front of foreigners, the sergeant tidied himself up on the way over. He put on his cap, dropped his cigarette and trod on it and then gave us a crashing salute. Not to be outdone I stood up, army fashion. 'Good day, officer,' I said. I shook his hand and after a glance round assured him that Kaloscopi was indeed one of the most beautiful places we had visited. Did he speak English?

He didn't reply directly but smiled as he said, '*Parakalo*, pliss. Your passports.'

Katie handed them over. He flicked through them perfunctorily, made a quick note and handed them back with a smile. He couldn't have been more cordial.

Where had we come from?

'From Amphissa,' Katie said; 'we are tourists from London.' To my relief he didn't ask us where we were heading for. Apparently he wanted to know whether we had seen a small yellow car.

'No cars at all,' she said, 'only big trucks. What sort of car?'

An old Fiat. One door smashed. It had been painted white. Katie translated. We considered the matter gravely and then both shook our heads.

The sergeant saluted. He took off his cap, shook my hand and hoped our journey would be a good one. Over Greek salad and warmish moussaka we decided he was as pleasant a cop as ever we'd met.

Katie yearned for what we'd eaten in Venice. I tried to cheer her up by observing that in Greece you get caught by the same old food whilst in Italy it's a case of the same old prices.

Katie sighed. Her feet were not at all good. More blisters, and she thought we might run out of talc and sticking-plaster. Madame had told her there was a small *maghazi* at the end of the street behind the tavern. 'I'll go take a look. See you back here in not much more than half an hour. And no more retsina! We've a long way to go.'

There wasn't much to see so I decided to take another look at the view through glasses. On the way I encountered Georgio who bounced down from the veranda, barking furiously. In a coarse phrase I bade him begone.

'He'll no fuck off if ye speak to him like *thaat*,' said Naval Jacket in the slurred vowels and clipped consonants of Glasgow.

Andy McFarlane, Chief Engineer at the Andrea Doria shipyard in Genoa, asked me to join them. Since Katie had only said retsina, I accepted a small brandy gratefully. With an airy wave of his hand he introduced me to Maria, his chubby girl-friend. 'The silly old cow can't speak much English, although I've been trying for years. Mind you, she understood that phrase of yours. I thought you were a Kraut or a Swede. Why didn't you speak out? What are you doing here?'

I told him, briefly. I didn't like the way the dog looked at me. 'And you?' I asked.

'We've got a place on the Passo di Bocca with a view as good as this. Half an hour's drive north of Genoa. Had it for years. Bought it cheap. Now Maria's got a great-aunt in a bonny village called Pira about twenty kilometres from here. There's a delicate question of inheritance, if you get me. We have to keep an eye on it fairly regularly.'

'So you intend to retire there?'

'Jesus Christ, no! I'd rather go back tae Glesga. Pira's a closed shop. They already resent us. They know what we're up to. Greek villagers are worse than the Wops in keeping foreigners out.'

'But surely they'd trust a relative of Maria's?'

'Trust!' he almost shouted. 'No Greek does *anything* without thinking what he can get out of it. It's self-interest right down the line.'

I thought, momentarily, about why he kept visiting Maria's old aunt but didn't want to stem the flow.

'Greeks are a predatory people incapable of real friendship unless it's within their clan, their extended family. Whenever they extend effusive hospitality they're hoping for involvement. Tourists, a substantial part of the national economy, are key figures in this process so long as they don't hang around too long. Hope you've never told them you're an author who used to be a journalist? They'll be after your London address. As soon as a Greek gets an apartment, a small bank balance and credit, he's thinking about becoming a bigtime property owner, a lawyer or a regional Deputy, even President. He's *never* satisfied with what he's got.'

'Pira's on our route,' I said. 'Any difficulty about getting there?'

'A dirt road. It shakes the hell out of our old Citroën but in boots you'll be able to skip along. Go straight up through the village here for about five kilometres and then fork left. Now listen, laddie. We could spend another night with the old lady. Why not come along with us?'

The ritual refusal expressed as courteously as possible. 'Thanks, but we're doing the whole jaunt of foot. We can cut corners off by following a track on our map.'

'What map?'

Somewhat diffidently I pulled out our tattered copy of 'Phokis Sheet 2'. 'Along this line,' I said. He glanced at the sheet, folded it up and handed it back.

'Haven't you found that Greek maps are just plain goddamned inaccurate? They don't even mention small roads. A hangover from the military dictatorship. Where you heading for after Pira?'

'Mavrolithari,' I said.

'The place of the black stones . . . yes, there's a track of sorts there. We've been down it in a Land Rover. It's about twelve kilometres from Pira.' He looked at the map. 'Now let's see what's next . . . H'm . . . After that Daphni, Marmara, Platanos. At least five villages, some of them falling to bits. You'll probably meet only a few old men. But when you get to Platanos you'll be more than two-thirds of the way to Karpenissi, a big market town.'

'*Brutto, brutto. Malagevole,*' murmured Maria.

'Shut up!' he said to her sharply. 'She's saying it's rough going and she's right. Still, if you're determined to kill yourselves remember those names. No, just a second. I'll put a ring round where at least they ought to be on this map. Why on earth didn't you buy the latest Michelin? Those tyre merchants have a vested interest in roads, and at least they can distinguish between left and right and don't rely on clusters of dots to confuse the credulous.'

'So you prefer your Italian neighbours?' I said.

'In our local village, yes. I've been there so long I'm near the top of the local pecking order. But not among the Genovese Mafia, who don't even trust each other. They drive flashy cars. They try to eat and drink with those who've got more power, more money than they have and they'll screw any wench in sight if it's not too much bother. I tell you, the Italians are a nation of artists. And with characteristic artistry they have managed to create a society that combines some of the least appealing aspects of socialism with nearly all the vices of the affluent society. I should know. I've lived there nearly half my life.

'For years they have suffered from a dreadful disease called *la dolce vita*. They invent marvellous words to cover up the vice, the suffering and the humiliation that lies under it all. And everybody knows it except the Italians. *Dolce vita*, my arse!'

I switched the subject to the cops and the interrogations. What was it all about? 'Some guy's escaped from a local glasshouse. Seems originally it was a political affair but he's been behind barbed wire for so long that he's had nothing better to do than turn it into a family feud. Now he's intent on blowing the shit out of his brother who fought for the other side. There's Greek love and trust for you!'

'Isn't the brother around here somewhere?'

'Well, I think he used to be.' He turned to Maria who'd been knitting as if we weren't there.

'She says Auntie told her the fellow got to hell out of it as soon as he heard that his brother had escaped. Now they're probably hunting each other. Beware of the Greeks when they're toting light artillery in the sacred names of politics.'

'We've been told that he escaped from Makronisos.'

'Never heard of it. I'll ask Maria.' He spoke to her again in bursts of Italian. 'She says Papandreou closed it down. The long-timers are somewhere up in the hills above Karpenissi.'

I asked him if he'd heard the sound of the rifle shot. A slight pause before he said, 'Sure I did and I know what the sergeant hit. It's in the back of his van over there. Georgio's been sniffing round it.'

'One of the brothers?'

He laughed. 'Not on your life. Just a wee staggie. The woods are full of 'em. You don't expect he'd come back empty-handed, do you? They're worth about 3,000 drachs in Lamia. If I could be sure of a haunch I'd gralloch it within half an hour.' He looked at me. 'It's best not to know too much around here.'

I turned over that piece of advice mentally. Had I been politely told to mind my own business? How did *he* know what was inside the van? For the first time he seemed to be thinking of something to say. He began to look at my face, closely, like an interrogating policeman.

'Your mouth,' he said. 'It's sort of drawn up at the corners; it's too tight. Haven't you got a girl-friend?'

'She's out shopping,' I said, 'and it's about time I got back.' His turn to look surprised, even slightly embarrassed.

'We didn't see you come in, and when you said "we" I thought you were with a fella. That's good. Every man needs a woman in bed.'

'I'm nearly seventy but can just about manage it twice a week.'

He glanced towards Maria. 'If I left it to her it would be every night. Wouldn't it, you silly old cow?'

She blinked. She looked puzzled. He glared at her. 'I said you like a *good fuck*, don't you?'

She laughed until she showed every gold tooth in her head. '*Si, si. Molto bene. Tutta notte, tutta notte.*'

He patted her hand. 'She's not a bad lassie,' he said.

*   *   *

'Thought you'd gone off with the town tart,' said Katie, who'd paid the bill and closed the rucksacks. 'Now, do we stay around or take to the hills?'

'Depends entirely on your feet, me darling. How do they feel?'

'Lots better,' she said. 'The local shop's a shed next to her husband's garage. Meat only on Fridays. Bread every other day from eight until about half-past ten, A real kindly soul. God knows what she does for the rest of her time, sitting down there surrounded by sacks of flour, beans and a few old potatoes. I looked over her shelves. Couldn't find much beyond your favourite squid in tomato sauce, sardines, tea and a bit of rice.'

'Nothing else?'

'Not unless we're in need of piles of detergents or *Peaudouce*, those disposable nappies.'

'No medicaments?'

'Iodine, aperients, Beecham's pills and liver salts. I couldn't put across sticking-plaster or talk in Greek, so I slipped off my slippers and pointed to the dressings and went through the motions of sprinkling them with flour. She went upstairs and came back with just what I wanted. As she wouldn't take anything for them I felt obliged to pay little enough for what's going to be your favourite standby. Tinned squid.'

'More weight?'

'Now what on earth *could* I do when, with a muttered blessing, she fumbled in a drawer, took out this little thing, and, without a word, slipped it into my pocket.'

A small plastic cross. I recalled what ex-Lieutenant Commander Andy McFarlane had said about what lay behind Greek friendliness and trust.

'Now, what's next?' said Katie.

'I'm all for pushing on for a few miles, maybe no further than the first reasonable place we come to for a dream home for the night. Let's try and have at least a couple of comfortable days. Apparently there's wooded country at the top of the hill. I've become a self-appointed authority on the district. That chap in a naval jacket wasn't an Italian, he's a pretty ferocious Scottish engineer. His girl-friend's got a relative in the next village, Pira. Wish you'd heard him. He trots out corrosive opinions on just about everything, but he's marked place-names I couldn't find on our map, which he thinks was printed during the Civil War. It seems that when we get to a village called Platanos we'll be more than two-thirds of the way to what seems a reasonable town, Karpenissi.'

Seen from above, Kaloscopi seemed far more fertile and prosperous than from the track beyond the quarry we had no wish to remember. Plenty of water, terraced holdings and a fine field of golden grain, perhaps barley, over which jackdaws flew in the way that inspired Van Gogh for his last picture, the one before he killed himself.

The banks of the hill were star-dappled with white flax, *vinca* the periwinkle, and asters which was appropriate since their name in English means 'a star'.

The junction at the top appeared as Andy predicted: left to Pira, right to Lamia. We struck left into an alpine landscape of immense rocks and pines, Aleppo, Cephalonian and, an old friend, a fine specimen of the Scottish species (*P. silvestris*), blue needles and rusty red at the cross trees. It might have been a long beleaguered consul from Edinburgh, waiting for news of the Jacobites.

In far less time than we could have hoped for we came across what we had sought at sundown for near a fortnight, that rare thing in the wilds of central Greece, a truly

185

comfortable haven for the night. There it stood, a plateau of reasonably soft ground, sufficient at least to hammer in the tent pegs without much effort.

Trees stood above a freshet of unclouded water. We could see enough dead wood for a small fire. We had a vista at our front door and the whole property stood just out of sight of a dust road. In his much-quoted 'Night among the Pines' in the Cevennes, R. L. Stevenson, supported, physically, by his 'diminutive she-ass Modestine', cannot have been better accommodated than we were an hour or two after the tensions of Kaloscopi.

Before we put the tent up, through field-glasses far below us I could just make out a line, maybe a dozen armed men in unidentifiable uniforms making their way up slowly through rough ground, like beaters on a grouse moor. I passed the glasses to Katie. 'What do you make of that?' I asked.

'Well, if your friend Andy's story is to be believed they take stag-shooting seriously around here. You're sure he isn't an informer?'

'A damned clever one if he is. As he seems to be against both Greeks and Italians, maybe he's a double agent. I just let him speak and I happen to know the village where they live. It's Montoggia in the Bocca di Leone. I walked through it on my Apennine jaunt.'

Then to our duties: mine to bring water and firewood, hers to do whatever industrious women do when left alone at home. The streamlet, about half a span in width, tinkled tunefully. A pity, I thought, to pollute its clarity with a wash pool, so I diverted a minute tribuary into a reed-lined depression with a conduit hacked out with my skinning knife. Great to replay in old age the games of our youth.

Among the Aleppo pines were pillars of rock preaching

in silent sounds to lesser brethren at their feet. The old bark of fallen trees was (to me) attractively riddled by recognizable bark beetles whose larvae had left behind strange hieroglyphs on the smooth wood below. Were they writing letters to mankind? I collected twigs for kindling and substantial pieces of wood for a modest fire in a protective hearth of rocks.

As Katie began to simmer a packetful of macaroni bought in the shop, to which she added the squid and tomato sauce, we heard the distant sound of a rifle shot, not below us but so far away to the north-west that I fancy we caught only the twice-repeated echo. It happened again, followed by what I took to be the faint chatter of a sub-machine gun. 'How far away do you think that is?' she asked.

I didn't know, maybe four or five miles. Things seemed to be happening all around.

The macaroni and squid *à la mode de Kaloscopi* began to bubble. Katie spooned it on to plates and garnished it with crumbled feta cheese and wild thyme locally picked.

After an interval for polite belches and a nip of Metaxas with coffee, Katie rustled about arranging the bedding and I shoved the last resinous log on the glowing embers. I settled down, looking at the flickering light reflected from the walls of the half-open tent. Nothing I can think of, certainly not television, can stir up a traveller's memories more vividly than the light of an open fire.

That tent of ours with its front open to disclose its articulated ribs reminded me not of the night of the tepees of Chipewyans nor the igloos of the Sea Indians. In my mind's eye I went back to the Little People of the Belgian Congo. Our hemispherical headquarters there was about six feet in diameter with a framework of bent saplings on which the pygmies of Epulu had laid the shiny green leaves of the

Mongongo trees used like overlapping shingles. More permanent huts were dirt cheap: they simply plastered the exterior with a skin of mud which promptly dried in the sun.

Given that limited floor space, a hut usually sheltered two clan-linked couples with maybe two or three children each. Seldom more. The responsibilities of fatherhood, taken very seriously, meant that the meat-providers had to spend valuable time pit-falling or netting deer, wild boar, small forest elephants and dangerous buffalo instead of indulging in what they loved most, that is the ceremonials of birth, circumcision, marriage, death and whatever their elders, the wise ones, dreamed up when, deprived of the joys of the chase, they felt like a night out with its prospects of free meat, home-made liquor and home-grown pot.

At the expense of Parcs Nationaux du Congo Belge I spent several months in the Congo, now Zaire. My guide through the Ituri forest and subsequently over the Ruwenzori, the Mountains of the Moon, was the late Jean de Heinzelan de Braucourt, a young Belgian aristocrat, a geologist and mountain-climber who preferred skipping about like a chamois, chipping away at rocks, to ritualized life in his family's elegant mansions. His excuse for taking me to Epulu was to find out, on behalf of PNCB, how many specimens of that rare forest giraffe, the okapi, with their velvet skins and short necks were being fall-trapped and eaten by the Little People instead of being delivered up for forest rights to the Belgians, who sold them to zoos. Devious are the ways of conservation.

More important than what I gleaned as a zoological correspondent were glimpses of the near-indescribable happiness of the Little People who among themselves spoke in a click language, Ki-Bira. Jean knew enough of the common language of The River, Ki-'ngwanna – which could be transmitted by drums – to pass on messages from village to village, and what they thought about life (*kicheko*), literally happiness and, without a shred of irony or envy, their attitude towards the *watu hakika*, the Real People, meaning everybody who didn't share their customs and philosophy.

I never discovered who were the gods of *kicheko* but everybody knew and feared the devil, *Bolozi*, the Evil Eye, overlord of all dark mysteries. He was omnipotent. During illness he was even more powerful than *dawa*, the medicaments of the Real People.

His name was attached to all fearful things that dwelt in the Great Forest. Man-killing leopards were *Bolozï*; Army ants, probably the most formidable insects in Africa, were *Bolozi sifu*. They advance through the night in columns of uncountable millions. They have no permanent nests. They never settle down. Like the Huns and the Tartars they sally forth on one raid after another. They have been known to kill and devour a tethered horse. Surely they were the little soldiers of *Bolozi*.

'What do they do about them?' I asked de Heinzelan.

'They can't do anything,' he said. 'They get up and go. Their huts are not permanent. They live as close as they can to where the living is easy.' We were staying at the time close to Camp Putnam where Anne Eisner Putnam spent eight years living among the Little People. This is what she said about them:

I looked at the men, strong, happy and unspoiled by the complexities of civilization. Then I looked at the women, so functionally female in their nakedness, so obviously pleased by their lot. There was no hypertension, no ulcer-breeding unrest here in the Ituri Forest. There was fire and there was meat and cover and love and laughter. They wanted nothing else.

Around midnight, or perhaps earlier, since we took to our warm cocoon before the little owls began their monotonous *pee-oo* at two-second intervals (timed), I awoke under the impression – as I so often did – that they knew what had upset my deep dreams of nothing in particular. With much anxious fiddling with two zips I stepped out naked into a warm bath of air, armed only with a small but powerful torch. I swung the beam round in a semi-circle to find the nearest trees reflected momentarily showers of sparks as if a pinch of iron filings had been dropped into the flame of a candle. The pines were drinking luminous drops of dew. Then back to bed and an even deeper sleep until dawn.

In the moisture and the coolness, the lingering relics of the night, I yawned my way through the trees, across the dirt road where, clad only in underpants, I hopped through the cold wet and prickly herbage to the pool channelled from the streamlet. Brimful.

A few minutes sufficed for a sponge-down and a brisk towelling from head to foot. Ashamed of the slightly soapy state of the water in which Katie intended to wash her hair, I dislodged the dam, temporarily, enabling the water to whoosh down into the swampy reedbed below. To my dismay an unseen colony of little frogs resented the pollution with a chorus of chirps, yelps, peeps, burps and sustained trills. A dozen or more leapt to safety, not into the parent streamlet but on to the broad leaves of waterside plants. Some clung to the twigs of willows.

With difficulty I managed to capture one little bright green elf about an inch and a half in length. I held it lightly between finger and thumb, intrigued to see that the end of its arms and feet were knobbly adhesive pads. I had captured one of the *Hylidae*, the family of tree frogs, the finest amphibious singers in Europe. It leapt away, but not before the little fellow had urinated into the palm of my hand.

★   ★   ★

Coming down the dirt road towards the village we had left the previous afternoon I came across as strange a trio as ever you might have encountered in the mountains of Tibet: a very old man with all the dignity of his circular wrinkles, seated on a donkey, the very model of Modestine, the colour of a mouse, with a proud bearing, conscious, one felt, of the green ribbons around the base of her hairy ears. In his right hand the old man held a switch of twigs, which he brought down almost mechanically on Modestine's flanks in the way the old men lightly flick over their worry-beads in the shifting shade of a tavern during the afternoon sun.

At the end of a soft rope tied to the pommel he led an old cream-coloured draught ox with the huge brown eyes of Hera. A well-looked-after animal. When the rope tightened as it stopped to nibble something to its fancy he reined in without turning round. Apart from raising his switch in salutation he scarcely noticed me. An elderly white-bearded man in underpants was just part of the landscape, like a surprised hare or a glimpse of a deer.

In *The Palatine Anthology** it is recorded that: 'Alkon did not lead his hard-working ox to the butcher's knife for he remembered with reverence his past toil. And now wandering at large through the deep meadow grass, he lows out his happiness at freedom from the plough.'

According to the translator Forrest Reid: 'Among the Greeks this scruple prevails. In Athens there was even a formal law forbidding a farmer to kill or allow to be killed a beast who had worked for him.' Katie, less romantically inclined, thought the beast was probably on its way to a butcher's knife in Kaloscopi.

A steep descent led us to Pira. The village of waterfalls announces itself in three languages; accommodation, food

---

*   *Tenth-century manuscripts deposited in Heidelberg University Library.*

and wine stores. One of us wondered why we couldn't have found a similar place at nightfall.

'Anything wrong with last night's pitch?' asked Katie.

I am intolerant of that sort of argument which didn't end there. Should we or should we not have a look at the place? It was, I agreed, not on our route. No, we couldn't have just a word with Maria's aunt! We didn't even know her name, and who would want to meet two complete strangers at eight o'clock in the morning?

If we were to keep our schedule we had, I reckoned, about seven or eight hours, allowing for a bit of food and a siesta on the way. Why did we have to keep to a schedule? Because we didn't want to arrive in Macedonia in time for Christmas.

It took us about half an hour to find out that the short cut of somebody's imagination led to a main road *above* the village; more time, incalculable, to wind through a maze of little houses with prosperous plantations watered by as many fountains and pools as you are likely to encounter in Versailles. Nothing needs to be said about disagreements over finding our way back to the notice-board. *Così fan tutte.*

Gradually the abundance of water, orchards, cultivated fields and a fine stand of trees began to disappear until with a progressive sense of desolation we were venturing an almost barren track hacked out of the side of a cliff. Had it not been for recent tyre marks we might have thought we had strayed on to a footway that led nowhere.

In places the serpentine path had been crevassed by flash floods which had left behind a scree of rocks and stones in the gulf below. What couldn't be imagined was how the gaps could have been shored up without dumping many tons of material. Surely it would have been more practical to have blasted into the right-hand wall of the cliff?

Katie walked ahead around a bend in the road whilst I paused to shake out a bit of grit from one of my boots. I hurried after her to find her cautiously looking down a subsidiary track. She motioned me to the inner side of the cliff. The police van stood some forty of fifty feet below. Through glasses I could make out the wreck of a yellow-coloured car lying on its side nearby. The sergeant was taking photographs of a half-open bullet-ridden door.

Whirlwinds and Water-nymphs

A pleasure always to find a priest with a glass of liquor in his hand. In this way he seems better equipped to grapple with the Devil than men of God armed only with cups of herb tea and biscuits. In the tavern at Mavrolithari we watched an old *papas* arrive on a donkey with the dignity of Our Saviour on his way to Jerusalem. Clearly he had much to say to his fellow topers, who addressed him affectionately as *Papouli*. Unfortunately he spoke too rapidly for us to make out what was most on his mind. With a nod and a smile to the company all round we took to the ale bench outside.

The village looked much smaller, much poorer, certainly less ostentatious than Pira except in one geological particular: Mavrolithari advertised itself. From the moment we switched off that arid track and climbed towards good timber on a hill and heard the sound of cicadas, the keynote of a botanically rich soil, we saw the small black stones, some highly polished by glacial action – obsidian perhaps or diorite, forms of volcanic lava. I may be wrong. We subsequently lost our specimens. Enough that we had arrived at what M. Théophane and the McFarlane of Renfrewshire had told us about: the Place of Black Stones.

After about half an hour on our own, a well-dressed

couple strolled across the square towards us; she short and Italianate, he tall and languid. Katie recalled them passing us in a caravan on our way up the hill. In fluent English Dora introduced herself and then her husband, Theo, a pleasant unparticular man, taciturn even when answering questions in Greek.

By contrast the Adorable Dora – as we referred to her afterwards – was rarely without something to say, an exuberant brimful-of-life person. Within minutes we learnt that 'himself' was an architect in Thebes where she taught English and French and 'some little time as a lecture person in University of Athens. I own small house here,' she said, correcting herself by adding, 'I mean *we* own it but only come for long weekends and school holiday times.'

Theo stood up and said, '*Signomi*,' before walking away. 'He has a customer here. What do you call it? A client for holiday home? He is specialist in *reconstruction*. What is that in idiomatic English?'

'Doing old places up so you can't see it from the front. Disguised modernization. It's what we call "putting in all mod cons", meaning all modern conveniences: indoor bathroom, lavatory and kitchen appliances. Sometimes a carefully concealed garage.'

She smiled, repeated 'all mod cons' and wrote it down before asking who could stop English people doing what they wanted to with what they owned.

'Local bye-laws,' I said. 'A complicated matter. They are different from place to place. *Byrlaw* is a very old word, perhaps Saxon. It means "according to local custom".'

Unexpectedly she asked, 'Why do you walk so far?'

The perennial question. The perennial answer. 'Because I can't imagine anything more exhilarating. When I'm in top gear or even slightly above it, it's almost indescribable, you might compare it with that gear called overdrive in a powerful car. I'm scarcely conscious that my arms and legs are working together. I keep up momentum by leaning forward very slightly.'

'Even with those huge things on your back?'

'Well, yes. That could be called a sore point. Without them there'd be no stopping us. But they mean almost complete independence. We don't worry too much about the weather or reaching somewhere to spend the night.'

'And how about you?' she asked, looking at Katie.

'I love it. I think I was born to be a tramp, or maybe a donkey.'

'Don't you get bored with nobody to talk to except each other?'

'I don't think so,' said Katie. 'He tends to go on a bit about his beloved beetles, frogs, diorites and things, but I spent fifteen years in Ceylon where nobody was interested in geology and natural history unless it had to do with growing high-grade tea. We both find things here which we have never seen before.'

Dora said she was much in the same position. In Thebes her husband spent most of his time at home in front of a drawing-board, planning alterations to old broken-down houses and buying building materials for his workmen. But, as she put it, 'I'm more interested in the sort of cement that holds people together, especially in a place like this. By buying and selling we can always go and live somewhere else. We've already had three places.'

'But what do you do when he's talking to his clients?' asked Katie.

'I know the people who live here permanently and I like to know what they really do. They seem to like us if only because we do some work for them when our builders are around, and I bring them odd things from the town that they can't buy locally. There are only about twenty families. In the 1940s there must have been a hundred or more.'

'Was the village occupied by the Germans?'

'Yes. They burnt the place down and the local people disappeared into those mountains you can see over there, the Vardoussia. Only one old house remained. Theo rebuilt it.'

'What do the villagers do in the winter?'

'They have a *maghazi*, a baker, the man who runs this place, a Civil Guard, two or three old Greeks who have come back here on a pension after years in America, a few odd-job people who act as caretakers for holiday homes such as ours, and a shepherd and his crippled son who look after almost everybody's sheep and goats. The old man knows them all by name, usually very rude names. He tries to make sure that the Vlachs don't drive in and steal their grazing by night. You know who the Vlachs are?'

I nodded and left it at that. Near two o'clock and we had miles to go before dusk.

'There's one thing we'd very much like to know,' I said. 'What do these old shepherds think about when they're up in the hills, alone, presumably for most of the year? We've seen a dozen or more, some of them two or three miles from the nearest village. When we've completely lost our bearings we've relied on them.'

Dora's face lit up. 'That's what I've wondered for a long time,' she said. 'Nobody in Athens seems interested, certainly not the anthropologists. Maybe one day I'll write a small thesis about it myself. What I'm much sure about is that they are people with great "sensitivities"; men all time in communication with nature. They can hear, they can see and even smell things a long way beyond what we can, like the sounds of small animals, even field mice, the talking to each other of birds, the marks they leave on the ground, the smell and the calls of jackals. They move about so that their sheep and goats don't eat everything down to the bare rocks. People here tell me that some of them chew the sticky stuff, the resin of wild cannabis and I think perhaps that makes them lose their sense of time except for the position of the sun. My theory is that the old shepherds have instincts that go back to people perhaps earlier than the Hellenes, those who worshipped Mother Earth.'

'And surely Artemis, Lady of the Wild Things?'

'Yes, that's her! Where did you come across her in Greece?'

'We felt that in spirit she wasn't very far away in the woods at the top of that enormous quarry on the way to Kaloscopi.'

'Surely the leader of the nymphs has never been honoured in your country?'

'Perhaps under a different name. Only fragments of our oral tradition survived long enough to be written down in the Roman alphabet by scholars such as Tacitus. Certainly not by Christians trying to lead people away from the old gods.'

I told her that we had found that shepherds sensed our presence when, looking at them through glasses, I felt almost certain that they couldn't see us. Dora thought their dogs knew that strangers were in the vicinity.

At that point Theo came back with a jug of wine and *mezedes*. It was somewhat embarrassing to learn that Dora assumed we would come back to their place, the one he had rebuilt. She expected that we would stay with them for a day or two. They'd so much to show us. We said . . .

Before we left I asked her about the wreck of the yellow car and whether they knew the story behind it. She looked surprised. They'd only arrived an hour ago. Surely, I suggested, they would know in the tavern? Theo went back to ask. While he was away Dora asked us where we proposed to stop for the night. Daphni, we told her – what sort of place was it? Could we get a bed there?

'A strange little place. Primitive,' she said, 'falling to pieces. We've only looked on what's left of the village from the road above, the one that comes up from the Gulf. It's not going to be easy if you stick to your dirt road. Don't wander down little tracks among trees; in the open you can see where you are going. You'll be climbing for most of the way. Are you *quite* sure you won't come back with us? On the top road we could run you there tomorrow in about half an hour. Why waste a whole afternoon over twelve kilometres?'

Theo came back smiling and shaking his head. The situation, as Dora explained it, was that the *papas* had seen the car and made enquiries. 'Priests', she said, 'get to know just about everything; it's their business and most of them are supposed to be politically neutral. They are like weather-vanes, they swing with the wind. As for this business of a political feud, it's nonsense. The kid was a bank robber. He and his brother were far too young to have known anything about the Civil War. The priest thinks the man in prison escaped to track down his brother who'd made off with most of the money.'

'But we were told the political story twice, the last time by a man we think was pretty close to the police.'

'Yes, and where do you suppose it all started?' She nodded towards the tavern. 'Probably in a place like that. You can't imagine what it's like in a small village where, because the oldsters haven't anything better to talk about, they sit around facing each other, each one knowing exactly where his companion used to stand. And their fathers before them. They are old soldiers, still fighting the war.'

'But why should the police get into the act on what looks like a political ticket?'

'Dead men often save the courts a lot of time and the police a lot of trouble. Isn't it called balancing the books? All Greeks are politicians at heart – and don't forget Greece was the birthplace of mythology.'

★   ★   ★

During walks through Europe and elsewhere I have often had the impression that I am a strolling player, privileged to look briefly into the acts, the minor dramas of others, pushing off before I get the hang of what it is all about.

As we struggled up one hill after another, climbing, always climbing until it seemed we were at the same altitude as some of the snow-capped peaks around us, we were obliged to stop, regain our breath and wonder what else had happened between Kaloscopi and Mavrolithari. Much of it seemed inconsistent if not improbable. Who had been shot? Was he the driver of the yellow car?

Dora certainly gave us comforting advice about that arduous trudge to Daphni: always keep high at junctions, she said. We kept high, ignoring what in the States are called 'tote roads for loggers', enticing tracks leading down to plantations of spruce and cypress with the regularity of corduroy. We were reminded forcefully of the Euclidean predilections of the British Forestry Commission.

In addition to the calls of cicadas, the belch of frogs and the sight of untidy old trees the odds in favour of encountering a concealed village are progressively doubled by increasing numbers of wayside shrines like birdcages on stilts, each with a burning wick in an oil-filled Pepsi-Cola bottle or a discarded jar still bearing a tattered label. The light flickers on a faded illustration of the Virgin with miniature bunches of still-fresh flowers at her feet, offered, one supposes, in the name of the recent dead.

Around a sharp bend in the track Daphni appeared as if, centuries ago, a once-prosperous hamlet had tumbled down a sunset-facing slope of abandoned terraces. No barking dogs, no blather of goats, no huckling of hens; nobody about except an old granny in black sitting on a doorstep with a Persian cat in her lap, knitting. She didn't look up when we greeted her. She was blind, but at the word 'taverna' she pointed limply to a huddle of buildings with a breakneck of stone steps to the upper floor.

I mounted them and knocked. The knocks echoed as if from an empty barn. Somebody called from the back. It wasn't easy to reach the back but whoever it was called again. A quadrangle of dilapidated buildings seemed to be clutching each other as if in shared grief. Impossible to guess their age. The hinges and scrolled metalwork of shutters on the ground floor had rusted and all but fallen down in wafers of speckled gold. Above them what had been windows in pairs were gaping holes, like eye-sockets in a row of skulls.

At the back stood a done-up building with a smack of Turkish-Greece about it, surely not much more than a century old, facing a wilderness of prickly grazing on an up-slope.

A young fellow, meaning fortyish, in jeans and jersey topped by a black beret, gave the impression of being brought back to life unexpectedly. He yawned prodigiously. In Greek Katie asked him if he could provide us with a small room and a bed for the night. At first he didn't seem at all keen on the prospect.

'*Mais c'est un mauvais moment.*' A few seconds' pause before he added, '*Alors! Peut-être je ferai des préparatifs.* You now have drink?' In an endearing mixture of French flavoured with English, 'Muzzi' (Mustapha) Androcles had everything to offer the hungry and thirsty if they were addicted largely to mutton stew and ouzo. It came out later that he was born in Cairo, before his parents came home to Lamia just before events in November 1973 when Greek army tanks and security forces crushed a non-violent demonstration at the Polytechnic in Athens. It was the Junta's mindless action over what later became a far more widely publicized eponym for self-styled leaders armed only with guns: the Hellenic equivalent of Tiananmen Square.

Muzzi led us upstairs into what was clearly the sleepy aftermath of a Bacchanal which had started the previous night. Two or three of a company of maybe seven or eight were leaning back, snoozing, mouths open, on wall benches behind tables bearing empty glasses. Others were playing a lethargic game of cards. Two, I seem to remember, were re-enacting the final goal of a national football match with their fingers dribbling a ball of screwed-up silver paper. Amiable disputes and much head-shaking about who had first tripped up somebody on the other side. Nobody, fortunately, seemed aware that strangers had arrived. Clearly a good time had been had by all.

Katie quietly asked our host where the toilet was and he pointed down into the yard where even half a dozen bantams appeared to be asleep. Time: seven o'clock. Would we eat with them in about an hour? Good! He put down two glasses, a quarter of ouzo and a jug of wine and went out. He came back with a bunch of keys, a brush and, I couldn't imagine why, an impressive felling axe.

Katie told me afterwards that the lavatory bowl was filled with dead leaves. She thought it best to scoop them out together with a lizard or two and a small salamander before she sat down, wondering, unimaginatively, what the company used.

From upstairs came the noise of a tremendous crash followed by much brushing before Muzzi returned to say our quarters were ready. On the way there he apologized for the state of the door, saying he couldn't find the right key. He had only been there for a week, looking after the place for his uncle and had been obliged to bust the lock open. A practical man.

The place looked makeshift but serviceable: a wire-framed bedstead and no linen, since we had told him we carried sleeping-bags. The permanently open windows were framed by swallows' nests and looked on to the courtyard.

Katie asked if we could have some water and he brought up two full canisters about half the size of dustbins.

After late supper in an almost empty bar we returned in the dark to find the floor wet. One canister was leaking incontinently. Only one thing to be done. To the consternation of the bantams I pitched the rest of the water out of the window. The birds squawked as if they'd been kicked, and flew off like misguided missiles. Maybe I saved their lives.

Towards midnight Katie nudged me and put her fingers across her lips. From below a most curious noise: muffled yelping as of puppies scrambling to get at their mother's teats, interspersed by a high-pitched whine. Foxes? Badgers? I couldn't make it out. I snapped on the small torch we keep at the ready. The beam lit up two reddish animals bigger than foxes, smaller than wolves. Jackals! One half-turned and bared its teeth before they both slipped away.

Though they are not among my familiars I had seen the Golden dogs (*Canis aureus*) on several occasions, especially in Khartoum after dark where packs emerge from the sewers and hunt down and eat anything edible by jackal standards.

I recall nothing else of that night, except that for hours on end swallows twitter in their sleep.

As crows fly in Evritani, the *nomos* we'd entered the previous night, we were about forty miles from Karpenissi, but we walked twice that distance in the four days it took us to get there. The first one, 17 May, opened with a dawn that wasn't so much rosy-fingered as riotous. The wind rose and cohorts of clouds were at odds with each other.

Far to the south the volcano-like peaks of the Vardoussia stood out as nipples against a ceiling of high cirrus, whilst from the down-slope to the north we saw puffs of low cumulus at intervals, like cannon smoke in a Victorian print of a battle-scene.

I never trust clouds moving in opposite directions in the mountains and when Katie asked what I thought we were in for I said rain with such conviction that I had to cheer her up by adding that unchanging weather is as dull as dining with a vegetarian.

In fact it didn't rain until we were almost within sight of Karpenissi and by then our only thoughts were upon reaching food and shelter before dusk.

We plodded along a wooded ridge at about 3,000 feet. Dora had told us that the down-slope marks the edge of the flood plain drained by the river Sperkios which flows due east from the Timfristos range above Karpenissi, then through Lamia to the Maliakos Gulf. The river is ten times older in the folklore of mythology than ever the Thames or the Tiber and the fertile plain is reputed to be the home of the river gods.

To get the hang of the ancestry of these gods we must accept what has been passed down from Homer and Hesiod. They sprang from the conjugation of Gaea or Ge, the personification of the earth, and Oceanus, the god of the waters which surrounded the earth. Dora could relate most of these improbabilities as easily as a child recalls much-loved fairy tales.

'Who believes in the nymphs nowadays?' I had asked Dora.

'More people than you think,' she said. 'Ask them. You'll be walking high above the Sperkios for several days. All the little streams you come to flow down to the parent river. The shepherds have their own names for them, although they're much alike. There's *Aspropotamus*, the white river or *Rematia*, the ravine, or the torrent of the old river, *Paleopotamus*. If they know of a spring or a secret supply of water they'll probably keep the name to themselves. When you were a boy didn't you have favourite places, somewhere where you found things that you thought only you knew about?'

Long after Amstel time we were still on that narrow peninsula with good timber on both sides and a ridge just ahead, at right angles to our track, but not a drop of water in sight for two travellers whose thirst matched that of Tantalus. Far from dropping rain, the high cirrus had disappeared but for no reason that could be accounted for a truly prodigious wind sprang up. At first I took it to be the Bora, that north wind that disrupted the Persian fleet at Salamis, an event which started a commemorative cult among the Athenians. But it was too warm. Distant landscapes shimmered in a heat-haze like a badly tuned TV picture. Unable to recall the name of the god of the south wind, I mentally composed a prayer to Zeus, Gatherer of Clouds, in the hope that he would take his rumbustious strays off somewhere else.

Could that prayer have been answered, obliquely? We rounded a slight bend where the wind seemed to be giving us a shove up our backsides instead of coming at us sideways as it had done earlier.

In earlier walks I have come up against several famous winds. The *ka-utcha* is known to the Athabascan red-men as the killer, the famine-bringer who drives the caribou south, right out of their territory. On the flood plains of the Nile you will meet the *haboob* and the *klamsin* so called because it blows for fifty days. Further south on the High Rewenzori I climbed up into the fury of the *masungu*, the one who beckons and cannot be gainsaid. In Europe I have been pushed backwards by the *sirocco*, and the *föhn* of the southern Alps which afflicts the temperamental, the Swiss say, with a particularly painful form of migraine. But all these were lateral winds coming from a known source. Never before had I experienced a wind that seemed to rise from the ground below.

It came from convection currents. Warm air is less dense than cold. We were trudging along a high causeway, and whatever the winds on the warm plains below were called they were rising to meet us in gusty squalls.

I had a premonition. Nothing paranormal. Just as a dog's nose twitches before he knows why, I sensed something ahead. Through a screen of trees on the far side of a sharp bend we looked down on a sorry collection of ancient buildings surrounded by cascades of musical water. How in the name of the blessed saints, not to mention the local gods and goddesses, the family Spirides and their few neighbours managed to survive in their shacks on stilts through the blast of winter is something we could scarcely imagine.

We had not only arrived there in the compassionate season of mid-May, but on a day of very special providence. From among the swaddlings of thick protective sheets of green canvas the men were unroping a large, metal, slightly rusted object about the size of the engine of a small car. Here indeed was the nearest they had ever been to *deus ex machina*, and their own machine too: an old electric generator.

Whether or not it was a communal cost-sharing enterprise for fuel we never discovered. What was certain from the centre of activity, a very small taverna-cum-*maghazi*, was that the fairy godmother was Aunt Eugenia, from what she called *Kairdiff* in South Wales. She appeared to be a relative of Kyria Koula, wife of the man of the house, and, temporarily at least, that kindly but stern-faced woman ran the place.

To us she spoke Welshified English with hesitancies and recourse to Greek words and gestures. Everyone else was addressed in rapid authoritative Greek. No questions about how or why we had got there. We were bidden to sit down. She extended her hand palm downwards and rapidly patted that invisible dog. Then she went on re-ordering the establishment, giving us time to look around. Their problem: the disposition of an old box-like television set in a fretted wooden frame which could never have been used and an equally ancient refrigerator, its enamelled door crazed and yellowed.

They tried to shove the fridge under the shelves of packets of biscuits and tins of chopped-up octopus, squid and sardines. Nothing else. Why not? We wondered what monopolist supplied the stuff, with its guaranteed shelf-life. We had run into his wares from Corfu to Cyprus and bought them only when there was nothing else. The fridge couldn't be accommodated without shifting the usual piles of boxes of detergents and disposable nappies. Result: impasse. Aunt Eugenia left the inert hardware to admiring neighbours and turned to us. Food? Anything they could offer, we said. Without a glance at the shelves she motioned us to the back of the house where from the top of a wood-fired stove she spooned out some tasty chicken with vegetables. This done she wished us good luck and went off somewhere else. We never saw her again.

Outside in the yard below the wind was giving a pretty fair imitation of a wind machine. The gusts had redoubled in strength, making conversation impossible with Katie who trudged close behind. We regained the ridge, striving to keep to the thickest avenues of sturdy pines. Without that intermittent shelter it would have been stupid to venture further.

As path-finder I tried to give the impression I had the whole affair under control, to memorize all our twists, turns and selected junctions so that we could, if necessary, retreat back to our friends awaiting almighty power from the generator. We certainly couldn't put our tent up on that tormented ridge, but I had the feeling that we might come across a loggers' hut or perhaps enough stacked timber to build a lean-to. As we were on the long axis of a formation that closely resembled a draughtsman's T-square I wondered what we should have to contend with on that high bare ridge due ahead.

Struggles against winds that come against you head on and hard can be overcome by leaning forward and lifting your feet up in the manner of a circus horse. For a mile or more this can be exhilarating, like walking in the fantasy of a dream or a space-fiction world without gravity, the essence of that fluid movement brought to theatrical perfection by Marcel Marceau.

This wind had no set pattern, no accustomed form. We were knocked about by an opponent who made up the rules as he swept towards us. An uppercut, but not a meaningful blow. A subtle feint. By the time we had counteracted one gust by leaning towards it a smart left from somewhere else all but knocked us over.

This was no nymph, no ward of the Mistress of the Wild Things. We were up against a malignant demon, protean in his different guises. With trepidation we approached the lateral ridge. Anti-climax. Far from climbing up on that local Table Mountain our wayward path slipped aside, down into an unseen ravine where on a road of sorts we were protected by cliffs of limestone hung about by garlands of red and white valerian. Within a quarter of a mile the wind gradually whimpered away until it became no more than the stertorous breathing of the sea heard from afar.

The ravine opened out into quiet and fertile country where, after our blustery bouts, we came to the conclusion that the story of Aeolus who, together with his six sons and six daughters, had tried to bottle up the four great winds was not a wholly improbable myth.

In Marmara, small rickety windmills clattering like plastic

toys profited that day from only light breezes. Goats with bloated udders were wandering among the new sprouts of vineyards. Nobody about except an angry middle-aged laundress who, pounding away at soiled clothes in a huge barrel of water with a paddle, was curiously abusive when we tried to ask her not only where the taverna was, but how to get into the village.

We walked through two narrow passageways only to find ourselves in the same cul-de-sac. We went back to the laundress where Katie repeated her questions in the kindest of voices and I resorted to sign-language by pulling a wry face, patting my parched lips and sawing my stomach in half. What she said we couldn't make out since she picked up her paddle again and whirled it round her head. I wonder which of us looked the most stupid?

On our second run we discovered that the village on that steep hillside was layered, with one long row of houses above another, three rows in all with a tavern and a shop in an isolated square. The four serious drinkers there were almost silent as if awaiting fatal news, but the landlord brought in the fellow from next door, an ironmonger and smith who spoke some English.

We drank Amstel and he ordered us *souvlaki* from the open-air stall outside. From the smith we learnt that the previous village, the one with the generator, was Paleohori, the old place, a name we encountered several times each week, and the streams around it were 'the Shining Ones', presumably more daughters of old Father Sperkios.

Further gossip was interrupted by a loud crash outside. A spirited donkey at the end of a trailing tether seemed wholly unable to stand on more than two legs at the same time. Called Pépé or Pipi, she had recently been shod and seemed to be trying to kick off her heavy shoes by plunging movements which brought sparks from the cobbled square. I tried to stand on the rope and was pulled off my feet to the amusement of a dozen or more people who had mysteriously appeared. The owner tried to throw a halter over her ears and they were last seen belting up the hillside.

Donkeys, in my view, have a hard time of it. They are beaten throughout their lives and at their death from exhaustion their skins are stretched across drums for celebrations and martial endeavour.

At the edge of dusk we settled beside a conversational stream, another tributary of the river below. If the citizenry of Marmara don't remember the white-haired couple who walked down and told them scarcely believable tales about where they had been, they will surely recall, we think, Pépé or Pipi who had the better of them all that afternoon.

The affairs of the butcher bird and the kind-hearted cop who misled us beyond measure began at half-past four in the morning when we could well have done with at least another hour or two of sleep. I woke up, as I so often did, at the sound of noises I couldn't make out. A bird, for sure, but what sort of bird? From somewhere only a few feet above our heads came a completely unmusical succession of broken, discordant sounds accompanied by a sustained high-pitched nasal whine like that of an indignant bumble-bee trapped in a matchbox.

Had an owl, I wondered, caught a huge stag beetle, or a magpie a field vole? Those are noises I have known since childhood, but this was unfamiliar, neither owls nor magpies. The awful racket continued for perhaps a quarter of an hour when, unable to ignore it further, I crept out into a clammy dawn.

An ashen grey and black creature rose like a sinister ghost from the topmost point of the bare branches of a stricken conifer. It hovered for several seconds like a kestrel in search of field mice before it gave a high-pitched yelp and floated off into the mist: the Great Grey shrike, largest of the European butcher birds, which from its watchful stance, sometimes maintained for half an hour or more, is precisely described by its scientific name, *Lanius excubitor*, the butcher's sentinel or watchman.

Although the bird had temporarily disappeared from sight I could still hear that high-pitched nasal whine, and traced it to a festoon of rusted barbed-wire on the spikes of which were impaled a seemingly dead grasshopper or two, a decapitated dormouse, a curiously blue bee and a large beetle, *Acanthocinus*, with antennae more than twice the length of its body. Both insects were moving feebly and squeaking, an unpleasant sight and sound even to an entomologist. The barbed-wire was the butcher bird's larder. Katie, clad only in her smalls, had finished paddling about in the stream and wanted to know what I thought about a breakfast of pilchards and potato crisps. I thought better not tell her about what was on the shrike's plate until we had finished our own. Before we were ready to pack up the sentinel bird flew back in a series of glides with extended wings and settled on a distant tree, where it behaved as noisily as before. We were hurrying. We were both tired and in need of re-creation.

At Amstel time we heard a church bell ringing at intervals somewhere down in the valley below, although there wasn't a tree to hide a building. Was it an omen? Up on high we were alone among the trees. I've known this from two long walks made years ago. It may have been an omen. I hold with De Quincey that not to be at least a little superstitious is to lack generosity of mind.

The ironmonger of Marmara had told us that some twelve kilometres beyond the fast stream, the one he called 'the noisy water', we should find ourselves at the foot of a steep track on the way to Nikolitsi where he recalled a small tavern. There he thought they would remember his name,

Gorgio, son of Otho, yes, like famous king of long time ago. His grandmother had made nine children. They all had famous names: Venizelos, Konstantine and Botsaris, after the liberty-fighter who had killed 'thousands of Turkish in time of your Lord Byron'. Gorgio's father 'thought it all much stupid. We were teached to work with our hands'. With an imaginary hammer and chisel he demonstrated how for many years his brother had worked in a marble quarry.

We walked to Nikolitsi with considerable pleasure on a carpet of Greek cowslips called *Elatior*, a rarity in Britain – but where on earth was the tavern? Two or three dilapidated buildings hadn't been used for years. Should we stick to our comfortable track or climb up to what looked like an old barn?

No need for decisions. Within minutes a Land Rover bounced down towards us with a smartly dressed policeman at the wheel. He left it outside what was presumably the local lock-up. He went inside, made a brief phone call and came out all smiles.

Problems? There were no problems. The tavern was the barn-like building above. He had just left it. How far? Why, we could see how far! Perhaps 200 metres. I pointed upwards. Could we reach the top of the hill from behind the tavern? He looked puzzled. Katie translated slowly. Why, yes! Easy! Through the trees. How far? On that point he was a shade uncertain. A kilometre, perhaps two or three. We should have given serious heed to two important words, *missos* (perhaps) and *ipano* (straight up).

With some reluctance the young fellow behind the bar put down his tabloid with its enormous headlines. He regretted he had no food to spare but agreed to put ice into our warm lager. On one point at least he offered some solace, and that was that as far as he knew the track at the back of the establishment joined a little road behind the top of the hill.

This wasn't true and what neither he nor the cop appeared to know was that after about a hundred yards the so-called track, a loggers' loop road, defeated by a wooded cliff, turned round and, as we discovered too late, came back to where we'd set off. That is, the track came back. We didn't. We soldiered on and, after a performance rarely seen outside a cage of gibbons in a zoo got to the top, tired out, sweating to our underpants and exasperated.

Carrying the worst part of thirty pounds, I climbed not one but several trees on a stretch of near vertical cliff by using arm- and foot-holds with the alacrity and circumspection of a thoughtful sloth. Trees which grow in precarious places endeavour to stabilize themselves by aerial roots and adventitious shoots at the points where the leader, the main branch emerges from the ground. These are the rungs of arboreal ladders, clumps of temporary foot support which enabled me to haul up our rucksacks and hang them on to something else higher up so that the step-by-step process could be repeated, *ad fatigationem.*

We kept up that ridiculous caper for over an hour through obstinacy, fortified by the misbelief that we should rejoin the track that didn't exist up there. Yet most bad things come to an end and we reached a hogback-like crest laudably bare on most of the down-slope but rather steep in places, where we were obliged to jogtrot, that staggering run you can't avoid when you are carrying something too heavy.

We sat down under a tree for a bite and a pot of tea. Our relief at getting there without more than a few scratches was tempered by the uneasy feeling that the track ahead meandered back to Nikolitsi. The prospect was no more pleasing to the right where the track seemed determined on swinging round in a south-easterly bearing, that is wholly in the wrong direction. I went to spy out the land.

It was damned hot on that winding track. What could lie

213

around the next corner? A lunarscape. Thin scrub. A few goats, some of them trying to climb up the ruins of trees. *The Waste Land*:

> . . . *where the sun beats,*
> *And the dead tree gives no shelter, the cricket no relief*
> *And the dry stone no sound of water.*

Behind a slight depression about half a mile to the north of the track I made for a spire of smoke as slender as a cypress. The Zeiss brought into focus the source – a modest fire at the centre of several angular tents, a few people, two or three trucks, and beyond a herd of sheep or goats on some tolerable grazing, perhaps the remains of somebody's crop.

Their dogs sensed me. They barked. Accompanied by a man with a slight limp they moved in my direction. I waited until they were quite near and then lifted up my arm in friendly greeting. What with the fire, the womenfolk and the goatherds in the background, the scene could have been the opening of the second act of *Il Trovatore* the one known best for the Anvil Chorus. '*Chi del gitano i giorno abbella?*'

Whether his days were ones of pleasure I shall never discover. It was a safe bet that they were not *gitani*, that is gypsies, a race with which the Vlachs are at odds in the manner of rival predators. The elderly fellow with his black cape and metal teeth was almost certainly on my side.

'Good day – *bunâ dzua*,' I began and shook his arm with enthusiasm. '*Eshti Vlachos?*'

He was for sure, and grinned, showing all his gold and silverware. He spoke rapidly. By frowning, touching my lips and holding an imaginary pea between my forefinger and thumb I sought to put across the fact that I knew about as much *Vlachos* as he *zburask Angliski*. As for being lost, I opened my arms limply. I looked up at the sky and slowly shuffled round in a circle. He understood. '*Dukesku,*' he said. '*Tsi loku?*' What village did we want?

'*Hori Platanos,*' I said.

More nods of comprehension. After pointing with his stick to an unusual hill to the north-west, he half crouched and peered deep down into a clump of daisies. There we should find a ravine and a torrent (ripple of fingers) and a *small* village (my gesture with the pea) and called as far as I could make out, 'Curious and curiouser.'

'*Graz,*' I said. '*Ashits*, yes. *Dukesku.*'

We embraced and in the best style of *opera buffa* yodelled, '*Adio, adio*' at intervals *da capo al fine*, until we were out of earshot.

What lay between Katie's shady nook and the Vlach's impression of a ravine and a noisy torrent is of no account except that we got there by turning off a track to the right which he had indicated by two fingers. Better by far his vigorous gestures than the cop's exuberant imagination.

But for two incidents we could have steered down that weird winding gorge in bath chairs without stopping. The first was an immense but harmless coiled snake like an outsize in Catherine wheels. Before it shimmered away Katie stopped, trembling slightly. She detests snakes of any kind, the outcome of her days as a young mother on Ceylon tea-plantations. She can't forget the day when the nanny allowed her first-born within arm's length of a family of baby cobras.

The second incident had to do with a mild argument about the name of the next village in Greek on a very old signpost. Katie decoded the letters aloud whilst I examined the map. '*Kappa, Omicron, Epsilon* . . .' she began.

'Curious and curiouser,' I said.

She looked up surprised. There are times when she underestimates my linguistic abilities.

Near the foot of the gorge two cataracts coalesced and crashed over a twenty-foot drop into a tree-shaded pool, the resort, if ever we saw one, of the naiades. Off came boots, pants and vests and we took to their sanctuary for ten minutes of sporty splashing. I rolled about in the deeps, floated on my back, duck-dived head down, and decided the water tasted somewhat sour. Magnesium perhaps. Knowing the effect on the bowels of that purgative stuff I treated it cautiously. Katie in the whirling froth of the shallows thought her skin felt somewhat soapy. Curious and curiouser.

Back on the bank, we dried on a small shared towel, lit the burner and ate something tinned flavoured with wild herbs. 'Tea tastes odd,' said Katie, firmly putting down half a mug full. 'Where did you draw the water?'

I nodded towards the shallows and, to confirm its clarity, I poured out about an eggcupful into a small transparent container. It looked a bit cloudy. 'Flocculent,' I said, loftily.

As I washed up the plates and cutlery I noticed that, after slowly whirling round and round, nearly all the foam eventually floated downstream but not all of it. In a backwater there was perhaps more foam than there should have been. Below that vortex the remains of an animal could just be made out, but only from its horns. I mentioned the matter to Katie, casually, a day or two later.

For two or three miles there was neither water to be seen anywhere nor a drop in our rolled-up plastic containers. My tongue felt as dry as a tram-driver's glove and Katie, salmon-pink about the arms and face, was perspiring profusely.

I heard a braying noise from afar and paused to ensure it wasn't a raucous crow or a malcontented goat. No – our old friend, a donkey, that audible emblem of a Greek village! As we had so often done before we tracked it down to a village in a hollow, the legacy of fugitive people. Perhaps something more subtle than the love-potion lay behind Titania's affection for that famous beast.

A half-cousin of the horse, the domesticated breed was uncommon in England until Gloriana came to the throne. Donkeys fascinated Darwin, and far from being stupid they have what a friend of mine who has kept a pair for years describes as quaint intelligence and strong affections. A Greek we met in Thebes who had for long been expatriated told us he almost cried for his native village when he saw one pulling a cart in Kansas City.

The tethered beast which beguiled us down to Curious and Curiouser deserved more than her two plump thistles with pricky leaves for a salad, and nibbled Katie's arm to have her ears pulled. To our dismay, as in Marmara, on our first foray up and down Main Street – perhaps a dozen unusually neat houses with fruit and vegetable gardens – the she-donkey appeared to be the only inhabitant, notwithstanding our uninhibited door-knocking and hallooing.

Had not the family Kyllini rushed down two flights of stone steps as if the upper floor were on fire at the first house we had come to on the way in, the one near the donkey, we might have helped ourselves from the hand-pumped well behind their gate, but it wasn't necessary. We were overwhelmed by irrepressible hospitality.

Our water-containers were filled to distension. In their large, comfortable living-room we were pushed, repeat pushed, into their best chairs by the affable mistress of the house, daughter of old, toothless and ever-smiling granny who on a chain next to her bosom fished out a small gold-framed photograph of her late departed in a military shako, class of 1940. He looked as if he were fairly old even then.

Madame reappeared with a pewter plate of goodies. Although far from hungry we selected two with calculated discrimination and even before I had swallowed mine she shoved another one, a bun dripping with honey, into my mouth. Never before had I been forcibly fed.

In came the master of the house, a young bearded fellow with a gentle face, who carried an earthenware pitcher of milk and a newly honed felling axe. We had heard him at it in the back garden. He bade me try its edge which I did with my forefinger, nodding and making out that I could shave with it. At this he went out and returned with a huge scythe over his shoulder, walking slowly, theatrically, as if the spectre of death.

This much tickled the whole family except granny who, not to be outdone, struggled to her feet and from among the relics and family likenesses on the mantelpiece under the crucifix took down a red-sealed glass bottle and shook the pebble-like contents vigorously. They were her gallstones, extracted, we were given to understand, about five years ago.

The master poured out the milk but only for us. An interesting drink, very slightly sugary and less cheesy than that of a cow. He watched me anxiously as I smacked my lips before going to the window and pointing out his donkey. I wanted to know the animal's name and ventured on *noma*. Puzzled looks. Katie – whom I'd introduced – pointed at the creature and said, '*Pos se léne?*' Laughter all round.

My turn to get into the act. 'Modestine?' I asked. 'Zoe? Poppaea?' At each suggestion they shouted, '*Ohi!*' Clearly they were building up to something. 'Delphine? Elena?' I shrugged, closed my eyes and raised my chin.

In a chorus they all shouted, '*Katerina!*'

The marvel is that we got away in just over an hour.

★   ★   ★

Under an atlas of stars that night we drank wine in the company of nightingales and cicadas. Rather sweet, distinctly alcoholic, Malvasia which Nico Kyllini had pressed upon us, saying it came from his native Crete.

In London about a year later I was ferreting through an anthology by Richard Stoneman for some elusive line about early travellers in Greece recommended to us by Our Man in Athens. In it I came across this intriguing paragraph from Robert Byron's *Europe in the Looking Glass* (London, 1926):

We ordered a bottle of syrupy brown wine named Malvasia, first manufactured at Monemvasia in Sparta. This wine, which we had also tasted at Ferrara, was the original Malmsey, exported to our notoriously drunken island, in which the Duke of Clarence, whose bones now hang in a glass case on the walls of the crypt of Tewkesbury Abbey, met his unfortunate end. It is a strange coincidence that not only did the wine of Malmsey have its birthplace in Greece but also the Dukedom of Clarence. One of the oldest titles of the English monarchy takes its name from a small town on the west coast of the Peloponnese . . . As the dinner progressed, enough Malmsey to have drowned a hundred Dukes of Clarence seemed to disappear. The small town is Kyllini, now called Glarentza.

If it's a true account, an extended record of travel on foot should reflect the changing moods of the narrator as surely as a cardiogram the movements of his heart. Of the two remaining days it took us to reach Karpenissi, where we expected to be up against different problems, in wild terrain we stumbled badly in the path-finding sense of the word. In brief, through misinformation which should have been double-checked at the start we failed to cross the capricious

River Sperkios at the nearest available bridge and were obliged to walk downstream and up again in an arduous loop of fifteen miles.

We were assured by an oil-merchant in Platanos that we could wade across the stream in a dozen or more places. All a matter of asking local fishermen where it could be done, he said and, as in the case of another local person, the cheerful cop at Nikolitsi, we took his word for it.

By lunchtime we were on the track to Pitsi which for those foolhardy enough to retread our trail for themselves lies at the very heart of the matter. In the tradition of young Lochinvar whose steed was the best, dust-polluted Pitsi should be renamed the Sperkios Leap.

Huge bulldozers were grubbing up cartloads of what looked like asbestos. White-faced and parched from the dust, we turned our backs on Pitsi and walked on. A dire decision. But, as we thought at the time, what did it matter? We could see an unexpectedly small stream which in places could have been jumped across.

An hour passed and then another, which brought us to Levkas and a mildly riotous wedding celebration in the village square. The groom and the bride went through ritual gestures of reluctance then were carried off, physically, on the shoulders of kinsfolk and may God bless their union. As for ourselves we needed solace beyond the drink so freely offered. A taxi-driver, a local man who volunteered to drive us anywhere we wanted to go, was authoritative, sympathetic but discouraging. He assured us that the stream below was the creamy-coloured Aspropotamus, a small tributary of the parent stream which looped north at the bridge eight kilometres below Pitsi of accursed memory. As for wading across the Sperkios, there had been storms over the Timfristos range and – as we should discover at the bridge far downstream – at no place was it less than about two metres deep in mid-current.

That sultry night – and it doesn't matter where it was – we saw only a few stars towards dawn. The next day we arrived in Karpenissi in torrential rain and wet to the skin.

Karpenissi

The last hundred yards of that unseemly baptism were watched with mild amusement by groups of students under the vast canopy of the Edelweiss, the leading *kafenio* in town. We scuttled towards it.

Karpenissi, pop. 5,000, is described in Michelin as 'majestically situated in a high alpine valley surrounded by snow-topped mountains and ski slopes'. The town itself, a higgledy-piggledy collection of busy little shops, bars and middle-grade hotels, commands the approach to the High Pindos and stands high in Greek estimation for its resounding victory in the days of Botsaris and Byron.

Katie promptly made for the women's quarters to tidy up, leaving me steaming gently in the company of two listless blondes from Sweden. They were there, they told me, to study silviculture at the local forestry college, the biggest in central Greece. I said I knew something about conifers and had once lectured at their home university. Their suggestion that we might meet again after supper became less enthusiastic, I felt, when I told them that my wife and I had just trudged in from a day-long scramble over Timfristos.

Without much enthusiasm I listened to the girls' gossip about college life and the lack of anything to do at night in a small market town. When Katie returned she enlisted the girls' help with what she calls the laundry lists, that is accommodation, shops, restaurants and the like.

We were joined by a young Swedish tutor, an expert on the classification of soils. This brought me back to what we were most in need of: large-scale maps. But I knew that it was as diplomatic to talk about them openly in Greece as about the sterling-rouble exchange rate in the centre of Moscow.

We learnt that for timber production and experimental purposes the college either owned or had been granted the right to use a large tract of forest, formerly a royal hunting-ground some ten or fifteen miles away. We should be wise not to go near it, our informant told us. It had been used as a large political prison and, for all he knew, the situation hadn't changed.

Between Karpenissi and that wholly unknown terrain, the range of Mount Olympos which harboured a military training-station and an airfield, our major obstacles were the Agrapha mountains ahead topped by a village and a rather mysterious place, Vlahogiania, the haunt of the Vlachs, some twenty-five miles east of Trikala.

According to the Royal Geographic Society in London there were neither rural roads nor marked tracks to either of these places; nor had we been allowed to take photo-copies of their detailed maps. Agrapha means the place without a name or more accurately 'unrecorded for taxation purposes', a toponymic dating from centuries of Turkish occupation when it was unsafe for a foreigner to venture up to a place five hours from the nearest road.

'How did you get here?' asked the tutor.

'Painfully,' I said. 'Mostly our own fault. Acting on local advice we clung to a spur of the Vardoussia although we all but got blown off the ridge above a place called Anatoli. Things went well until we reached Pitsi where, not knowing about the new by-pass, we took some fool's advice that we could wade across the Sperkios. Perhaps we could have if we'd been on stilts but the river was in full flood and it cost us a day via the bridge east of Vitoli where we spent the night. Then Timfristos. Have you any idea how many loops there are in that little road up to the village?

He shook his head.

'We counted about twenty before we discovered there were as many or more on the down-slope to Agios Nikolaos where I would have stopped in an old barn as it began to piss down but, fortunately I suppose, before we unpacked our gear I found that the hovel crawled with more scorpions than I've seen before.'

'What were your reactions?'

'As a naturalist they intrigued me, the first I'd ever seen in Europe. In Kenya I was once stung on my thumb. Damned painful. If I'd been alone in that hut at the foot of Timfristos I think I'd have stopped for at least long enough to have collected a specimen or two, but as things were Katie was tired and she doesn't much like the sight of the creatures, so off we trudged, here, through about twelve kilometres of suburban slums.'

He smiled sympathetically. 'I tell my class that if they want to learn about soils they should taste them for acidity and get the feel of them under their feet.'

'Soils, yes, but ferro-concrete, no. We're tackling no more roads.'

'Where are you off to next?'

'According to the little we were told by the tourist board in Athens it's the Agraphiotis river with a tributary that rises under the village of Agrapha.'

This came near to the truth. Shelley held that basic truth is imageless though Saint-Exupéry considered that truths as he saw them might clash without contradicting each other.

Katie reckoned it about time that we found an hotel. Benta, one of the students, said she knew the management of a comfortable one nearby and offered to take her there whilst I stayed with the tutor, who gave the impression he was solidly on our side. Katie said if she liked the place she'd book in, take a bath and change, and I could join her – but I hadn't to be too long, she added.

Speaking slowly as if he'd been turning over the ins and outs of the matter, Palinurus the Pilot, as I shall call him, repeated the word 'Agraphiotis'. 'For the last two or three days we've been hit by some very strong easterlies,' he said. 'Flash floods have cut the track in several places.'

'What do you suggest we do?'

'To start with, you'd be advised not to tell anyone you've been talking to me about getting through the hills. They don't encourage it around here. The Agraphiotis, I know, is the shortest route but at this time of the year when the snow is melting it's much the most difficult. Make for the Tavropos river at Megdova bridge and see what conditions are like when you get there. If the bridge hasn't been damaged, as it was last year, follow the little road to Hrisso and Agios Dimitrios. You're carrying a small tent? Good! Then you needn't rely on anyone for accommodation.

'If I were you I'd climb up to the ridge where there are few trees and not much scrub, even for goats. Nobody takes sheep up there any more, not even the Vlachs, but on the high tops there are small tracks, hundreds of them, which have been used for centuries. What's important is that something more than general directions should be clear in your mind. Watch your compass. The little village you must ask about is Marathos. It lies deep down in a valley to the north-west. You will have to climb out of it and then from the very top you will see Agrapha village.'

'And beyond that?'

'I don't know,' he said. 'I've never been there but you'll find many people over the age of sixty in this town who were taken up into the mountains as children during the

German Occupation. When they're not engaged in local feuds Greeks will go to extraordinary lengths to help each other. They say you can put your Greek in a jug, boil off a dozen barbarian strains and the essential Greekness will be left at the bottom, like salt evaporated from sea-water. Mind you, I wouldn't say as much for their flashy multi-millionaires nor the modern descendants of the old families like Tsaldaris and Venizelos who are always at each others' throats in what they call the *politikos kosmos.*

'Listen! If you really want to see the boss at the forestry school, phone his secretary at this number and ask for an appointment. If you get one, be careful what you say. He's more than somewhat devious. *Don't* say you've had a word with me.' He paused. 'Your wife, I see, is coming back with my friend Benta.'

He promptly switched the conversation to the growth rate and peculiarities of various kinds of pines (*Pinus*) which, as he pronounced the word to rhyme with Venus, sounded mildly Rabelaisian. He rose to go. 'I'll see you later,' he said. 'Remember! Be careful what you say at the school.'

I went back with Katie.

'It's called the Elvetia,' she said. 'A quiet sort of family place, also used by the leading traders in town as an unofficial Chamber of Commerce. I think we've struck gold. There's half a dozen of them in there now. They couldn't be more friendly. One of them called George – can't remember his other name – is a warm-hearted person, a tailor and draper. Take your rucksack up to our room and change that filthy shirt. Come down as soon as you can, as George has got something he strongly recommends for my feet. I'll tell you about it later. There's a lot of goodwill in this place.'

George Papadopoulos, a name about as common in Greece as Paddy Doyle in Dublin and Dai Jones in South Wales, offered me a coffee and, turning to his friends, merely said, 'This is Mister John, Madame's husband.' No formalities. A short man with spectacles and a moustache, he looked the very essence of ordinariness, but he gave us one of our two keys to Karpenissi.

'So this is your first visit here?'

'Yes, but I heard about it before we left London.'

'Really! What are we famous for?'

'Marcos Botsaris,' I said.

Delighted looks all round. The master tailor smiled. 'His statue is in the market place. Tell me more when you come to the shop tomorrow. Madame has my card.' He shook hands with us and the company filed out.

Katie looked at me. 'Crafty husband,' she said. 'What do you know about Botsaris?'

'Quite a lot,' I said. Perhaps as much as he does. 'I've done my homework.'

'Uncharitable thought: you only spent five minutes with him. His daughter is studying history and English. He was in Australia for fifteen years and went to night school to learn the language. The old man with him, the one with the grizzled beard, is a pharmacist, and the wife of the one with the bad scar is a hairdresser. George has given us the address of two restaurants where he says we have only to mention his name.'

We ate that evening in the place next door, underground and as cool as a church crypt, and pooled what we'd been able to find out about the forestry school.

Katie's theory was that the student, Benta, was very fond of and might even be the mistress of the temporary director.

'That complicates things,' I suggested. 'The lecturer's also very fond of Benta and I've given him my card to pass on to a secretary with a view to meeting this man. I'm going to phone tomorrow. I wonder if by "secretary" he really

meant Benta? Hope you didn't tell her I write for a living:
that won't go down well with civil servants.'

We saw George Papadopoulos at his best in the morning
when, from behind metre-ruled counters backed by bolts
of cloth and made-up suits he could lay his hands on shirts,
chemises, fine fabrics and fents for two or three customers
at the same time; a man, one had the impression, fully in
charge of an environment of his own making. The picture
of all-round competence was enlarged considerably that
night when we, guests in a house as well organized as his
workplace, saw him go down into the wine-cellar to milk
an affectionate nanny goat.

By that time we felt that the events of the day were running
in our favour. The soles of Katie's feet were still painful but
Grizzlebeard, an apothecary of the old school, could find no
evidence of sepsis and agreed with George that, under layers
of lint and gauze, a light touch of pure olive oil, the best in
Evritania, would do more for her abraded skin than dabbling
about with antibiotics – although we might carry some as a
form of insurance. He and George also agreed that cotton
socks were better for her feet than the woollen ones of the
type I had clung to since childhood.

The man at the school put me through to an extension
number where somebody, certainly not Benta, read from
what seemed a prepared statement. It said that the acting
director hoped to be able to speak to the distinguished
Englishman at half-past eleven the next morning. Yes pliss?
Unsure about that qualification I asked if I could visit him
at any time that day.

A three-second pause before the message was repeated as
if on an 'Ansaphone'. Perhaps it was. 'Thank you,' I said.

'Yes pliss. Yes pliss, *ne parakalo, efharisto. Yiasas,*' adding, 'Cheerio,' on behalf of all distinguished Englishmen.

I put the call through from a *periptero*, one of those social lighthouses on street corners for the sale of anything from newspapers, magazines and stamps down to chocolate, soft drinks, toothpaste and diarrhoea pills. To discourage their use as a public library the daily papers profusely displayed outside are hung up latitudinally, but to no avail. The locals queue up to scan them at risk of ricking their necks.

The one we used regularly was run by another adopted Chicagoan who, whenever we appeared, even on the opposite side of the street, popped his head out of the dark recess and bawled, 'Hiya, folks! What's cookin'?' This together with our association with Grizzlebeard and Scarface who ran a sophisticated wine and pastry shop, and above all with George the tailor made us feel as if we'd been granted honorary citizenship. But there were hermetic undertones to this sociability. Only the affluent traders joined in with a sprinkling of lawyers and agents in a subterranean resort of their own. The group Katie introduced me to in a back room of the Elvetia would no more mix with the students and travellers in the Edelweiss, where we had met Benta and Palinurus, than they would be seen among the alcoholics at tables inside and outside two or three taverns almost next door to each other.

My regard for trees dates from childhood when I escaped to a lair among the branches of an old lime in our garden in Leeds. Long afterwards, with my younger brother Joe, an historian with a home in the Forest of Dean, I was threatened with libel when I wrote about some of Britain's arboreal slums. As a professional critic I visited government forestry stations in several countries but never one more depressing in appearance nor unhelpful on the part of the management than that place on the road into the Greek mountains.

The acting director and his secretary had gone out for the day and nobody knew where. Could they find out who was in charge of the place? Apparently not since they shunted me into a back room until, fed up with being ignored, I walked out and looked round on my own. Next to nobody about, certainly nobody who knew English until, accidentally, I walked into the library to find Palinurus the Pilot at work on a pile of examination papers. He looked up, surprised.

'Why did you come today? He's gone down to Athens. I could have told you that.'

'He invited me to be here at half-past eleven. At least the person I took to be his secretary did.'

'And what did she say?'

'She didn't say anything except repeat what sounded like a dictated message. I thought she didn't know much English and didn't understand my suggestion.'

'Yes, that's always useful when you're faced with an awkward question.' He drummed with his fingers and then picked up the phone and spoke to someone whom from the tone of his voice I took to be a colleague.

He put the phone down and sighed. 'I was going to suggest you came round tomorrow but a friend of mine here says the old bastard has left word that he may be away tomorrow as well. I don't believe him because he sometimes lies when it would be in his own interest to tell the truth. Chronic deception is a progressive disorder. Well, my friend, I'm afraid you've been swept off. No! That's not good English. I mean brushed off. Stood up. Tell me, what did you *really* want to see him about?'

'I wanted to look at your maps. Ours are almost useless.'

He lifted up both arms and then pointed to a cabinet of long narrow shelves. 'But they're all here. Why on earth didn't you ask me?'

'I didn't know who you were. We've been brushed off

so many times by Greek officials I thought I'd try an oblique approach, that of forestry.'

'*He's* not a bloody forester, he's a small-time politician. That's our problem or, rather, the problem of the Greek forestry service. The elections are coming up. Do you suppose that even PASOK dares risk losing votes by reducing subsidies to those who scrape a living by keeping uncontrolled sheep and goats, the foresters' worst enemies? Now, what can I show you? I've got to be away in about half an hour. More politics. I'm trying to brief a man who I hope will get the top job here, a Greek who was trained at your place at Rothamsted. But what does it mean to me? By then I hope to be back in Stockholm.'

The maps were 1:50,000 which I took to be two centimetres to the kilometre. They showed alleged water-courses and springs dampened or dried up long ago. They were old maps surveyed by the UK Ministry of Defence in 1972. Under the supervision of the Pilot I made copious notes and a quick breakdown of the Greek soil situation based on the work of one of his fellow countrymen. Palinurus suggested we should take a drink together that night. I said he'd already played his part as the Button-moulder. He laughed. 'No,' he said, 'I have no casting ladle. This is the market-place of the Balkans, not Scandinavia.'

Between half-past one and five o'clock Karpenissi closes up like a bed of oysters at low tide. The resting time, the Hellenic siesta. Shutters have clattered down, their owners resting on their verandas at home. Watchdogs sleep in the shade. An old tom-cat with frayed ears, too tired seriously to stalk its favourite playthings, bright splotched butterflies on the pots of flowers, watched them flicker from one nectary to another. The tip of his tail still twitched. No predator is ever really asleep, and his back feet opened and closed like a parrot's claws when it's washing. His toothy jaws opened and closed in a soundless miaou.

All this I saw when, leaving Katie asleep at the Evetia, I made my way up the street, past the apothecary's place and the hairdresser's shop to an uncompromising statue of Marcos Botsaris which smacked of official Russian portraiture in the days of Stalin.

Marcos Botsaris was a Vlach. We had learnt this from Nacu Zdru, on that day when the *Flying Tortoise* was smashed to pieces. He led the Greek Resistance forces against the Turks during one of their attacks on Missolonghi. 'Allah! Allah!' they shouted as they rushed forward and planted ladders to climb on the trenches, but the Greeks' musket-shots and sabre-strokes made them fall 'as thick as frogs'. The town with its low defence wall finally fell to the Turks. Ibrahim Pasha, who led the victorious army, boasted that his men collected 3,000 heads, and that ten barrels of salted human ears were sent to Constantinople for the Sultan's delectation.

The sequel to that story was told to me by Loula, the attractive teenage daughter of our friend, George the town tailor. She said Botsaris escaped and that when Byron arrived in Greece in 1823 he brought a letter given to him in London by Ignatius, the Orthodox bishop, with the request that it should be handed to Botsaris. Presumably it commended Byron's intelligence, his organizing abilities, his wealth and European reputation for backing the Greek struggle for independence. Unsure of the whereabout of Botsaris, Byron, then in Cephalonia, sent it by messenger to Missolonghi, adding a note about how much he yearned to meet the famous fighter. But Botsaris had left when the messenger arrived.

How he managed to trace him to Karpenissi, 'that Khyber Pass of the Pindos' doesn't seem to be known but he did receive the letter and was 'much flattered by the commendations of the champion of revolt'. He had much on his mind. The Greeks were disunited. Botsaris had been through the grinding mill of oppression. He was born at Suli in Albania, and his father Kitzaris had been murdered by that suave, enormously rich puppet-master, Ali Pasha who had confided to a concubine with a good memory that he could double-cross the Devil.

This Botsaris knew. How best then to double-cross a double-crosser? He joined the hugely patriotic Greek society, the Hetairia Philike. Together with other Suliots he made common cause with Ali against the Ottomans and with the instincts of a good aggressive general sensed strong support around Karpenissi. Under his leadership a mere 300 Suliots won an outstanding victory against more than ten times that number of Albanians paid with Turkish gold. But Botsaris died in the battle on 9 August 1823. Among the great ifs of history is what might have been achieved had he and Byron met earlier, when Byron was bouncing in bed with the Countess Teresa Guiccioli and Botsaris complaining about the inadequate earthworks of Missolonghi.

The pop-up man in the *periptero* took some time to tell me a mildly obscene story I'd heard years ago, before he confided that my 'Swedish friend' was in a little place on the opposite side of the street. Palinurus and I had a few drinks there. 'It seems he's just had a helluva row with Benta,' I told Katie who, kneeling on the bedroom floor, was examining the seams and buttons of our jackets and pants with the zealotry of an old-clothes dealer. We intended to pull out early the next day.

'We'd been talking about all sorts of matters from Botsaris to wolves and bears before I happened to ask, perhaps incautiously, how Benta was. He didn't answer for a moment or two and then said he'd never in his life been closer to smacking a woman's face, hard. Apparently about an hour after I'd left the forestry school the ambitious bastard, as he called him, came back in one of their Land Rovers. Benta got out first. Far from going down to Athens they'd been out for an afternoon spin to where, with any luck, we'll be tomorrow – Megdova bridge over the river Tavropos which, incidentally, he thinks has been poisoned.'

'And then what?'

'He first asked Benta why she hadn't been about her work and then, when she waffled, whether she thought being screwed by the boss might advance her diploma for forestry. I'm compressing this, of course, but he was rather excited. You can imagine the confrontation.'

'Has Palinurus spoken to the boss?'

'Yes, he told him he thought it unwise to ignore an appointment with a man who might have got him a job in England! Perhaps, unintentionally, I've bust up a beautiful romance, but if so Palinurus doesn't hold it against me. He's convinced Benta's a go-getter who could go a long way with a man in the same league.'

'What's this about bears and wolves?'

'Bears, to quote him, are "very rare except in bad weather on the Albanian border". He heard there used to be one near Arvanitovlach, now Kedrona – I've got the details on the recorder. It's a village in Macedonia where Nacu Zdru comes from. The old creature turned up regularly in winter and the villagers loved it. They left their garbage outside at night. Then some Austrian arrived with a high-speed rifle and shot it. I wonder if it could be our friend on the train, the man who got on in Venice? Palinurus says he was lucky they didn't shoot him. He got out quick.

'He doesn't think wolves are particularly rare but natives – who get a bounty for knocking them off – exaggerate their numbers. He thinks it should be paid only if they can produce the whole corpse. He says if we ever get into a claimant's territory we should try to examine so-called wolf-kills to see if the bodies are badly torn or were born dead. Wolves kill lambs by seizing the belly flesh or the hams; dogs that go wild grab the ears. And wolf and dog tracks are quite different. Wolves' hind legs normally swing in the same line as their forefeet: as he puts it, "They single foot like foxes do." But he doesn't know anyone else in his Department who cares a damn about them apart from the opportunity they afford for a few days out in the mountains.'

The Place Without a Name

To master what mileage we could before the sky became a burning-glass we turned our backs on Karpenissi at cock crow. On a gritty road I switched to loose thoughts on what the cocks were crowing about. If the theory is valid that intelligence among animals, including birds and man, can be correlated with brain size compared with body weight, the so-called galliform birds which include turkeys, pheasants and domestic poultry are a nut-brained lot but likable in eccentric manners and edibility.

We've often said, Katie and I, that if ever we get that place in the Howardian Hills we'll have a dog or two and a flock of free-ranging fowls, preferably bantams, but they must be persuaded to spend the early hours out of earshot of our bedroom.

At some 4,000 feet that morning the cries of the Karpenissi flocks became fainter, but from isolated holdings around us the soloists seemed to be in intermittent touch with rivals far away.

One outstanding Caruso among the cockerels, lording it about among his drab harem on a mound of garbage, selected a vantage point, shook his blood-red comb and golden hackles and, after some throat-clearing, vented a slightly cracked top C. Then, the effort over, he appeared to be listening. Back came a call and then another. The repetitions were so marked in their phrasing that they might have been echoes. But were they? We heard several more. Could it be that the dialects of cockdom were being thrown across the length and breadth of Evritania? Perhaps even further, to where there are different accents in Phokis and Thessaly?

I was reminded that many years ago my friend, the late Alan Civil that superb horn-player, told me that he and his family, also professional players, were on holiday in Switzerland where, on some platform, a few native tourist-trappers got up in feathered hats and lederhosen were demonstrating their virtuosity with one of those immense alpenhorns used originally, it is said, to summon cattle for feeding. They offered a small prize to anyone who could produce a coherent sound on the instrument. Its echo, they said, could be heard from many miles away.

From the curiously regular time-intervals and his knowledge of acoustics, Alan felt reasonably certain they were in league with players in a distant valley on a strictly timed basis. Seconds before the crucial blow he managed to delay the performance on a technicality, to the point where the echo was heard first. To the delight of a small crowd, Alan's daughter, their youngest, played the elements of a popular tune in harmonics which is all these musical dinosaurs are capable of.

Things seemed to be going far too well for complacency. The corner we cut off diagonally gained us an unexpected bonus in terms of altitude. To the tune of 'Old Macdonald had a Farm' we versified extempore farewells to the peaks and ski slopes of old Timfristos which, seen far away to the east, looked contemptible. We advanced, cautiously, *allentamento*. Rough country ahead from which no cocks crew.

Shortly before midday we were within a few hundred yards of two shacks surrounded by pubic-hair-like bushes on the crest of an almost wholly bare mound. Not a tree in sight. A situation to be dealt with, *presto*. We were hot, tired and thirsty. The first shack stood under a palisade of scaffolding, the hallmark of a Greek lodging-house on the way up. An old man whom we took to be a roadsweeper was still sweeping up the same patch he had been when we first saw him ten minutes earlier. There seemed to be no reason for this: the patch appeared no different from what we'd been walking on since we'd trudged out of the aromatic conifers. Neither gruff nor affable, this ill-dressed fellow would have looked better with a shave the previous week. Ritual greetings were reciprocated. Then my standard follow-up in hilly country: rarely, I said, mendaciously, had I seen a finer view. This pleased him hugely. He nodded, vigorously. But where, I asked, smacking my lips, could we get a drop of water?

He looked surprised, and pointed authoritatively at the shack almost next door which could be charitably described as a tavern of sorts. Unqualified thanks on our side. We waved farewells and left him to his rhythmic brushwork.

The door was locked. After repeated bangs a wholesome-looking young girl appeared with a very small suckling noisily engaged in finishing its lunch.

Food? Yes but *ligos*, only a little until her good cousin arrived. As for drink, they had plenty. She waved towards four or five bottles and the refrigerator.

A flashy car pulled up outside. The driver, as vulgarly dressed as the flags and stickers on his vehicle, immediately began to shout at the nondescript sweeper-up who shouted back and shook his brush in mock-aggression. They were obviously acquainted, but on what terms? Difficult to tell among argumentative Greeks. The driver strode in laughing, pausing only to shout something over his shoulder.

We learnt that all three were related. The newcomer held the honoured rank of godfather (*koumbaros*) to the baby which he squeezed, clumsily, until it cried. No matter: it would be rich one day he told us, twice within five minutes. He owned property locally and abroad. He had recently returned from South Africa where he paid niggers to work for him for gardammed next to nothing. Different from the five years in Arkansas where they had gotten uppity. Did we know Hollywood? Great place! His boasted close association with Tom Mix and Marilyn Monroe made it clear that we were dealing with a highly imaginative traveller.

Before the sweeper-up, his cousin, joined us and he modified his extravagances, we learnt 'that the poor bastard's chief fault was that he'd always worked for someone else'. That way he wouldn't get nowhere. Now he was working for *him*, and he smacked his chest. He owned the house in embryo, the bar and another one in Athens.

'But what's he sweeping up for?' I asked.

'Waiting for a load of sand and lime. He's been waiting for days. He's got a concrete-mixer at the back. All he's done is oil it. That's what I'm here for, just to get him off his ass. Some guys are coming up here tomorrow and I want two floors on that joint by the fall.'

We ate there. We ought to have stayed there for at least another hour or two but in trying to bang the table he shared with the compulsive sweeper-up, the friend of Tom Mix nearly fell over. He had already drunk too much. We walked out into the ferocious heat.

A bad afternoon, that. The road just beyond the tavern dipped sharply, not in a series of loops but in one downward plunge which we could follow with our eyes until it disappeared into the haze. We carried, we thought, all we required: salt tablets and a litre of water that sploshed about in my pack with an annoying *ploonk ploonk plop* in time with our walking. With Katie in front to set the pace we trudged along, some twenty-five yards apart.

Since there was nothing of interest to look at – scrub vegetation with next to no bird life – I couldn't take my mind off that diabolical heat. I tried to recall what I had done in the deserts of North Kenya when even my almost nude native Turkana were obliged to wear plaited crowns and epaulettes of palm leaves. As for diversion, there came back the memory of when, for want of something better to do, I had tried to work out the time of the day from the length of my shadow but had become irritated because I couldn't cope with simple geometry.

At nine o'clock in the morning my shadow was almost exactly equal to my own height. At ten o'clock it was a little longer than half my height, and at precisely midday – within two degrees of the equator – I had no visible shadow unless I stood with my legs apart or jumped into the air. Mezek, my young cook and personal servant who had previously been employed there by Wilfred Thesiger, watched these antics with ill-concealed amusement. Why had I felt in better trim then than now? Simple answer: I was younger, fitter and carrying only a 30.06 on a sling.

We trudged on: *ploonk ploonk plop.*

We were suffering from hyperthermia, which is basically the release of nitrogen into the blood tissues. I had learnt this before I left for Lake Rudolf from Peter Preston, fellow clubman and former head of a RN research establishment at Portsmouth. He had been in charge of affairs in Malta when word came through that a team of Japs had bought an oil-diving concession in deep water off the coast of Libya. Wanted immediately were gear and instructions about how to treat the 'bends', their local consul said. A caisson and cylinders of compressed air were shipped off at once. They were handled incompetently.

When word came through, weeks later, that two men had died in the chamber, the British team in Malta assumed that the divers had been treated too late. At news of yet another death soon afterwards, an expert flew to Bizerta. His radio report was notably brief, Navy-style. He glanced at the blood-red corpse. He felt the cylinders. They were hot. They had been left uncovered in the sun. The victims had been boiled to death.

This incident is on medical record. Others are of questionable verity. When Charles Sturt, the British explorer took one of the first parties of white men into a desert of South Australia in the summer of 1845, he reported it so hot that the screws on their wooden boxes fell out, their hair stopped growing, and one full but badly stoppered barrel of water, hauled on a cart by Aborigines, was reduced to a few pints in twelve hours. Except for one incident in yet another filthy hut we had nothing to match this, but we felt downright uncomfortable and occasionally dizzy.

The going was downhill. No shade from either rocks or trees. No signposts. Because we didn't know the distance to the next hamlet we rationed our water. The friend of Tom Mix had told us that the river was about ten kilometres away, a gross understatement. We had already been on our feet for several hours.

From a typically curt statement by the late Humphrey Bogart ('You'll fry') when he predicted that a girlfriend of his would wind up on the hot seat for murder, we still refer to that hovel as 'Bogy's place'.

About the size and condition of an abandoned bus shelter, the floor fouled with droppings from goats, shepherds and recent travellers. With an armful of twigs still called broom we swept up enough space to put down our rucksacks, and leaned up against them. Katie lit the butane stove to make tea with the rest of our water whilst I fumbled in an outside pocket of my pack into which I'd incautiously dropped two pens. My fingers came out bright blue. The biros had blown their balls out.

Salvation ahead. A mile or two below that sordid shelter we saw a rich pasture refreshed by a stream that wove in and out of the shade of trees and a cliff of soft grey dolorite. Small cataracts talked in a variety of tongues. An ideal caravanserai, we thought. *Carpe diem*. Should we call it a day? Had there been a single tin or packet in our meagre stores which we didn't dislike deeply we should have stopped there. Outcome: compromise. Katie bathed whilst I explored the stream. An hour later we ambled down through avenues of acacias, planes, and pink-flowered *Cercis* to Megdova bridge which spans the river Tavropos.

A friendly place. A lotus land. We were neither ignored nor interrogated. Women nodded and smiled. Their menfolk outside taverns stroked their worry beads. We settled for a camp-site that couldn't be seen from the road; a comfortable corner on a carpet of pine needles in the shadow of a ruined chapel.

The evening was marked by two incidents, one of them heart-touching in its simplicity and the other downright macabre. An old man who looked as though he were merely out for his evening stroll among the riverside willows walked towards us. In one hand he grasped a tall stick with a carved head of the kind used by shepherds, and in the other two long-stemmed roses. We greeted him and he replied cordially. He walked round our zipped-open tent with mild curiosity. He didn't peer into anything. He paused for a moment before handing us each a rose, the first, almost ceremonially, for Katie.

She talked to him for a few moments – where did the road lead to? How far was the next village? Apart from his sociability it seemed clear that he'd come to tell us that the river water wasn't drinkable. He pointed towards it, moistened his lips and shook his head. We showed him our container, filled at the village tap. 'May your night be a good one,' he said, and walked back as sedately as he arrived.

Our first sight of the Tavropos had been from the bridge, a metal one surely modernized from a military construction, which forced the water into the narrows where it ran fast and deep flecked by streaks of yellowish foam, the detritus of the recent floods. We walked back along it and struck upstream where, as we neared our camp-site, we heard the clamour of sea-birds as on an urban garbage dump or in the wake of a harbour-bound fishing boat. That evening I made for where the sound seemed to be coming from.

A fearful sight. During the spring floods the Tavropos had carved out a basin about a hundred yards in diameter, marked by bone-white islands and substantial holdings of more trees and scrub. Among them dribbled streamlets which coalesced in deeper channels lower down.

At my appearance a vortex of scavenging birds took to the air screaming and croaking – crows, gulls, fork-tailed kites, ospreys and a few buzzards, some of them carrying the whole bodies of fish. The islets were tenanted by rats and other animals impossible to identify in the fading light, possibly catfish which had come ashore for the stranded spoil.

If anybody knew what had really happened to the river they weren't prepared to say much in the adjacent hamlet of Parkio, where in the tavern restaurant we ate that night. Katie left early with a friendly local woman, leaving me to gossip with a bus driver who spoke English. No, he wasn't a local, he said. His mate would pick him up there in the morning. Unable to tell him anything about the fate of Spurs and the Arsenal, I did rather better on the amenities of Coventry where his youngest brother drove a truck. I asked him bluntly what had happened to the river.

'Poison,' he said, cryptically. 'A lot of it.'

'Pesticides?'

As he didn't understand the word I whirled my finger around and buzzed like a helicopter. He knew what I was getting at.

No, it wasn't that. The police had been talking to a man in a village not far away.

'What was the poison?' I asked. He shook his head.

Did the local people know?

If so, he said, quietly, they wouldn't say anything.

The full moon had about it the colour of a corpse. The jagged silhouette of the chapel looked sinister, but before we turned in I noticed that we were almost surrounded by an old ditch in which grew those handsome plants of our native hedgerows, the mulleins, with their woolly foliage and butter-yellow flowers which 'sheweth like to a wax candle or taper cunningly wrought'.* In both Britain and abroad the folk names of these plants range from Our Virgin's Candle to Snakebane. 'If a man beareth with him just one twig of the powerful wort he will not be strucke with any awe of wilde beaste or the horned one.' Hermes is reputed to have given mullein to Odysseus before he encountered Circe, and after that he 'dreaded none of her evil works'.

During the night, turning uneasily at the shriek of a bird, I discovered that the mullein, also known as Velvet Dock, wasn't proof against marauding ants from the pine needles under our sleeping-bags, which we were using as a mattress.

When the first light made the downy mulleins glow like incandescent fire we were ready for the road, but abandoned

* *Henry Lyte.*

it for a serpentine track which we found ran alongside the
river where:

> . . . *the very deep did rot, O Christ*
> *That ever this should be!*
> *Yea, slimy things did crawl* . . .*

Upon that slimy lea. We never discovered how or why the
river had been poisoned.

We knew that a famous stream close to our moorland
cottage had been virtually sterilized when a local farmer
flushed the remains of half a gallon of DDT into his lavatory.
Eels in their thousands were seen trying to climb out of the
water.

The new village of Viniani is indistinguishable from any
other recently built out of concrete blocks, except for a sadly
impressive civil war memorial and a locked-up *periptero*, the
paper shop which must have been sheer hell between ten
in the morning and five in the evening.

Some jolly, well-dressed schoolchildren were waiting for
the bus. They tried out their English homework on us. We
said we loved them all, and waved as they boarded.
We trudged on towards Agrapha, uphill nearly the whole
way.

That grim monument in the square at Viniani, like others,
scores of them throughout the length of the country, is a
testament to the Greeks' predilection for slaughtering each
other. The repetitions of surnames in groups on those
memorials showed that whole families – particularly the
youngsters – must have been wiped out within a bracket of
two or three years. It's possible that the slaughter itself may
not have been quite so dreadful as the wholesale and

* '*The Rime of the Ancient Mariner*', S. T. Coleridge.

nationwide distortion of values for which such wars are directly responsible. I am borrowing freely from *The Flight of Ikaros* by the late Kevin Andrews* who, as a much travelled archaeologist, fell in love with the country and became a naturalized Greek citizen.

He was there ostensibly to study medieval fortresses but his life changed when he went walkabout and became the godfather of the young, the charming and violent Andoni Kostandi from the village of Agrapha, who had forgotten how many people he had killed and when bored and ill in hospital, as he so often was, admitted to his *koumbaros* that he yearned to go out and kill someone else. This is how the author described him to a fisherman he met in Kalamata:

As we sat over our coffee I said, 'One thing I have learned on my travels recently is that very few people have any inner life at all. I am thinking of a friend of mine – the most completely likeable person I have ever met. As I know him, he's good through and through. Apart from terrific courage, he's the best husband and the kindest father: a person who hates to cause embarrassment or unhappiness or even disappointment to anyone he's fond of, yet he has slaughtered so many people that he's lost count of the number. I even hesitate to say how many. Anyhow the number doesn't matter. And he's not even anxious.'

'How do you know?'
'Because he's proud of it!'
'How do you know?'
'Because he has no other standard.'
'He won't always be proud of it.'
'And how do you know?' I asked.
'Because you can't always stay with the outer forms

* *Penguin Travel Library, 1984.*

246

of things – things like honour, power, revenge. Some day he'll come to a crossroad, a moment of crisis, of judgement. Everyone meets it sooner or later. And then he won't be able to escape himself. That's when his life may begin.'

At Amstel time in yet another village without a name we leaned back and admired the view, which might have been Bournemouth before Branksome Chine was doomed to popularity. The mountains were out of sight. Before we tackled them we made a number of resolutions. First, no more mad-dog stuff under the midday sun unless trees were as plentiful as in that nicely disordered grove of Oriental spruce. This giant is not as exotic as its name sounds. An admirable tree, a native of the Caucasian mountains, its strength lies in its neatness. It has short needles that'sit tidily on its twigs, a model of arboreal grooming. Had we that manor house on the Howardian Hills and the means to keep it up, we decided we'd plant *P. orientalis* around the back of the heather garden.

We also agreed that it was downright stupidity to try and walk for more than two hours, say six miles given reasonably easy going, without at least half a litre of water to spare. Last resolution: we needed at least one good meal each day. No more trying to sweat things out from dawn to dusk on tea and tinned stuff. Dehydration and rubbery squid had reduced our bowel movements to much straining for meagre reward. We paid and left.

By contrast with the barren country we had seen in the past few days, our upland trail now led us through diversified landscape. Some of the abandoned terraces of vines and other fruit trees were coming back to life. This puzzled us. Before we left Karpenissi, Palinurus had told me that Greece had lost more than nintey per cent of her original soil. He had learned this, he said, from Karl Fries, his father's tutor at Nordiska Museet and Skansen in Stockholm. Fries had worked out erosion rates from the richest soils of other Balkan countries, which have always been less densely populated than Greece, and then extrapolated backwards.

'How far back?'

'To prehistoric times. In the *Critias*, which was written about 2,500 years ago, Plato deplored the fate of Arcadia. The process was well under way even in those days. He said it was sad to see the old soil which had broken away from the high lands, sliding away ceaselessly and disappearing into the dark sea. By comparison with what used to be there, Plato said, 'They were looking at the skeleton of a sick man. Their soft fertile earth had wasted away.'

To judge from the height of the trees, about eighty feet, and their close-knit uniformity, the hallmark of a man-made plantation, some foresters who perhaps fought under the flag of Venizelos, the man who made Crete a part of greater Greece, had planted that most adaptable of 'the great family of conifers, the Macedonian pine, whose dark, well-furnished spires shaded where we walked that afternoon. This Balkan tree is supremely adaptable. Given a little encouragement it can grow in almost any soil, including those with a touch of lime.

Up we went, contouring, not worrying over much where we were heading for as long as it was a few points west by north. The Macedonian pine was interrupted by a carbonized waste of timber laid low by fire. 'Impossible to control,' Palinurus had said, 'until mankind can control lightning.' Then a glade. A pocket of Arcadia had come back to life. Bright yellow broom, *Genista*, 'young Harry's nosegay', with some umbelliferous plant like cow parsley at its feet and thyme, too, inching up, anxious for a look at the burning sun.

Butterflies were in love with the place. Blues, Clouded yellows and among them the Tiger swallowtail, most beautiful of the European race flickered over the ground. 'Here', said Katie with the determination of a woman who'd found a tea-room during a wearisome shopping day, 'we are going to stop.'

With probing tongues like watchsprings, butterflies are delicate feeders. Some groups, however, have an indelicate regard – by human standards – for urea, excrement and putrescent carrion, which is used by collectors to tempt the Purple Emperor down from the tops of trees in old forests. Putting to work a trick picked up from a game warden in the tropics, I took off my sweaty shirt and waved it about gently. Mild response.

A little encouraged, I rubbed my hands under my armpits and held them up as if in an invocation. To my huge delight and Katie's surprise a swallowtail whirled up into the air, sweeping in wild curves, soaring in splendid circles until, gliding with extended wings, it settled on my slightly moist fingers. Of such are the simple pleasures of itinerant naturalists.

That warden had told me how one morning his headman came to tell him that a young girl had been found dead in a nearby forest glade. She had been raped and strangled. She lay on her back with one arm behind her head. Her posture, the warden said, was so peaceful that for a moment he thought she had fallen asleep. What surprised him most was the sight of her eyes, for below the lids two large blue butterflies had settled and were slowly opening and closing their wings.

Time we were off. In that fine profusion of forestry the trail led us up to a platform some five or six feet wide near the upper limits of the conifers. There we ambled along with neither prevention nor peril, except a five-hundred-foot drop on the sinister side.

Hours passed. The sun sets precociously in high places. The walking rhythm established earlier had become almost monotonic, and we felt as if we were on a comfortable upgoing elevator on which the scenery on one side, the right, seemed to be forever higher and higher. Glimpses of bleak hills through the thinning trees afforded no comfort and there was no sound of water. By seven o'clock, or it could have been eight, we were in need of somewhere to put at least our mattress down. But the trail was insistent, like a single railtrack. There was nowhere else to go.

It began to grow dark. I left Katie in a stony embayment and scuttled ahead. Two short blasts on my whistle meant that at least I'd found a refuge of sorts.

Around a sharp bend the trail narrowed as it swung round a sheer drop of some hundreds of feet. Nothing for it but to scramble up the bank above. I took off my rucksack. Hard going on what on Dartmoor is called clitter, that is banks of loose shale. Pausing for breath I looked around. The whole defile to the left was spanned by four power-lines, supported on our side by an immense pylon standing four-square on a grassy platform about a hundred yards ahead. I made for it. Satisfactory, I thought; that is, if I could rejoin the track below without much effort and together we could both scramble up. I whistled, she answered, and we spent the night there, comfortably.

Not long before dawn I awoke to the distant sound of a melodic howl. In degrees of probability a dog on the loose, I reckoned, or a jackal or, less likely, that eerie but most glorious of mammalian calls of the wild, the rising and falling glissandos of a wolf. Katie stirred and we both leaned forward listening.

Minutes passed. Another call, further away by far and from a different quarter. I decided we should try to take a compass fix on where the sound seemed to be coming from, but we heard no more for a time, and drifted back to sleep.

During that trip to Uranium City* on the border of North Saskatchewan I had heard a great deal about wolves from trappers who hated their guts. They tore the precious ermine, mink and silver fox out of their claw traps, but the men admitted that for their sledge-teams there couldn't be better leaders than a cross betweeen a husky bitch and a wolf.

I had seen wolves from the air when flying over mile-long herds of caribou migrating north towards the snow line to escape the skeeters and No-see-ums. Those wolves, though supreme predators, ran alongside the herds in twos and threes like Cossacks shadowing Napoleon's retreating army. Without the wolves to keep them on the move and tightly packed, the caribou – relatively brainless ungulates – tend to 'yard', as the Scottish call that movement among Red deer: they stop and moon about where the living is easy. In the case of the caribou dependent on a moss, technically a lichen, they will stop on their return trip in the fall until the snow closes round them and they are done for.

I decided to make recordings of wolf calls, and asked a trapper how to get close enough to a pack without a parabolic reflector around the microphone. Easy, said that fruity-voiced Québecois; come with us next week when we peg out our husky bitches on heat. Their erotic cries will bring them eager lovers from many miles around. It came out that way. A spectacular performance.

The scene: a clearing among Jack pine scrub above Lake Athabasca. The time: near midnight with the sky ablaze with the shimmering blue, green and purple light of the aurora

---

* *See page 134-5.*

borealis. Everything we touched produced a shower of sparks in that log cabin. I worried about the tubes, the thermionic valves in that heavy recorder. I turned it on for a test run. The playback sounded as if I were speaking within earshot of the Niagara Falls. We insulated the thing in a nest of blankets. Reception? Tolerable.

Five or six huskies were staked out at intervals of about fifty yards. Even before the pegs were hammered down they announced their sexual condition by copious urination and heart-throbbing calls.

In complete silence, like a commando operation or a spoonful of mercury splashed on corrugated cardboard, the wolves slipped through the trees, a pack of maybe a dozen animals.

They assembled around their leader, the king dog. He tiptoed forward towards the nearest excited bitch, but stopped on his haunches to announce his seigneurial rights with a howl that began slowly and rose and fell within an octave. Apart from much vigorous tail-wagging the pack was quiet and still.

As far as I can recall the scene – I carried both a stopwatch and field glasses in addition to a notebook and tape-recorder – he covered that bitch in two minutes sixteen seconds. This done, he rolled aside, licked himself, stood up and howled again, this time more softly and in a different key.

At this, what must have been one of the best lupine choral societies around Lake Athabasca responded with a group howl before, with remarkable orderliness, they set about pleasuring their chosen partners. Those low in the pecking order hung about obediently, as if in an exclusive bordello.

That concerto between the king dog and his pack became the overture and leitmotif of a series of radio programmes called 'Men of the North' for what was then the BBC Light Programme, the popular rival to the austerities of the Third.

Some years later Dilys Breese, doyenne of the

Corporation's Natural History Unit, phoned to ask if I would care to come down to Bristol and comment 'live' on the language of wolves, accompanied by somebody who, as she put it, politely, 'understood music'. I knew the best man in the business, that maestro of the French horn Alan Civil. We went down to Bristol together and not knowing what he was in for he stole the show.

Before we arrived BBC technicians had edited representative recordings accompanied by spectographs, that is electronic charts in terms of pitch, frequency and time in split seconds.

The programme opened with that superb howl by the king dog; the producer described briefly what it was all about, handed one of the sonograms to Alan and asked if it meant anything to him. Not knowing that it was upside-down, he scanned it and shook his head, saying he was not surprised as he'd played first performances by Birtwistle and Stockhausen. Could he hear some more?

There were times when I thought that Dilys, a pro to her fingertips, looked a bit anxious when the unscripted half an hour bore some resemblance to the 'Goon Show'. We had agreed, she and I, that I shouldn't dwell over-much on the biometrics of canine copulation. Alan only mentioned the word 'mounting' twice, and sang the rest.

He pointed out that the howls of the king dog, the virtuoso, contained 'at least five harmonics either a little above or a little below an octave'. He thought it interesting that although most if not all the wolves started *pianissimo*, only the pack leader had the ability to rise to a *messa di voce*, apparently on one breath, before sliding down a bit incoherently to where he had started 'within the tonic'. This threw us completely.

He explained that by *messa* he didn't mean a 'sung mass' nor even a *mezza*, a half-voice; the virtuoso could hold or, as Alan put it, 'place' his voice in a *crescendo e diminuendo* on one long sustained note, something popular in the palmy days of Italian *bel canto* in the eighteenth century. Could that be where the wolves had originally picked it up?

Very unlikely, I thought, but a darned sight more interesting and, I suspect, intellectually more productive than dreary biochemical analyses of canine urine on wolves' well known pissing-points at the foot of trees. To illustrate his point Alan asked for the soloist's best piece to be replayed at half speed, where he analysed the modes, quietly, and then added his own voice, harmonically, so that we were given an impression of how the king dog carried – as it were – half a dozen calling-cards which had to be acknowledged by his underdogs. Trappers around Athabasca had assured me that wolves very rarely fight amongst themselves. Dominance has been ritualized by their musical howls.

A blood-red dawn. Katie had poured the tea out. I had begun to shake the dew off the outer fly when a noise that resembled someone tearing a sheet of old calico ended in a double explosion as if both barrels of a shotgun had been fired almost simultaneously. Situated as we were at the foot of the highest lightning conductor in the Pindos, we had to get out quick. On the scree down to the track we again heard that howl which rose and fell within an octave. It came from somewhere on the floor of the valley invisible to us. The howls were repeated, twice. Perhaps the animals were as concerned about the gathering storm as we were.

No rain at first, but the wind rose and among a forest of conifers it had as many voices as the sea. Gusts of increasing violence carried greyish-white dust. It partly obscured the sun which appeared and disappeared like a lemon behind a tumultuous wrack of clouds. The dust was loess, a geologist's term for sun-dried earth and sand which may have been carried for many hundreds of miles. Unlike the case of the *meltemi*, this is not the ground-up floor of the Balkans. The chances are high that, originally, it blew down from central Asia.

On the track to Marathos, the last habitation before the village of Agrapha, we were bustled, buffeted and then towards midday drenched to the skin by rain that came at us in stair-rods.

Looking back on the affair I think we rather enjoyed our sense of invincibility. No matter that we were soaked through and through; our much battered rucksacks, we knew, were porous but all spare clothing, our maps, passports, cash, credit cards and the like were doubly insulated in plastic bags within the cocoon of the tent.

Emotions are curiously inexplicable affairs. At the very height of that storm, when we were mostly preoccupied with keeping below the tree-line, Katie told me, afterwards, that she had been thinking about one particular tea-estate with a lot of exposed rock, at Menikdiwela in Ceylon, when with two small youngsters in the nursery she became aware that during a violent display of lightning, blue flashes were coming from the power-points.

At the seige of Sebastopol, Tolstoy jumped out of the trenches and ran towards the bastion under heavy fire from the enemy. He was horribly afraid of rats and had just seen one.

My own thoughts that day went back to the Congo, the Mother of Rivers where in an antiquated stern-wheeler we were carrying two precious pairs of okapi between Bumba and Stanleyville, now Kisangani. On the first day out we ran into an apocalyptic storm. For twenty hours we were showered with lightning that wiped out the difference between dusk and dawn. It could have been a coronation fireworks display.

On the bridge the handsome Kabala tribesman held the mahogany wheel between his fingers and thumbs. In his eyes, in the delicacy of his touch one could see what Joseph Conrad so admired. On either side a fellow tribesman operated searchlights, trying to pick up reflectors on islands in that continental drain which, thereabouts, is some ten miles wide. Showers of lightning reduced huge forest trees to blood-red pillars of charcoal.

The ship, the *Lieutenant Lippens*, was shoring two barges ahead. The storm had blown the generator in the galley but somehow they had managed to get the refrigerators going with auxiliary gear. Captain Jean-Paul Marin occupied a cabin just aft of the bridge, whilst five of us, myself and a Methodist missionary with his unhappy-looking wife and two howling children, shared the rest of the space on the top deck. About 800 blacks swarmed in the bowels of the boat. They sang, they drank and kicked up a hell of a cheerful noise.

Jean-Paul had more than his share of worries. He had run headlong into a bank of problems, personal and professional. By far the worst was that someone in the Company had told his wife 'way back in Brussels that he shared his cabin on the *Lippens* with a beautiful black bird, a young Kabala girl with breasts like chocolate ice-cream cones. This I knew, since she had come aboard the previous day, her name long forgotten but unquestionably an eyeful.

Mme Marin had gone to OTRACO,* Jean-Paul's employers, and demanded to be flown to the Congo to sort things out. He had heard this by radio but was partly excommunicated by chronic static. He couldn't reply and had a pretty shrewd idea she would be waiting for him at Stanleyville. He was already a day and a half late on course. We had run into enormous banks of water weed, *Eichornia*,

---

* *Office d'Exploitation des Transports Coloniaux, Voies Fluviales*.

the so-called Devil's lilac, some of it two or three hundred yards wide. This meant reduction to half speed, sometimes running astern, and churning up the river into soapy froth before the helmsman managed to forge ahead through narrow weed-free channels.

That night I quit our antiquated ship at Yangambi in the company of the Captain's consort; me for a three-day journey by Land Rover to the foot of the Ruwenzori, the Mountains of the Moon and she, presumably, back to her father. At moon-rise, next to no sound on the great river except for the 'talking' two-toned drums of the Lokali tribesmen, the Congolese equivalent of the Morse code. For me, at least, the storm was over. I never discovered what happened to Jean-Paul.

Seen through the weeping trees a small mosaic of roofs appeared and disappeared far below us, like a glimpse of Lilliput. We heard a roaring noise as of escaping steam from a ruptured boiler. It came from an invisible cascade about half a mile away. Later we saw where quicksilver streamlets poured over a cliff to float down behind the topmost screen of conifers.

Marathos has been rebuilt out of a huddle of ancient, perhaps seventeenth-century houses on the scree of a landslide. The inhabitants, about five or six families, are no more deprived of water than a community on an offshoot of the Niagara Falls but, unlike fertile and equally well watered Pira where we saw the bullet-ridden car, the place looked as if it were falling apart, dependent only on small crops of vegetables and herds of goats.

I knocked on the open door of the first ramshackle house we came to. Inside a middle-aged man with a long sad face like a horse sat at a table taking an ancient alarm clock, an Ingersoll, to pieces with the aid of a tin-opener and a small screwdriver. Without a shred of curiosity he looked up, said '*Yass*' in a faraway voice and went on with his tinkering. Somewhat put off by almost total disregard, I asked if there was a tavern in the village. He sighed and pointed down the cobbled passage which served as a main street, and we heard the sound of uproarious laughter.

Instant hospitality. A small card school broke up. Chairs were pushed towards us. Impossible at first to guess who the landlord was. The company helped themselves and tossed the reckoning on the top of a barrel. The usual questions: where had we left our car? Did we want a drink, food? The feeling of apprehension which had beset us since we caught our first glimpse of the village flooded away in the house of 'Kaiser' Kapodistrio, native of Aetolia, the ancient region north of where Byron died. A good, a very whiskery fellow with handlebar moustaches and huge side-chops. In addition to some English and German he spoke his native Greek slowly for our benefit.

Within half an hour we learnt that Kaiser ran not only the pub-cum-grocery store but was regarded as the headman of that cheerful little hamlet. He and his plump wife looked after us from the moment we walked in.

After lingering over the first meal we had eaten since we left the electric pylon in a hurry, I asked if they could put us up. At this he shrugged his shoulders, pulled a wry face and pointed upstairs. It came through in polyglot accompanied by gestures of mock discomfort that his father and mother-in-law had arrived and they had only two *schlafzimmer*.

Was there no other place?

He nodded slowly. '*Ja, ja. Jawohl*, a good man, a kind man but strange, *wunderlich*.' He pointed up the narrow passage to the first house we'd called at, the man with a passion for pulling mechanical things to bits. He called to his plump wife who took us back to the house of Nico

Notopolos, the melancholic fellow who seemed to live in a world of his own making. He floated ghost-like from room to room, showing us his curious treasures.

Above the ruins of the alarm clock on his work bench stood the tarnished components of a brass astrolabe, an instrument for measuring the altitude of stars. In one piece or even in bits it must have been worth a lot. On the walls of our bedroom were shelves of dusty, ancient, fretworked radio sets, Murphy, Mullard, Ferranti, Pye, Ekco, Cossor and others we couldn't make out. Nico bounced on our bed. *Kalos, kalos*, a very good bed, yes? As for the radio sets, especially the Pye with its price-tag (19 guineas) still stuck on to the veneered walnut, we told him, truthfully, we had never seen a finer collection.

As we left for the tavern at dusk he stood in the open doorway, shading his eyes against the sun, looking up at the immense defile. Without turning round he said: 'Look! There she is. My wife.' Through glasses we saw a woman driving a herd of goats down a track steeper than anything we had encountered that morning. She never faltered. She walked slowly but she walked straight down, shouting at the laggards. The morning's rain had given way to a glowing evening.

In the tavern Marcos, a customer who had just driven up with supplies from Karpenissi, said in almost word-perfect English: 'A strange one, that; he lives too much inside his head and that's bad for anyone.' He took another pull at a handrolled cigarette made from raw local tobacco, spat on the floor and repeated in Greek his opinion of the man who took things to pieces. The company nodded. They had heard it all before.

'But he's got a wife,' I said. 'We saw her coming down the track about half an hour ago. Doesn't she look after him?'

'Yes, but the question is who looks after her?'

I couldn't understand what Kaiser said which brought a laugh all round and I caught a glance from Katie that meant enough is enough.

We ate and drank there, laughed at bits of the conversation translated by Marcos, and we managed to get a quarter of an hour with him alone before going back to the bedroom of fifteen radio sets.

Though he had met Nico regularly for several years, seen his strange objects and had bought one of his bone flutes made from an eagle's wing, he said he didn't know what made him tick. Who could tell what went on in other people's minds? 'The sad one', as he called him, believed in witches, demons and the spirits of the woods and the streams, particularly one we'd met before called the *daouti* who, from the stories about how this creature terrifies the shepherds and their flocks, I took to be Pan.

'Do you believe in these things?'

He half smiled and shrugged his shoulders. '*Mystika pragmata, kala pragmata?*' Secret things, perhaps good things: who knew?

'What does the village think about Nicos?'

He leaned forward confidentially. 'They are sorry for him, he was here before the *makaronades*, those Italian bastards. As most of the villagers are from outside and don't really know what went on in the old days, I think most of them respect him – at least they did before he married that goddamned Vlach.'

'Do you really think she is one?'

'Course I do. Who else could walk down a hillside like that?'

The story was that when the village was bigger than Agrapha, he had met her when, like all the other lads, he took his turn at looking after the communal herds of goats. After his father's death he inherited the house and saw more of her. It came as a surprise to everyone to learn they were married. There was a small band of Vlachs above the village who took up their winter quarters around Trikala and Larissa when the snows began to fall in mid-October. The strangest part of the story was that Nico had hinted to someone that even when she went away he could keep in touch with her. Nobody knew how he managed it.

The village of Agrapha sits on a steep slope amidst a range of peaks a little more than 6,000 feet in altitude. It took us nearly ten hours to get there, probably our most difficult day, marred only by unsuccessful efforts to cut off the loops of tracks trodden by those who knew far more about short-cuts than we did. Viewed in the round, the dramatic moments of life are apt to fall singularly flat.

E. M. Forster has pointed out that life is full of false clues and signposts that lead nowhere. He says that 'often with infinite effort we nerve ourselves to a crisis which never comes. The most successful career must show a waste of strength that might have moved mountains and the most unsuccessful is not that of a man who is taken unprepared, but of him who has prepared and is never taken.'

Strange that in isolated villages such as Marathos enquiries about how to get to the next place were usually answered in terms of the nearest road, even though we tried to explain it would probably be double the distance that we should have to walk if we could cling to paths. Was this, we wondered, concern for our safety or for some reason of their own? Kaiser knew quite a lot about the track over the top and, we thought rather begrudgingly, told us that if we got into trouble we could follow the waterfall to get up on to the bare plateau.

The day started well. We were weaving through good timber. A loud deep bark. A bright red roe-deer, a female with two wobbly fawns at foot, stared at us for a second or two with upturned muzzle and then plunged down through tiers of trees which had taken us at least half an hour's walking time. Katie mopped her forehead and wished that for that day at least she had been born a deer. My eyes were on a patch of slightly moist sun-dappled mud on which half a dozen butterflies were almost invisible until they rose in the air together, fluttering like a spotted handkerchief in a breeze. We saw that feeder on grasses, the Great Banded grayling in hot pursuit of a would-be mate. Again we watched the beautiful Apollon whose floppy flight makes it easy prey for collectors.

Most people with a slight interest in natural history seem satisfied if they merely know the name of a bird, a plant or an animal. Could there be, I wonder, some lingering element of word-magic here, some feeling that knowing the name gives one power over the creature specified, the sort of feeling that leads primitive people to conceal their personal names from all except their intimates? An enemy, learning their name, might be able to use that power for evil purpose. Unless the creature is a useless parasite or a predator the most difficult question of all to answer is: 'What good does it do?' This presumably is a hangover from the anthropocentric universe of the Middle Ages when everything had a purpose in relation to Man with a capital M. Today, against a background of countless galaxies, astronauts walking on the moon, geological time and hosts of wild creatures, there is still no answer to the function of, say, dragonflies, water-skaters and mayflies, except that they add marvels to days in the country.

The sun told us that it was somewhere between about ten and eleven o'clock and I didn't like the look of our progressively worsening nature reserve. The shady conifers were being invaded by acacias, the spurious blush of Judas trees, and more and more of that impenetrable scrub oak.

The track broke up into occasional branches. We clung

to what looked the most trampled down. Where was Kaiser's waterfall? No cicadas, no butterflies nor songbirds for comfort, only skittery Crested larks on patches of sand.

At one point the track divided purposively. There was no way of choosing between them. Both to the left and the right we caught glimpses of the bare ravine. We put our packs down, took out our whistles and trudged off in opposite directions. I felt reasonably sure we should cling to a north-west, not a north-east bearing.

My path wavered uncertainly before it swung round a bend where due ahead I saw it had been cut by a waterfall, small but too precipitous to be waded across. Yet immediately above there stood an alternative track, almost a staircase with a series of steps about fifty yards in length. Thereafter it moved steeply but steadily from side to side to another bend from which could be seen a down-trodden path through a sparse wood. I reckoned we could climb from one level to another without much difficulty. The whistle had scarcely touched my lips when I heard a short toot from Katie. I went back to where we had left our packs. She had not even walked out of sight and beckoned excitedly and pointed when she saw me.

In a hidden depression of bare rock and loose shale below us we saw the nut-brown woman, old Nico's wife, driving her herd of goats directly up the dry bed of a stream. Her steps put me in mind of a sleep-walker. With her eyes apparently fixed on the ground she never hesitated except to throw a stone just below a group of strays. They bleated and scampered up in front of her in a ragged line, starting a small avalanche of stones. We needed a rest. We sat down and watched. No trained sheepdog in a trial could have bettered her. From past experience we sensed that she knew she was being watched but she never looked up.

Impossible to calculate her speed of ascent, but I guessed it equalled ours on our laborious zigzag upwards. In terms of altitude gained in feet per hour we were probably outclassed by three or more to one. A born mountaineer. Seemingly without effort on something close to a cliff, she could match in speed and agility a reasonably good walker on the side of a hill. A Vlach in her natural environment.

She switched to a diagonal traverse and we left her to it, going back for our packs and on to the waterfall where we drank, washed our feet and took to the upper track. A stumble here and there. A resolute pull up for Katie when both our loads were safely perched, and we were off again. On the wildlife front we were much on our own except for prickly stuff and dreary asphodel which rattled in the breeze. A rather large grass snake (*Natrix*), a harmless creature although it may reach a length of eight feet in the Balkans, uncoiled as if heavily oiled before it slid away. I looked round: there might be many more in cavities in the scrub. The species is remarkable for its polygamous habits. In the breeding season it collects up to a dozen females and as many as a thousand eggs can be found in rotting vegetation. A pair of ravens or a jackal could wipe them out in half an hour.

Above us, more difficult to make out even through glasses, we again saw the mysterious warden of goats, always referred to by the women of Marathos as Nicolaina, using the feminine form of her husband's name as one might say she-Tom or she-Carlos. Going in the same direction as we were, she was moving towards a small plateau of grazing at a height of probably four or five thousand feet. We both heard and saw the by-product of her relentless drive minutes before we caught a glimpse of her.

A boulder crashed down, leaped into the air and bounced off a projecting rock where it split into fragments that tinkled down like a kind of spray, considerably wide of our track but near enough to compel a sharp look-out.

We paused to watch. Anxious for a fresh bite amidst that

barren waste, the goats scampered ahead stirring up small avalanches that progressively increased in force. They put up a variety of creatures from red-winged grasshoppers to a pair of mountain hares and a bare-necked vulture, the Griffon, which, hitherto unseen, arose from behind a rock like a genie from the earth's interior, circled the disturbance and flapped off, disconsolately, I should imagine. When the goats and their warden settled on that patch of coherent grazing all became quiet again.

What we couldn't make out was why Nicolaina had literally clambered up to a small and isolated pasture when, as we had seen on the forested trail to the place where Katie had first spotted her, she had outflanked shady glades more than fit for omnivorous goats. Could the explanation lie in Kaiser's marked reluctance to support our plan to scramble over the arduous but more direct track to Agrapha? Was that Arcadian haunt of roe-deer, perhaps wild boar and those ridiculously small doves we had heard a small communal hunting-ground? On what was their economy based? Almost certainly not entirely on sheep and goats, although old Nico and his agile wife may have been responsible for grazing the common stock of the village. Was that the way in which Nicolaina made some reparation for her irregular association with the local band of her fellow countrymen, the Vlachs, those Ishmaels regarded by some extremists as scarcely mammalian? This is odd because although most Greeks fear the countries around their northern border, as a nation they are singularly free from that distressing and almost universal complaint, xenophobia. That morning Nicolaina may have been on her way to rejoin them, temporarily. We had no direct evidence one way or the other except that she was heading for the barrens and not the next village. Speculation and curiosity about what we saw was what always kept us going.

On a narrow track still within sight of that talkative stream we were obliged to walk one behind the other, with me in the role of path-finder some forty yards ahead. Uncompanionable but necessary when there was the danger of starting more avalanches. When I reckoned we were within an hour of reaching what had been uppermost in my mind, the top of the ridge and what lay beyond it, we stopped for a rest and a drink where I asked Katie what she had been thinking about.

She paused for a moment and said the remarkably deep blue colour of the sky, emphasized on all horizons except the one immediately ahead by the ring of unmelted snow. She didn't recall it when she used to live at a similar altitude in Ceylon. The grotesque towers of jagged rock surprised her: why hadn't they been flattened and smoothed like most of the others? She admitted being scared by the shower of stones dislodged by the goats but not as much as by vertigo when she daren't look down to where the track narrowed around a sharp turn in the rock face. Did I think there would be more of them ahead?

At heart I didn't know since crests are not uncommonly false ones, but Kaiser, I told her, had assured me that when we got over the ridge we should be able to see the village of Agrapha.

Nicolaina and her flock were out of sight. As far as we could see we were the only human inhabitants of the central Pindos, that vast arena of marauding hordes, bloodshed, brigandage, foreign invasions, mass slaughter, the destruction of whole villages, internecine strife, treachery, family feuds and heroic resistance, all enacted within lunar landscapes. The mountains were strangely quiet. Could it be that with hindsight they were listening?

In asking Katie what was uppermost in her thoughts, I really wanted to know how long she felt capable of pressing on, of enduring long stretches under fierce sunlight with about thirty pounds on her back. Her feet, I knew, were blistered, certainly worse than they had been. Perhaps she read my thoughts. Among other matters she told me more about her feet. We were two of a kind. I had a pain like toothache at the base of the spine when cautiously I lifted up my pack as we started off in the morning, which sometimes never wholly disappeared during the rest of the day. Would it not be advisable to get down to the plain and come back in the autumn, I wondered. Or should we finish the whole venture then and there? Was it sheer age on my part? Perhaps. Even the Flying Dutchman came at last to port.

Dark thoughts were quietly recorded soon after we set off again. They were sparked off by a glimpse of yet another horizon far behind that gap in the immediate snow-line. Not a mirage. It didn't lie between our line of march and the sun, but whenever I looked it appeared to have risen by a few degrees. Two dome-shaped crests in colour somewhere between blue and violet, as if we were being peered at through the eyes of an old whore.

We could have done with a touch of the old stuff. We hadn't one. A song, then. With a throat that felt like warm cottonwool I croaked out: 'Beer, boys, and bugger the Band of Hope' to a tune a quaver or two from the 'Soldiers' Chorus' from *Faust*. Katie smiled wanly, so, taking the lead again, I got back to thinking about something to think about.

The ancient custom of transhumation, the taking of flocks up to the high pastures in the spring when the plains were as dry as sunbaked stubble and bringing them down before the snow started to fall, was the third stage in the evolution of man's activities – that is, before the coming of fertilizers. For millions of years bands of shaggy-looking fellows ate anything they could find from fruits and berries to carrion filched from agile predators, especially big cats, and what could be picked up on the seashore including flotsam such as dead seals and whales. Then came Man the Toolmaker, the artificer of weaponry, flint axes, spears of bone and yew wood, and metallic products culminating in the atomic bomb. Before they dabbled in intertribal slaughter on a big scale, the wisest hunters found they could fill their bellies most easily by cooperation. They could scarcely fail to notice that wolves were in the same line of business.

Wolves, the outright enemies of mankind? Far from it. From the abandoned young of those sagacious animals that, like themselves, hunted in packs under undisputed leadership and discipline, primitive man acquired the domesticated dog, that vital first step on the road to pastorilism. This took place some ten or eleven thousand years ago. Man had reared an obedient hunting companion with sharp teeth, a creature who could run much faster than he could. Goats and sheep were probably domesticated from their wild ancestors some two or three thousand years later and that nicely balanced partnership between man, dog, goats and sheep has persisted until the present day.

Paradise is somewhere in the Near East; Jerusalem is the centre of all countries and nations, and the world itself is a flat disc, surrounded by oceans of water; so the monks, the mapmakers of the Middle Ages, saw the world they lived in. Towards three o'clock on that afternoon blaze, our own horizons were slowly but enormously enlarged. We topped the crest and immediately opposite us, at our level but separated by an immensity of air, stood the village of Agrapha. It took us three hours to get there.

Tavropos, Tortoises and Trikala

When at last we got to grips with a large-scale mountain-climbers' map it became clear that the dominant village of the Agrapha range is surrounded by peaks within circles of peaks all of which are close to – or rather more than – 7,000 feet in height. For centuries, probably millennia, invaders from the west or the north would have had to thread their way through the gorges and foothills of Mount Delidemi; those from the north would have had to cope with the sprawl around the sharp nose of Borlero and the saddle of Plaka whilst, as we discovered for ourselves, the southern approaches stand high above the Agraphiotis river. Like eagles from their eyries, the Agraphiotes could have seen enemies advancing across the void around the place called the Village Without a Name; more appropriately it might have been known as *Aproseetos*, the Inaccessible, isolated but not aloof.

Before we got there we recalled our friend George Papadopoulos from Karpenissi telling us that as a boy he and his family and friends had been whisked up into the range when invasion threatened their home town; he scarcely remembered it except with gratitude. Others had had much the same story to tell. Could it be that we had arrived at the Geneva of the Central Pindos, a constant refuge for people or nations at odds with each other, or

269

another Marathos dependent primarily on a great gush of sparkling water?

Difficult to say, but what we were sure of by the nods and smiles of the people around the cafés and restaurants from the moment we walked down their narrow main street at right angles to a cultivated slope of Mount Koukourountsos was that they were on our side.

We were the first strangers they had seen that year. Were we mountaineers? It seemed easier to say yes.

An old man, Carlos with the map, who seemed to be in charge of the place offered us a drink and directed us to the house of a kindly soul who promptly adopted Katie. She insisted on kneeling down and washing her feet; she offered us a pleasant room and suggested a meal, an omelette with those Greek beans we enjoy so much.

As we sat on the veranda feeling at peace with the world we heard the sound of eggs being broken and the sizzle of boiling oil. Nearly twenty minutes passed. Wasn't it ready? Under the pretext of ordering another carafe of wine I wandered through to the kitchen, saw the big omelette on a plate and asked if I might take it back to our table. 'Oh no,' she said, 'it's still hot. Hot food is bad for the stomach.'

I forget how I managed to get round that one without seeming impolite, but it explained much that we'd had to put up with in Greek kitchens until we'd learnt the necessity of saying, 'Hot, hot, please,' – '*Zestos zestos, parakalo*,' when we pointed to trays of food that had been kept lukewarm for hours.

Carlos strolled up to ask if we were satisfied with the house, and stayed to catechize me gently, presumably on behalf of the village. The usual questions: where had we come from? How had we got to Agrapha on foot? Our age? Had I been in the army? This enabled me to ask about what had happened locally.

He was eighty, he told me. One of the few remaining natives. His contemporaries had either been killed, died or moved away. Those there today were mostly refugees from the Italians who had just stayed on. The Germans hadn't thought it worth while to send their armour into the thinly populated mountains but had bombed the village, twice. He chuckled when he said that on the second occasion there was nobody there. They had scattered. After the Occupation all the mountains of Greece were in the hands of one Resistance band or another. ELAS ruled Agrapha, and that was a bad, bad time. Members of families had hunted each other.

Against those terrible stories of half a century ago, the Agrapha of today had about it an air of serenity, a touch of Shangri-la. An ancient priest in full canonicals had a benign smile for everybody, an immoderate thirst and a flowing white beard which would have got him a job as Father Christmas in any Western store. Oldsters gossiped in the tavernas, clicking their worry beads. Worry was man's function: women hadn't the time. Those not scurrying about carrying things knitted furiously.

We stayed only a couple of nights. On a route he was familiar with Carlos showed us on his map how we could work our way round Borlero and Plaka, those twin domes which earlier I had likened to the eyes of a whore. He assured us that once up there it was downhill through forested country to Kastania and Lake Tavropos. Easy words for hard going on which I don't intend to dwell since it was largely a two-day repetition of that breath-taker up from Marathos, but downhill.

Tavropos. Now that was different. A ten-mile long, narrow, mostly artificial lake, presumably a reservoir fed by that river beside which we had walked on that hell-hot day, our first out of faraway Karpenissi. But that Megdova, or Tavropos, had flowed south, this one north. The two names, we learnt, were synonymous; one ancient, if not classical, the other modern. Gravity being what it is, somewhere along the flow line there must be a common source.

With a carrier bag of cold meat, bread, tomatoes and wine bought in Kastania we strolled round the ins and outs of the lake's shore-line, looking for the ideal camp-site. We found one under some alders reflected in the water. During the evening we heard some fearful shrieks which came, it amused us to imagine, from those hell-horn birds the Stymphalides with their brazen beaks and iron claws, considered by Pausanias to prey on mankind. Among a host of other monsters they were killed by Herakles, most celebrated of the heroes of antiquity. They were, in fact, Loons or Great Northern divers which for many weeks had been my companions on the Appalachian Trail.

Within a couple of days of Trikala we managed to lose ourselves close to Mouzaki and slept in the open among bales of maize stubble, but were fortified by glimpses to the north-east of the great Plain of Thessaly. As we inched round the edge of that steam bath we kept as high as we could. We found tortoises which, here in their native environment, can scuttle away on the tips of their claws. No wonder these heat-loving animals, captured generally in their hundreds of thousands in North Africa, Turkey and the Balkans for export as pets, rarely survive an English winter. Criminal destruction.

We lunched in a humble place where with apologies the lady of the house seated us near an unkempt priest who could be heard eating his daily free meal two or three tables in front of us. Before each mouthful he crossed himself as if swatting flies. He knocked things over and asked for another plateful. Our hostess flung down what she had been crocheting, a fine shawl in unbleached homespun wool, and stamped off. Katie asked if she might continue the intricate pattern. Instant friendship.

That night we found a grassy knoll as smooth as the Sussex Downs with a few flat-topped boulders on which we could lay out our gear. A shepherd approached. We greeted each other. I told him we were sleeping there. Just for one night. Was it in order? '*Endaxi*,' he said. He accepted a cigarette with dignity adding two significant words, '*Adio, graz*,' before walking down the hillside as surely as he had walked up. The words mean 'thank you' and 'goodbye' in Vlach. Thereafter all was quiet as we lay on the ground, our eyes impressed with the diamonds of the poor, which are the stars.

A curious awakening about five o'clock in the morning. *Clack, clack, clunk*, repeated as if temple blocks were being struck by a child. I rolled over to see a large tortoise attacking another one almost concealed under a boulder, with its head withdrawn. The aggressor was butting the edge of its shell with its own shield. It turned, saw me and ran away as fast as a rat, to be followed by the other tortoise. What were they up to? Two rivals fighting it out or a courtship pattern peculiar to a very ancient group of animals whose relatives on equatorial islands weigh up to half a ton? Quite simply I don't know.

The Plain of Thessaly, 'mother of flocks and homeland of horses for Olympic charioteers'. We had seen the statue of the most famous one in the museum at Delphi. He wears the expressionless expression of cab-drivers throughout the world. Here were horses in straw hats, donkeys in diapers, carts with solid eccentric wheels, cheerful peasants on ancient tricycles, and rows and rows of brightly painted beehives.

Trikala, tricolour. Fascinated by all we saw, from the white-washed walls of the old Turkish-style houses pleached with blue clematis and the bright red of ramblers, we made philological play with the name as we walked down to the trickling river. We recalled *Roumeli* by Mr Leigh Fermor, to whose sensitive ear the word 'Dodecanese' seems a sea-song sung by twelve sponge-fishers, 'Athens' a canticle of columns, 'Thrace' the beat of a drum, 'Hymettus' the hum of bees and 'Trikala' the stork's beak rattling from a broken minaret.

We saw pairs of those symbols of fertility only in Pigi and Parapotamus, two suburbs we should have forgotten but for our disgraceful conduct there.

In both places pretty young girls in their very best embroidered dresses slipped out of their homes carrying basket-work trays of all manner of dainties. Shyly they dropped a curtsey and offered them to us with a phrase we couldn't understand. Thinking they were for sale and having already eaten, we smiled, thanked them, said something simple, and hurried on. They looked wholly taken aback, saddened. We learnt later, I don't know where, that on behalf of the Mother of Jesus they were the gifts of virgins to strangers, in a ceremony which probably has something to do with the Gateway of the Virgin, the Porta Panagia, by which one enters the town. May the Mother Herself and those young girls forgive us. We wholly misinterpreted a heart-touching custom.

Above the trickling river, the Pinios, and close to the old quarter and the bus station, we made for the comfortable Hotel Divani, where, as he had said he would, M. Théophane had left a message. Would I please phone him after ten at night at Metsovo, some forty miles away in the mountains of Epirus? Katie sniffed. 'As far as he knows we haven't arrived,' she said. 'Let's go take a bath and pretend to be civilized.'

This is easy in Trikala, once famous for the oldest known sanctuary to Ascelpius, the god of the medical art and recreation. To Homer he was not a divinity but simply 'the blameless physician of deep knowledge'.

On our side of the river, we were flanked by narrow streets of craftsmen's shops and tavernas with trays of aromatic vegetables and slowly turning roasts over beds of glowing charcoal.

On the other side, across a choice of brightly painted bridges and a public garden, are restaurants and glittering shops designed to empty the wallets of visitors.

Towards sundown the principal thoroughfare is closed to all wheeled traffic for the *volta*. This slow parade for lovers, would-be lovers and families with their young all done up in their best was as a royal performance for which we'd seen the rehearsal in Amphissa. Music was played but it was quiet music from several sources, mostly cafés and restaurants, and there was orderliness almost everywhere. Crowds, yes, but mostly in twos, threes or fours sauntering up and down, then round again, unwinding between everyday work and the ordinariness of life at home.

Note the word 'almost'. That night two Greeks, one less a considerable portion of one ear, were hauled off to the cooler for fighting with lethal cutlery outside the doors of our highly respectable lodgings. The night porter Basilides (Bassy for short), an energetic old man, had called the cops. Katie was ready for sleep so she told me not to be long, and under cover of getting some useful information Bassy and I shared one or two stiff ones.

The two combatants, youngsters by his standard (he admitted to being on the wrong side of eighty), were the grandsons of two political chieftains, Royalist and Communist (ELAS during the War of Independence), who had

been threatening to kill each other since they had first
handled rifles misguidedly supplied by the British in Cairo.
The one deprived of part of his ear was the grandson of
Velhouiotis who, as even I knew, under the *nom de guerre*
of Ares had boasted, rightfully it seemed, that he had killed
hundreds of men, potential allies who had disputed his right
to run a private army in the mountainous Albanian border
region. They had been cornered and killed in the Pindos
by the Rightist forces, the Colonels. His head had been cut
off and displayed on a lamp post in the square just below
our bedroom window. Bassy had seen it. It proved such a
popular attraction that it was taken down and pickled for
exhibition in Lamia, where Velhouiotis came from, and in
other centres of unrest.

'A bit late, weren't you?' said Katie the next morning.

'Yes, but I heard a lot more about the fight from the night
porter. It's a feud, goes back to the Occupation and the
War of Independence.'

'But they must have been in prams at the time.'

'Maybe, but their grandfathers were big-time Resistance
leaders who fell out about what they were fighting for, and
they're good at hating each other. Anyway, I have news for
you: I got through to Théophane and he's going to take us
for a joy-ride in the mountains. He's sending us his car.'

'You mean *you* are. I've got an appointment with the best
hairdresser in town at midday, and I want to do some
shopping. He's your friend; you go off with him.'

'I didn't say today. It's coming after breakfast tomorrow.'

Some argument ensued. From the very start of the trip
we'd agreed that whenever we stopped for two or three
nights in a town such as Thebes or Delphi we should spend
a day on our own. We had been in each other's company
from dawn to dusk for days. Théophane had been quite

explicit: he couldn't come to Trikala himself, he had business in Metsovo, a Vlach village, he said. He'd send his good young friend from Crete, Kalonaros, to pick me up.

'Madame might prove difficult,' I had suggested. As if he'd read my thoughts he'd said, 'Afford yourselves then a little vacation. There are excellent shops in Trikala. No, wait! Another idea. Perhaps she too would also like to go sightseeing. On the way here one goes through Kalambaka and Meteora with its columns of rock, the skyscrapers of nature. Kalo, as you must call him, will introduce her to a lady friend of mine there, and at whatever hour pleases her we will pick her up on the way back to the Divani. One word, though: Kalo has some difficulty in speaking, he has had an operation to the throat. You will come, then?'

'I told him I would phone him back after I'd spoken to you,' I told Katie. 'How do you feel about it?'

'Good idea,' she said. 'Théophane and I have not met each other. All I know about him is what you've told me. He's clearly not interested in meeting me, and I'm much of the same mind. How do you explain that?' Not wishing to go into the obvious, I suggested negative telepathy.

If it hadn't been for a procession of mule-drawn carts carrying vegetables on the long straight road to Kalambaka I had the impression that Kalonaros at the wheel of the Mercedes would have covered the twenty-five miles in less than half that number of minutes. An extremely good-looking man with hair in glistening ringlets. He was, I should guess, about forty years old and a very courteous driver, permitting himself only a gentle hoot as he purred past other vehicles in that air-conditioned mobile armchair. His limitations in speech were made up for by a wealth of gestures.

We saw the skyscrapers of nature long before we got

among them. These extraordinary rocks have been likened to the decayed and irregular dentures of gigantic mammoths. Katie, confident in her new hairdo, had picked up the literature the previous day. The vertical monasteries have earned three stars from the Guide Michelin. Originally, that is during the sixteenth century, there were twenty-four of them. The monks were hauled up in rope webs like netted trout. Today only four are inhabited.

The days of jointed ladders pulled up in an emergency are no more, and the nets are now strictly limited to hauling up supplies. Occasional romantics who misguidedly hanker after the good old days when the traveller was pulled up uncomfortably squeezed into an outsize string bag are quickly cured of their rash desire by one look at the rusty windlass, especially if told the gruesome story that the rope was never changed until it broke.

Kalo circled the cobbled town before pulling up – as I had anticipated – at the door of an expensive restaurant. Madame was waiting to greet Katie, warmly. Kalo touched his watch and raised his eyebrows. What time should he return? Katie said quietly, 'Thank M. Théophane warmly. Tell him I should have loved to have met him but must return to Trikala by taxi for another appointment. Perhaps another day . . .' Ahem. We were off again.

Next to no traffic beyond the town. At eighty or ninety miles an hour in that almost silent car, the sensation was of floating landscapes by Turner. Miniature villages appeared far below on the snow-topped landslides, Tringia, Kastania and Kerassea. With a map on my knees I followed their slow progression. Minutes passed and they slid away to be replaced by others, all much alike. How many, I wondered, were among the last resorts of the Vlachs? Field glasses showed that all the lower houses stood on stilts, and were reached from the floors of valleys by sinuous tracks.

We swung up the highest road pass in Greece, 1,690 metres, and passed a ski villa used in summer to house the snowploughs. Another loop, and then down the other side to the tourist-populated show town of Metsovo. All the way a splendid road, shown off by a splendid driver.

'Kyr' Ioanni,' he greeted me, his hands on my shoulders. '*Nous sommes les oiseaux de passage, eh? Comment ça va?* How well you look! But too thin, perhaps. Is it that you do not eat well in the mountains?'

Disinclined to tell him about tinned squid, biscuits, fruit and coffee in remote villages, I sketched in our route briefly, mentioning the manhunt and the bullet-ridden car between Kaloscopi and Piri. The thought occurred to me that questions almost always came from this shrewd collector of objects and ideas. What I wanted to know was what he had been up to and what was he doing in Metsovo?

Théophane airily waved the bullet-ridden car incident aside. 'When Greeks are not engaged in national wars, and then only with enormous help from the big nations such as yours to get them out of troubles – mostly which they make for themselves, they are fighting each other on the political edges of old antagonisms. It is within their nature, as a small nation of large ambitions and, *au fond*, supreme opportunists.'

'But you told me you came from Famagusta. Surely that is – or at least it used to be – part of Greater Greece?'

'Allow me to correct you, *mon ami*. I said that was where I was born, a different matter. It may be that I could have said that I am a Cretan Jew, or a part Vlach. Birth certificates are part of the *bataclan* of bureaucrats. The large family of my father came from a ghetto in Smyrna. Why is it, do you suppose, that I know so much about Anatolia and the Taurus mountains? But *qu'importe*? In *Enosis* I do not believe.

Fundamentally, that is to say on the paternal side, I am of the race of Ottomans who blocked the advance of the Mongols in the thirteenth century.'

He changed the subject. '*Dites-moi*, did you attain Mavrolithari, the place of the black stones? Is there any news of the Temple of *Hercule*?'

'No one knew. I think it's merely a village tradition. But what are you doing here?'

'I am trading, *naturellement*. It is in my blood. I love beautiful *objets*, and here and in nearby Ioanina, the city of the Ali Pasha, there are for sale icons and ancient Turkish rugs.'

'Who's selling them?'

'Rich Greeks, who because of the oil and the shipping difficulties have not much money in hand. I have a very important engagement in Ioanina this afternoon. Please to come with me. It will not be a long time.'

The sinuous road through Metsovo wriggles down a steep hill. On both sides of the approach to the square are solid two-storey buildings with well spaced windows, and gardens at the back. They are, M. Théophane assured me, typical of several townships in Epirus.

We were sitting on a balcony. Down the road waddled old men in blue serge tunics, with long white woollen stockings and wooden shoes adorned with pom-poms.

'Do you know who they are?' he asked.

'Yes, Vlachs. We met one of their chiefs on the train from Venice to Thessaloniki. We've seen them up in the hills. I know a few words of their language.' His turn to look surprised.

'What I didn't know', I admitted, 'is that in this town at least they look so prosperous.'

'Prosperous! These are only *les petits bourgeois* entertaining the tourists. They are paid to do it. However, there are Vlach millionaires. They are among the people from whom

I am buying *objets d'art*. Come now! First a little lunch, then Ioanina. We have much to tak about.'

If Kalonaros, our chauffeur from Trikala, may be compared with the charioteers at Delphi, Théophane, seemingly so worldly wise, had something in common with Phaethon who was notable in mythology for atrocious driving. Like a badly trained stable lad trying to show off on a thoroughbred, he flung the Mercedes around hairpin bends at an appalling speed and usually on the wrong side of the road. When, immediately ahead of us, sanguine motorists – rare among Greeks – refused to let us through, he hooted incessantly, and all the time he talked whilst I did my best to answer through clenched teeth.

Did I not know that the Vlach, Averof, was so rich that he had presented Greece with her only heavy cruiser, which was named after him? Answer: no. Had anyone told me that one of Greece's prime ministers, Ioan Koleti was also *un roumain*? Same answer. And so on until, to my heartfelt relief, he pointed far down to an immense lake on the shores of which stood Ioanina, the capital of Epirus – relief because we then encountered a military convoy which clung resolutely to the middle of the road.

Ioanina is a modern town except for the old district near the lake, which embraces a bazaar, a huge fortress and several minarets and mosques. We entered one or two of them to see icons similar to those Théophane intended to buy from private collectors. What did I think of them?

'Fine,' I said, mendaciously. They looked too bright, too colourful and too fussy. My inclination was to tell him that whilst masterpieces speak for themselves relatively few intelligent people can recognize bad art, but thought better of it.

As I was left alone whilst he was about his business, the thought occurred that many small mosques with their domes, pendentives and squinches are unimaginative miniatures of parts of the glory of Saint Sophia. One recalls Sydney Smith's comment on the Brighton Pavilion: 'It is as though St Paul's had gone down to the sea and pupped.'

Théophane returned with a large, heavily protected parcel which he locked up in the boot of his car. 'Seven pictures,' he said. 'About them I have been thinking since I last saw you. This is a matter for champagne. Let us drink where we can see the lake.'

'*D'abord*,' he began, 'Agrapha. What do you think? Totally isolated, eh? Primitive?'

'Not at all. Difficult to get there, though. Perhaps stupidly, we went over the mountains. We learnt too late that there is a passably good road that follows the river, the Agraphiotis, but as a professional I don't follow rivers. They are deceptively easy and I was told it was flooded. When in doubt you walk high, across the knuckles of the landscape.'

'But the village itself?'

'Among the best we met in the mountains. The woman of the house we stayed in adopted my wife. She washed her feet. As for the rest, hospitable. A mixed lot, Greek and Balkan refugees. A *stetl*, if you know the word.'

He smiled. 'Among other racial mixes, I am part Jewish,' he said. 'Any Vlachs there?'

'I don't know. We were both tired as hell. I remember the head man, a pleasant old chap with an upturned white moustache, big enough for three. My idea of a Klepht. It was he who recommended the house of the Magdalen. Also an old priest who, we were told, did next to nothing except drink and dispense platitudes. Apart from the women who, like everywhere else in the mountains, seemed always busy, the male Agraphiotes just lolled about and gossiped.'

'And you are going to write about the unwritten place,

which will bring tourists to where they have never been before?'

'That's my business, just as yours is driving about collecting ideas and things you don't really want. Has Ioanina anything to offer the packagers, the pedlars of tourism, as you call them?'

'*Eh bien*, that is a matter of one's taste. One has to be curious about excessive villainy as I am. Does the name Ali Pasha have a meaning for you?'

'Yes. I've read that by an awful mish-mash of intrigue, fraud and homicide he came pretty close to stealing most of continental Greece from the Turks. In fact, I recall a picture of him,' I said. 'A very old man with a long white beard, leaning back in a boat smoking a hookah. He looks like a stage villain – too sinister to be true.'

'So! The sketch by Louis Dupré. It is to be found in the Bibliothèque Nationale in Paris. His ancestors were compatriots of the family of my father,' he added with what seemed a touch of pride. 'What else do you know about him?'

As I recalled the story, Ali Pasha, the man who murdered Botsaris's father, was the descendant of an Anatolian Dervish who settled in that area, and from whom he usurped authority in Ioanina. He was supposed to have had a harem of 400 women, to have been constantly in the company of a retinue of semi-naked boys with hair down to their waists, and the court was guarded by trained assassins. He was allied to the French, but when the truce broke up he sent one of his sons-in-law to Constantinople as an envoy, and he died there, some believed by poison.

'That is true. Ali Pasha was fond on public spectacles. When he heard the news he pretended it had been contrived by his enemies. He rounded up all the immediate family, including Euphrosyne, his son-in-law's favourite mistress, and had all fifteen of them, naked and lightly bound, drowned one after another as a diversion during the intervals of a banquet.'

Théophane told me how Ali Pasha's eldest son, Mikhtar had such uncontrollable lust that he frequently raped women in the public street in broad daylight, and his younger son, an exquisite called Veli, boasted that he possessed the largest library of pornography in the Near East.

Surprisingly, this bizarre court was visited not only by Byron but by other members of the intelligentsia who happened to be in the area. Théophane wondered how they reacted to being entertained amongst concubines and catamites in a palace decorated with the skewered heads of their host's enemies?

Remarkably, considering his many enemies, Ali Pasha lived on to be over eighty, but in the end, abandoned by all his former allies, he fled to the island of Nissi Ioanina in the lake below the town, where he took refuge in the upstairs room of a pavilion. Soldiers broke in and started firing through the ceiling. A chance shot caught him in the groin, and he died screaming in agony as he'd heard so many of his own victims die before him.

I could see a dozen or more egrets circling and circling, slowly, their wings bright white but unmoving in an uplift of warm air.

'Who', I asked Théophane, 'is your good friend, Kalo, Kyrie Kalonaros?'

'A compatriot. It is many years that I have known him. Now, *hélas*, the dear man has operation on the throat. He has much knowledge about art. Once he was a valuer for Christie's in New York. Also, he drives the car for me when my mind is on other matters, and together we play the game of chess.'

'Who usually wins?'

'*C'est moi.* My business it is to think far ahead. Do you play?'

'I scarcely know the moves, but you are perhaps aware that the game was the basis of yet another of Freud's ridiculous ideas? Since the object of the game is to check-mate, which is the symbolic killing or castration of the enemy king (father figure), and since a player's strongest piece is his queen (mother figure), good players are often motivated by parricidal urges and mother love.'

Théophane thought the matter over for a moment before saying: 'I loved very much my father and my mother. You were in *contre*-Freud mood when we talked together at Amphissa, *n'est-ce-pas*? Have you any explanation?'

'It's a subject I know quite a lot about. My late wife, my beloved Tilly, died of cancer soon after she became a senior analyst of the Anna Freud Clinic in Hampstead.'

'Could it be that you are constantly walking away from reality?'

'Not at all. I have been fond of walking since I was eight years old.'

'*Eh bien.* And what is your route from Trikala?'

'Due east in the general direction of Larissa, but after about twenty kilometres we hope to climb up to some place called Vlahogiania where as far as I can make out there aren't any roads. With any luck we'll be at Elassona at the foot of Mount Olympos within four or five days. I'd better be getting back; we're setting off at dawn.'

'Always on the move?' To my relief he added, '*Entendu!* I will drive you back to Metsovo where Kalo will take over. One last question: have you met many Vlachs in the Pindos?'

'A few here and there. We've seen their trucks several times. Perhaps the strangest person was a woman at Marathos, the last place before Agrapha. She was married to a local man, and they say she came from a group which camped out high above the village. Each day she took a herd of goats almost straight up the mountain where, we think, she joined them. I have an idea that in some curious way the husband managed to keep in touch with her wherever she was. Others have told us that these people still revere nature gods, the spirits of streams and forests.'

'That is not a surprise for me. Man worships what he knows best. If triangles invented gods, they would imagine them to be three-sided.'

'You seem to be uncommonly interested in these people. What's the reason?'

'The best of reasons,' Théophane said. 'Before her marriage in Smyrna, my mother was a Vlach, originally from Albania.'

The Mountain

Not a good start. At dawn a thick white mist. The moist plains of Thessaly were breathing heavily. We ventured out into the empty square. All that could be heard an hour before Prime were arguments between local cats and the incessant bleep of frogs from the river Pinios. At the start of our long looked-forward-to assault on the summer home of the gods the augurs of good fortune could have served us better.

We swung out of town on the Larissa highway. We had been told that somewhere close by a derelict mosque marked the turn off to the *paleodhromos*, the classical turnpike to ancient Trikala. But it was difficult to find. We were among half-seen garages, shoddy shops and the dumps of the suburbs. Damn the frogs! We were too near their riverside romping place. Suddenly out of the murk there loomed the remains of an ivy-gripped pendentive with spandrels and narrow windows with semi-circular eyebrows. I regretted what I'd said about Ottoman architecture! It looked fine. A path ran alongside the rubble of broken pantiles and stone and beyond it a Thessalian farm where tethered cows were being milked on sun-baked dung among a gabble of guinea-fowl. Two girls and their mamma in kerchiefs must have been surprised at our exuberant greeting.

The old road? Why it was over there! As an actor peers

through the curtains at his audience before the show begins, a lemon-coloured sun emerged through the thinning mist. We could see the gate and the lane and we were on our way in an ever-brightening landscape.

For insecticidal purposes the lower portions of the trunks of fruit trees are painted as white as the stockings of men at Metsovo, which brought us back to the enigmatic M. Théophane. Did I think that Kalo was his resident boy-friend, asked Katie.

I thought not. In my opinion the compulsive collector was of that class rarely recognized or talked about in Britain, a capon, an affectionate neuter with a penchant for horrend-ous stories. A sadistic substitute for sexuality?

'He talked with what seemed enthusiasm about the dreadful goings-on of Ali Pasha; he described how a bishop of Trikala who had stepped out of the official line was flayed alive and his body stuffed with straw before the Turks took him round in a cart on an exhibition tour.' I told her how as we hurtled down to Ioanina Théophane said it was on that route that Curzon had a macabre encounter with an unfortunate traveller strapped to the side of a mule in a small box. He assumed he was a dwarf until somebody explained that his particular mode of travel was because the man had just had both his legs cut off by robbers.

To change the subject Katie bent down to examine an exquisite bunch of Madonna lilies on the banks of an irrigation ditch. Even in well-watered Thessaly the hot dry summer was well under way. Nearly all the annual species of plants had already set seed and were drying up. Never-theless we saw Greek trefoils shimmering with blue butter-flies and valerian, Love-in-a-mist, cornflowers, mulleins, St John's Wort and on sandy land the Spanish oyster plant, a thistle-like herb with golden flowers. The ancients dug it up for its edible tap-root which, according to Dioscorides

'is good for such as have the arme pits and other parts of
ye body foule smellie'.

We began to climb. The sun poured down fiercely. The
farmsteads were falling away. On open land the natives build
wattle shelters like Masai *manyattas* around isolated trees to
protect their sheep and goats from the heat. Estimated animal
population within each compound about fifty.

Here we began to get some idea of the economics of rural
pastoralism. In Trikala a butcher had told me that graziers
received an annual subsidy of 3,000 drachs, a little more
then £12 for each animal. What for? To reduce the scrubby
vegetation to the deserts seen on most of the high tops?
Ignorance is a basic problem. It is, unfortunately, possible
for people to live on a rapidly eroding landscape and be
almost unaware of it.

The country became hilly. We had been walking for
hours and were too parched to eat what little food we had
bought as emergency supplies. There were no changes in
the contour lines on the last of our almost useless maps. We
had imagined we should spend the greater part of the day
on the plain but to the north-east we saw, faintly, a huge
range of hills, and to the south the Larissa highway.

We made for a compound around the only tree in sight,
a withered evergreen where a score or more of curiously
mottled sheep huddled around a young lad under a thick
woollen cape. We asked him about the nearest village.
'Neohori,' he said, and by holding up all his fingers and
then those on one hand indicated it was about fifteen
kilometres to the north. We trudged on with bloodshot
eyes, tired and with no enthusiasm.

Sod's law again. Unless rectified promptly discontent-
ments tend to be cumulative. With the plain far below us
we clambered up a track, the wrong track, came back, tried
another and at eight o'clock that night arrived at the small
but sophisticated village of Neohori, where a well-stocked

supermarket had been closed for about an hour, and the taverna was about a mile away up the road. We gazed longingly through the shop window.

Up came a young girl who asked if she could help. The shop closed? No problem. The owner lived nearby. She would fetch him. He seemed delighted to see us, and with the girl, a student of the guide school in Thessaloniki as interpreter we chose a supper of everything we could wish for including fresh fruit, pastries and a litre of the best white wine in the shop. Could our friend recommend anywhere beyond the village where we could put our tent down for the night? We liked soft ground.

She spoke to the shopkeeper at some length. Presumably there were alternatives. There was one phrase, *ine steeheeomonos*, which she asked him to repeat and then, turning to us, said, 'Many places just beyond the bridge where a wood has been cut down for new buildings, but there is one place marked by a monument in front of an old stone wall avoided by most of the villagers. They say there used to be an ancient place of holiness there. It is *Steeheeomonos*. I don't know how you say in English.'

An evil place, I suggested.

She shrugged her shoulders and sighed. 'Perhaps. The Germans murdered many people there, including some of my father's family, during the Occupation.'

By contrast with the gauntlet of stares we had so often endured, the citizenry of Neohori were filled with goodwill. We had invitations to stop for coffee and answer their questions. We shook hands and passed the time of night with everybody who greeted us. The bent figure of an elderly man with a black eye-patch who spoke good English insisted on finding out where we were heading for. To Elassona, I told him, by way of Diasello and Vlahogiania. 'There is a bus from Larissa to Elassona,' he said. 'You can pick it up anywhere on the main road.' Because we suspect that places which rural Greeks haven't visited don't exist, we left it at that.

Beyond a number of squares were neat suburbs, each with a pump on a plinth. We filled our plastic water-container and felt the householders would not have refused us a bath in their garden.

The site we chose in the almost dark backed on to an incomplete building of red brick immediately beyond the town limits. Owls halloo-ed sadly and wraiths of mist floated up from an invisible streamlet. With gear up and in order we drank to the outcome of the day, *and* to the next one when, with any luck, we should be at least within sight of the almost unimaginable, a glimpse of our objective, the throne of Zeus.

'To us,' we said, and again to the fruit of Gaia, an excellent wine made the better by what we had sipped in the village of hospitality.

'Who's that?' Katie asked, quietly, pointing.

A scarecrow of a figure, slightly lame. Not making towards us. He moved backwards and forwards, peering under tarpaulins at builders' gear, piles of sand and a cement-mixer.

'Better have a word with him,' I said.

I followed him. I don't think he had seen us. Surprise on both sides. It was Captain Hook, the man with the black eye-patch from the village. What were we doing there, he asked. I told him we were camping near the stream. If we wanted to, we could sleep in the school, he said, pointing to the red brick building. It was empty, and as caretaker he had the key. Did we want to use the toilets and the taps at the back? If so, he would turn the water on. Yes? Then would we please follow him.

Where had we come from? Not wanting to go into a long, tedious explanation, I told him Trikala. On foot? I nodded. That was a long way. Had I been a soldier? Yes. He thought so. Sergeants taught a man how to walk. In the war he had been wounded, and touched his eye-patch. I asked him where that had been. 'Here,' he said, 'in Neohori, but I was lucky. I got away. Look!'

In front of an old stone wall stood a cenotaph inscribed with twenty or more names. All the men the Germans captured had been stood up in front of that wall and shot one after another. The bullet marks, concave depressions as if pitted out by a chisel, could still be seen in the uppermost stones. Then, as a reprisal for guerilla activities thought to have been supported by local people, the invaders had burned the village down. I could think of nothing to say. The name Neohori, the new place, occurs throughout Greece.

The caretaker showed me the water taps in the shed. I thanked him. We shook hands warmly and I went back to Katie.

Hours before dawn she woke me up at the sound of a sustained howl from somewhere near by.

'Wolf, dog or evil spirit on the prowl?' she asked.

'Dog,' I said firmly. 'It's been barking on and off since you went to sleep. No matter what they said in the village, I don't believe in the supernatural.' I had been haunted by the thought of the old stone wall and the men who had died there.

Years ago during the Spanish Civil War an old friend of mine, Arthur Lerner, the economist and philosopher, faced death with three other members of the International Brigade. For some reason they were reprieved, and a dispatch rider arrived when they had already been lined up facing the firing-squad. 'What were your last thoughts?' I asked him. He said it had happened in a farmyard, and he recalled looking down to find that he was almost standing in fresh cowpats. Feeling that it was indecent to die there he managed to inch away, nearer to one of his companions.

The next day: Monday 4 June. Because of the uncertainty about the country ahead and the thirst-provoking heat, I felt distinctly out of sorts. Our last day but one on that laborious stage is a confusion of tape-recorded impressions, starting with a shrine that became a pock-marked wall of death, and ending with egrets and the travellers through the night.

Almost the only figures in those immense landscapes were old women in black, mostly alone, hoeing away in the stubble of old tobacco plants. They were glad to be greeted; they waved their hoes and shouted back, '*Kalo taxidi.*' Working on a presumed position of Diasello due north, we struck up a sinuous track in that direction, fortified by the opinion of a shepherd and his goats, two or three of which had climbed up thorn trees, that the village was '*Makria makria*', further up, further up. At least he had heard of the place. Somebody we had asked not far from Neohori had pointed in an entirely different direction and said something we didn't quite catch but which we took to mean 'difficult to find'.

Eleven o'clock. Another hour had passed. It had become hot. Expecting to pass through at least one small village before Diasello, we had cut down on weight by carrying only about a pint of water in a plastic bottle. We had drunk half of it and could hear the rest splashing about in my rucksack, tantalizingly.

It took me back to the deserts of North Kenya where, with a dozen camels and four men in my care, water was a constant problem during stages of three or four days. On several occasions there wasn't enough for a wash at night nor the next morning, since I wasn't prepared to rinse my hands and face in camel urine, straight from the pump so to speak, as the boys did. With time to spare before dusk we sometimes unloaded the camels and allowed them to wander free in hummocky country with nothing visible except a complete circle of sand. There was just a chance that in an almost straight line they would make for a patch of scrub in a depression unseen by us, where they would begin to browse. At this the men would plunge their spears deep into the ground and examine the blades when they pulled them out. If just a few particles clung to the metal they concentrated on that area until they struck slightly moist sand. Then they began to dig with the exuberation of dogs which had smelt buried bones. They were looking for the line of an extremely small underground spring – enough sometimes for cooking, but with the reasonable certainty that there would be much more in that hole by the morning.

Another hour passed. Through glasses Diasello appeared as a dot on the horizon with, behind it, horizontal clouds on a mountain range. We were elated. We drank the rest of the water. For reasons I can't explain in terms of estimated distances between horizons, landscape-reading in Greece is more deceptive than in any other country I know. Perhaps it's the light. For every mile we walked Diasello enlarged in size; it looked lower than when we first saw it; our pace quickened and our packs felt lighter too. Friends have said of me that I'm frequently surprised by the obvious. As we neared the buildings on that steep slope and saw far beyond them the white-topped peaks of the Olympos range all became clear. Another dragon of the imagination had been slain.

From the old squat buildings in layers on the way into town it looked as if the high-perched hamlet had at one time been a Turkish fort. The little streets were labyrinthine and the local folk gracious. There was none of that 'Hiya feller' stuff of middle-aged Greeks who had spent their early years and their family's patrimony in the slaughter-houses of Sydney or Chicago. The place breathed self-respect. We wondered if we had climbed into another Vlach village.

We settled down and, seeing me poring over the last of our tattered maps, a well-dressed young fellow in his mid-twenties asked, simply, if he could be of any help.

Vyronos (Byron) and his brother Veni, presumably short for Venizelos, the two sons of Papastavros, apparently a rich man, had been beguiled away from studying economics in Athens to help their father during a local labour shortage. Although they didn't say so, both seemed bored to hell with life in the northernmost part of the *nomos* of Trikala. Did I really imagine they liked ordering kilolitres of *venzini* for the truck and sacks of fertilizer, when they could have been in the students' club in Panepistimiou? Would we come to their home for something to eat? Five kilometres; they would take us there and bring us back in the pick-up. No? Then perhaps another drink? We were the first tourists they had ever seen at home.

The most important question, as I put it to him, was how to get down to the floor of the valley and reach Elassona without touching the central highway from Larissa. There were not even any small roads on our map.

We were joined by his brother and together they looked at the sheet with some surprise. 'A very old map,' said Veni. 'I have never seen one like it. True, there is no road but there is a shepherd's track. Would you like a lift down there? No? Then look. Come down in this direction,' and with his pen he drew a serpentine line. 'That is a tributary of the Titarissios which joins the Pinios.' In the other, the northerly direction, we were told, it flows through Elassona.

'How far will that be from here?'

'All the way? Perhaps twenty-five kilometres or a little more.' And in answer to my final question: yes, we could drink from the stream. They had drunk a great deal of it when out shooting, but it was greatly improved by a touch of ouzo.

We were conducted to the edge of the escarpment where, below us, swinging down in the form of an immense letter S through a mosaic of pasturage and farmland interspersed with trees, we could see the track. This, coupled with the local advice from the brothers, set our spirits soaring.

We talked about the name Vyronos which in Greece still has a charismatic quality. Even in small villages, from Athens to Trikala, we had seen the tribute paid to him in the names of streets, cafés and restaurants. Thousands of children are baptized in his name. In town squares where inscriptions under statues have been smudged by time, some Greeks seem unable to distinguish between heroic representations of the *lordos*, or perhaps Marcos Botsaris, or even a ferocious old Klepht in battle-dress. This point is nicely made by Patrick Leigh Fermor.

Poets, he says, have strange posthumous careers. When Rupert Brooke died aged about twenty-seven in 1915, he was buried in Skyros, an island he'd never visited in his life. The Skyriots are proud of him and he is greatly honoured there. A few years ago a visitor was admiring the olive grove where the poet's grave lies, and reading the inscription on the tomb, when an old shepherd spoke to him saying he'd noticed that he was admiring the grave of *O Broukis*: 'We are glad to have him with us. He was a good man.' On questioning, the shepherd admitted that he was not strong on letters and had never read any of the poetry, but said you could tell he was a great man, adding, 'You see that olive tree over there? That was his tree.'

'How do you mean?'

'He used to sit under it every day and write poetry.'

Not wanting to contradict him, the visitor asked if he was sure they were talking about the same person. The shepherd was quite sure.

'What did he look like?'

'Magnificent, sir. Tall, dignified, flowing hair, burning eyes and a long white beard.'

Late in the afternoon we reached what could have been a line-and-wash sketch for a picture of Arcadia by Edward Lear or Claude. Classical landscape with figures. The stream, one of the innumerable tributaries of the Pinios, the nymphs of yet another river-god, gurgled through an arcade of tall, light-dappled plane trees and willows. A dozen or more cheerful young men whom we took to be Vlachs were watering and milking goats and sheep, the latter by throwing the ewes over on to their backs and straddling them to reach their swollen teats. Some old shepherds with intricately carved crooks stood around, together with two or three women, knitting or finger-spinning on a distaff.

We didn't stay long. They had work to do; as for us, to keep up with that damned implacable task-master The Schedule, we felt we ought to tread down a few more kilometres. We shouted goodbyes and left in the company of that talkative stream.

It let us down, we felt, by swinging away from the track on the left bank which led us into flat moist country inhabited by aggressive horse-flies and mosquitoes. No chance of a peaceful night there. The ground became slightly steeper; the dirt track, joined by another, looked more used. Wheel-marks and sheep- and goat-droppings. Surrounded by hills on three sides, we came out into a grassy plateau perhaps a mile in diameter with some curious wooden contraption immediately ahead.

A long feeding-trough on trestles with at one end a metal cistern partly set into the ground and fed by a dribbling tap. 'Home from home,' said Katie: I was less enthusiastic. A cardinal rule for anyone who sets up camp in the bush is never to be too near to, or even within sight of, a water-hole, the focal point of tribesmen, animals and their predators.

Leaving Katie to unstrap our packs and draw more water than we had been able to squander in days, I took a turn round where the plateau began to slope. The sight of a flock of snowy-white birds, egrets, circling above where we took the stream to be, disclosed a patch of flat ground where we couldn't be seen. Katie, meanwhile had found a litre bottle of white wine in the cistern, presumably left there by somebody who would be coming back for it. Footprints were still visible in the moist sand.

We walked over to the egrets' hunting ground. After sitting with our feet in lukewarm water we supped and stretched out luxuriously, listening to the calls of owls. They weren't the species we had become accustomed to, Scops owl which murmurs *pee-oo, pee-oo*. These were Little owls (*Athena noctua*), the symbol of the city, created according to legend by the Goddess of Wisdom. Scops are remarkable for a loud ringing cry that puts us in mind of the opening sequence of the bird we know so well from our northern moors, the curlew. The Greek equivalent of coals to Newcastle is that anything commonplace is like sending owls to Athens or priests to Athos where they used to swarm like bees. When Curzon became Under-Secretary for Foreign Affairs at the end of the last century he received word that the heavily bearded brethren on that peninsula were violating their vows. Unfortunately, in cipher, the word vows became cows. In the margin of the despatch Curzon simply scribbled, 'Send them a papal bull.'

That night we listened and gazed up at the owl-like moon until we slept. At about two in the morning I woke with a start. I heard a truck, and then another. The noise grew louder. Four or five vehicles without lights made their way toward the cistern. There they stopped. Men got out. Goats and sheep bleated. Much laughter and loud talk in the clipped vowels of the Black Departers. Were they about to release their flocks with dogs? To our immense relief they kept them penned up and off they went. 'How long will it take us to reach Elassona?' asked Katie in a tense voice. I thought about five or six hours. 'Thank God,' she said.

I underestimated the number of loops in that serpentine track. It took us from first light until five in the afternoon. Ahead of us for most of the way like a mirage that came and went we saw the immense ridge that marked our journey's end.

On Thursday 7 June we were hanging our washing on the balcony of a hotel remarkable only for the fact that our bedroom overlooked a pair of nesting storks, which, when they exchanged incubating duties, made a noise like dice rattling in a box.

Over supper that night we talked about how far we should venture up towards the visibly snow-capped platform of the range. Katie argued, forcibly, that from the moment we decided to make this trip we had chosen the foot of Mount Olympos as merely a tangible objective to head for. Well, surely we had arrived there, hadn't we? She pointed out that we could see the slopes from the roof of the hotel and thought they looked less inviting each time she saw them. In the Agrapha we had already done more mountain-storming than we had bargained for. Enough was enough. Didn't I remember that night under an electric pylon when the thunderstorm started to brew up?

Had the small market town of Elassona looked more attractive I might have agreed to haul the flag down then and there. Homer mentioned the ancient place, since demolished, which is more than Michelin does today. Strange, this, since for thousands of years Elassona has stood watch and ward between the rich Plain of Larissa and the mountain pass, the *Elassonitikos*, the classic invasion route of Thracians, Persians, Slavs, Huns and Turks.

Katie sighed at my intention of eventually pushing on and asked, 'Well, then, what next?' I suggested that for a few days we should enjoy ourselves doing nothing in particular, and then perhaps a modest venture into those nebulous slopes to the north-east, which were under a cloud that morning. Could it be that the gods had pulled down their blinds?

I was up and about earlier than Katie and came upon several thirsty souls in a taverna beyond the market-place. The company included Spiro, a local tobacco merchant who had served his time in Richmond, Virginia; Grego, a cab-driver with a fine Mercedes bought from his earnings in Detroit; and a butcher with a South African wife. They spoke English in a variety of accents and I heard their stories out before getting down to ways of reaching the *Elassonitikos*.

Grego, their spokesman, told the story, strange to my ears but far from uncommon in Greece, about how, within a year of his getting a hard but well paid job on the Chrysler assembly line, his father sent him three photographs of a girl he had never seen, with more than a suggestion that he should marry her. Unknown to him the parents had been discussing the subject for months. He met her for the first time when she stepped off the boat. He showed me several coloured photographs. A striking-looking girl with a wry smile whom many a man might have run off with even without the property his father had told him about, together with an attestation from the best-known lawyer in Elassona.

'Gardammit, never did a better deal in my life,' said Grego, and the others who had known the family for years nodded their approval. Together with his taxi business they now have a house and a small vineyard just outside town, and three daughters, one already engaged.

The others told their stories. All of them had worked abroad, helping to keep their parents until they collected their short-term pensions. The man with the flashy rings and watch who owned the tavern still had four sons in Germany, they told me.

This nation-wide propensity for emigration stems from centuries of Turkish oppression when Greeks in their millions, especially in the north, became refugees, deprived of their family holdings. Lord Curzon said there was 'no precedent in modern times for this gigantic transference of populations'. The problem was exacerbated after the Convention of Lausanne in 1923 where the Allies sought unsuccessfully to straighten out compulsory Graeco-Turkish exchanges. The housing shortage was such that for two or three years each box in the municipal theatre in Athens was occupied by a whole family of Greeks, their only living space.

Grego recalled stories his grandfather had told him of the road between southern Bulgaria and Macedonia which was solidly blocked by hordes of home-bound families trying to move in opposite directions, obliged to live on herb tea and roots which they dug up and boiled, together with anything else they could find. Grandpa had said that for two years his relatives close to the sea came round begging for anything they could offer the refugees, but 'not those lousy Bulgars,' he added.

Mention of that road brought me to what I really wanted to know about: how did one get up into the mountains from Elassona? Grego made no bones about it. We were on what he called 'the wrong side of the big haul', the highest part of the *massif*. By far the easiest way was from Litohoro – that place we had seen on the bus on our way south from Thessaloniki over a month ago. There, as he put it, if you took a cab up to the half-way house, a little hamlet called Prionia, you could get to a *refuge* and then the summit in two or three hours. There really wasn't much to it.

I recalled the peaks: the highest point, Mytikas, the Throne of Zeus, with Skolio and Skala on one side and Stefani and Toumba on the other. I could repeat their names like a litany. What I hadn't realized until that morning was that due largely to perspective and the extensive plateau immediately below the utterly bare peaks, the whole vista couldn't be seen from Elassona, which is some thirty miles to the south-west. The bulk of the range extended for some forty or fifty miles to the north-east.

'Why can't we go straight over the top from here?' I asked. For answer Grego slowly raised an invisible rifle and shot me through the head. 'There's a small army up there at the garrison of Olimbiada,' he said. Sometimes they let civilians through in a closed truck but not often and not without special passes from the Greek Alpine Club.

'Can't we work our way round the rim of the fortifications?'

We might, he thought, if we were lucky and prepared to slip a sentry a few notes. But he admitted he didn't really know. Neither he nor his friends had ever been beyond the gates at the garrison. It was a roundabout route by a little road, but he could run us there in about an hour.

'About how far is it across country?'

He hadn't thought about it. Maybe fifteen kilometres, but very steep in places. I left it at that.

I found Katie sitting on our balcony, poring over the crossword in a month-old copy of *The Times*. 'Where did you get that?' I asked.

'At the bus station,' she said.

'*What* were you doing there?'

'Just talking to the Inspector, darling. Don't be so snappy. Look! Overnight we've had an addition to the family,' and she passed me the field glasses.

Peering from beneath the outstretched wing of one of its parents – storks are difficult to sex – could be seen a stumpy white chick staggering about making a clicking noise in imitation of the adults. To its evident satisfaction the parent leaned over, touched its small black bill and heaved, slightly. The process is called regurgitation. Temporarily satisfied, it rolled over on its back and stopped clicking.

During the chick-rearing season storks develop prodigious appetites. Within an hour one banded specimen watched by a professional ornithologist devoured forty-four mice, two hamsters and a frog. Normally they gorge themselves on insects and amphibious dainties. Owing perhaps to the fact that the birds are regarded as emblems of fertility and worthy of protection there are still about 2,500 pairs in Greece, although as in other countries their numbers are declining.

Over drinks that evening I recounted all I had learnt from the cab-driver, emphasizing that the garrison, Olimbiada, was far higher than anything we had originally intended to essay. As I saw it, if we reduced everything we had been carrying to irreducible necessities, far from achieving the lower slopes from a respectable height we should be able to see where the gods were reputed to live during the summer. Wasn't that worth another stage or two?

There were arguments and counter-arguments against the alternatives. No, I didn't want to see what the northern flanks of the range looked like through the windows of a bus on its way to Katerini on the coast. We had already been there on the way in. Outspoken friends have said of us that on important matters Katie and I are one and she is the one, but on this issue I won hands down on a local map provided by that good fellow who gave us his radio-cab number and offered to haul us back. Could he give us the garrison number? Like hell he could, he said.

Relieved of part of our load we felt buoyant, almost cushioned on air as we strode through lark-infested stubble some two or three days later. Visually tedious until the contours began to squeeze together at something over 2,000 feet. Thereafter the dry irrigation canals became first damp and then slow-moving streamlets fed by melting snow and enlivened by banks of flowers. A botanical peculiarity about plants on steep slopes is that the higher they grow the later they flower. Their spring is delayed. Those which were beginning to look desiccated on the plains, such as a variety of gentians, saxifrages and orchids with luscious 'lips', had only just achieved full sexual vigour around us.

Orchid fertilization is so complicated and varied that in their efforts to attract pollinators this huge family of some 30,000 species has been described as a floral *Kama Sutra*. Their rounded tubers resemble testicles, which is *orchis* in Greek, hence their name. Anthony Huxley, a son of the late Sir Julian relates how in medieval England orchids were known as dogs' stones or bulls' bags. Shakespeare wrote of Ophelia's 'long purples' to which 'the liberal shepherds give a grosser name', a phrase which must have had them rolling about in the pit.

Guileful orchids both protect and advertise their generative parts in the form of scents which usually happen to be very attractive to our senses, such as lily-of-the-valley. Several Dendrobiums offer heliotrope in the morning and lilac after dark. More remarkable from an evolutionary point of view is the way in which their lips and purses resemble the female bodies of bees, flies, small moths and other insects on which they are almost entirely dependent for fertilization.

In all this erotic chambering there is more than a touch

of sadism and prostitution. A beguiled pollinator, let us say a dull but extremely diligent bumble bee, is forced into ridiculous postures, often upside down to satisfy his misplaced lust. He may be physically drugged, trapped in narrow passages from which there is no escape unless he enlivens the moist ovules (ovaries) of his heavily disguised temptress. When it eventually escapes, 'groggy and wet-winged' as Huxley puts it, the insect can't be aware that it has visited the wrong house, that of a sex-deficient group of plants remarkable for florid beauty and bizarre bodies which in some cases actually smell like the legitimate mates of their pollinators.

Despite the erratic nature of tracks between holdings we made good progress, climbing steadily. The sight of an old fellow leaning on a stick watching his goats brought to mind our first glimpses of those solitaries in distant Boeotia.

What did Katie recall most vividly at the start of the trip? Without hesitation she said the *Flying Tortoise*, the wreck of the trains; two monsters smashed into small pieces. She'd never forget it, and often wondered how many people had been killed.

'Yes. But what would you pick out on the plus side?'

She thought for a moment.

'Good will. The hospitality of everyone out to enjoy themselves on the first of May but most especially those exhausted young men at the taverna that night who left their sweeping to put a wrap round my shoulders.'

We mentally spooled back to other memorable times. One of Katie's recollections was her joy at the profusion of flowers in the early part of the walk; mine were of the poverty of land at the end of its tether, Arcadia reduced to an irrecoverable wilderness through lack of water and the improvidence of landowners intent only on their current income. We thought of rigours scarcely talked about at the time and were at one about that gorge, the Devil's Arse, its heat and its hurts, nicely smoothed out before night by the chance encounter with the gallant Legionnaire from Sidi bel Abbes.

About the Agrapha and its narrow cliff-hangers some hundreds of feet above the noisy torrent, the Agraphiotis, I have no mind to say more than that I might have turned back if it hadn't been easier and more prudent to press on. What I can't explain is how we were able to expend so much energy walking up to eight or nine hours most days with very little food yet rarely feeling hungry.

Thirst now, that was something different. We were often chronically dehydrated. At the sight of moist earth at the foot of a scree I had dug like a starving ant-eater. As somebody put it, you can get used to anything – which has always seemed to me a cogent argument against the minatory prospect of Hell. But where now? *Pou-pou-pou*, as hoopoes say.

No hoopoes on the stairs to Olympos, only squeaky quails, twittery larks and now and again melodious warblers which warbled in bird language wholly unknown to me.

Almost immediately above us we could make out a line of battlements partly obscured by the Gatherer of Clouds. We were within sight of our destination. It certainly looked mysterious, but I was in no mood for the supernatural. We had clambered up there to see the place believed by the ancient Greeks to be the summer home of the gods. That day the wind from the heights felt somewhat chilly.

It seems to me that myths of creation and eventual extinction vary according to the climate. In our cold north the first human beings were said to have sprung from the licking of frozen stones by a divine cow-like creature named Audumla. The Northern afterworld was a bare, misty, featureless plain where ghosts wandered hungry and shivering. Those unpleasant places were destined for serfs and commoners: the nobility with paid bards to sing about what splendid fellows they were could look forward to warm celestial mead-halls in Valhalla, and Elysian fields in Greece.

According to a myth from the kinder climate of Greece, the human race derived from a Titan named Prometheus kneading mud on a flowery riverbank, which he made into human statuettes and Athene brought to life. Without a hope in hell, the ordinary run of Greek ghosts went to a sunless, flowerless underground cavern.

Our long journey ended on the authentic note of anti-climax echoing from peak to peak. A military helicopter clattered over and encircled us twice.

The sentry at the gates of the garrison knew enough English to say plainly but politely that nobody without a military pass could enter whilst they were engaged in manoeuvres. 'How long would that be? A few days? A week?' He didn't know.

Hoping for a glimpse of what that high platform looked like from behind the gates, I asked if we could speak to the commander.

He shook his head. He had been given his instructions when he first saw us approaching about an hour earlier – and he pointed to an almost concealed pylon inside the enclosure. On the top of it could just be made out the slowly revolving arm of a radar scanner. Before he closed the gate, decisively he saluted and wished us a good journey. '*Kalo taxidi.*'

★   ★   ★

Most journeys end more abruptly than they begin. We tramped down to a village, Kallithea, from which after a telephone call, Grego hauled us back to where the storks, both parents, were clattering excitedly over the emergence of their second storkling.

Among the Gods

Nearly four months later I flew from Heathrow to Thessaloniki, alone. Thoughts about the eastern face of the famous peaks on the skyline above Litohoro had become something of an obsession. As soon as we had turned our backs on Elassona I regretted we hadn't stayed on, rested for maybe another week, and then tried to add a few Olympian laurel leaves to our last long walk. But in addition to family affairs far too much work had to be attended to in London even to think of going back in the summer.

About mid-September, or maybe it could have been a little later, I put a call through to the Hellenic Alpine Club in Athens to ask what was the latest date one could be reasonably sure of getting up to the *refuge* above Litohoro without whooshing about on skis. I don't think I can ski. I've never tried. They thought mid-October or the beginning of November. They gave me the telephone number of their local manager and guide, Costas Zolotas. That helpful fellow – who speaks both German and English with curiously inverted phrases – was much of the same opinion. '*Korrekt,*' he said. With him I should be there about mid-October, it had been a hot dry summer followed by much rain. In the northern Balkans clouds were already piling up.

Katie agreed to stay at home until I phoned her, first

before I started the scramble and then again when I returned to the hotel. She could rejoin me in either Corfu or Metsovo. She packed spartan gear for me – tent, sleeping-bag and woollies – and demurred when I slipped in a miniature camera and a short-wave radio the size of a pack of cards. Total weight far less than half of what we had lugged through Greece. She was apprehensive. No need to worry, I assured her. After all, I said immodestly, I had scrambled over the Mountains of the Moon in Central Africa to nearly 15,000 feet. Tim Salmon who has done a lot of walking in Greece has described Mount Olympos as a mere pimple by Himalayan standards.

Litohoro is a Chamonix or Bourg-St Maurice in miniature, a small township at the top of a hill from which serious climbers, scramblers or indolent scenery seekers can stroll up towards the youth hostel, turn sharp right to a comfortable open-air restaurant and sit down the better to have their breath taken away by one of the greatest views in Greece. Immediately ahead lies an immense V-shaped gorge of grey rock, the spectacular outflow of a torrent, the Enippeas which flows into the Aegean some five miles below the town.

Lording it over the landscape at a height of a little over 10,000 feet are the peaks subordinate to Mytikas, the very throne of the Gatherer of Clouds. In the curiously green light they stood out that morning like dark stones in a bright necklace of snow.

Zolotas turned out to be a hairy, square-shouldered fellow who looked as if he could carry one of his own mules. They were quartered, he told me, at Prionia at the very top of the gorge. This is the half-way house up to the skyline. It could be reached most easily, he assured me, by local taxis on a twelve-mile loop of the forest road. Alternatively he could run me up there in his Land Rover the next day, since his wife ran the *refuge* about six kilometres above Prionia. If I held to what he called the '*Zeek sack*' of the *podidhromos*, a foot-track through the last of the trees, I could make my way up to the crest of Olympos in maybe two and a half hours. The verticals were for serious climbers.

A genial fellow, but his proposals sounded too much like a conducted tour for self-satisfaction. I told him I proposed to scramble up through the gorge on a DIY.

He looked puzzled. '*Allein*,' I said. 'Alone – by myself.'

'*Gar nicht leicht.*' In his opinion it wouldn't be easy.

On a large-scale map he pointed to places where there were overhangs of rocks. At those points it was necessary either to take a path up to the top near the road and scramble down the other side, or to cross the stream at various points.

'*In diesem augenblick*' – just at the moment the snow was melting and the stream flooded. Now if only a week or two earlier I had come . . .

'When will you leave here?' he asked.

'Maybe in a day or two. First I want to have a look at the gorge.'

'Before you depart come and see me,' he said. 'Then if we don't see you at the *refuge* we shall know where to look.'

It looked formidable. For two or three hundred yards the left wall above the torrent is paving-stoned with blocks of ferro-concrete. These end abruptly in a confusion of screes, foot-pointed in various directions. I took to an up-going diagonal with little confidence, confirmed by the tinkle of dislodged pebbles the size of gravel. Seeing a traverse on more substantial stuff several feet above my left shoulder I soldiered on towards the apex of the first of the overhangs I had been told about.

Much more of that local lithology and I would have

accepted the offer of the lift up to Prionia but the Devil, having been at his game for a long time, deals slowly, offering small rewards to ventures on the slippery stones to peradventure.

It looked fine on the down-slope – a dribble of a long track down to the torrent. What could be better after that initial survey? Surely a drink or two back in Litohoro? And so passed that day and the next.

In that time I met the trim young Mayor whose father had been with ELAS in the mountains, his chief clerk, who was interested in botany, and the charming French-speaking woman from the Information Bureau, from whom I learnt in order of importance that the weather prospects weren't too good but avalanches were rare because of the bangs from the bombs on the range on the top – meaning, presumably, behind Olimbiada – and that, to my surprise, it wasn't until 1913 that a local guide, Christos Kakkalos had helped two Swiss climbers, Baud-Bovy and Boissonas to climb to the summit of Mytikas. The operative word here is climb. They scaled an almost vertical face with overhangs. Nowadays it's done regularly by professionals but each year thousands of other summit-seekers scramble between the verticals, and I hoped to be among them. Madame said near the top of the gorge I should probably see the priest in charge of the Monastery of St Dionysius.

In the sixteenth century this saint, one of three of that name and the founder of the rule, had written somewhat sceptically about the 'so-called gods' who were reputed to have lived above his retreat from 'worldly affairs'.

That evening I phoned Katie to say that I intended to set off the next day. Not alone, she hoped. There'd been some talk on the radio and TV about worsening weather advancing on the Balkans from the Ukraine. Thick snow in northern Yugoslavia.

'No talk of it here in the Hotel Aphrodite,' I said. 'In any case, I'm scrambling up with three lusty Australians to-morrow. Right now they're whooping it up in some nightspot on the coast.'

'Take care, darling,' she said. 'Phone me as soon as you can. *Kalo taxidi.*'

Worsening weather? I combed the air with my short-wave radio. Nothing but the sound of tearing calico from the BBC World Service, Thessaloniki, Belgrade, Zagreb and Ljubljana. Electronic black-out? Had it anything to do with the snow?

The manager of the Aphrodite was several shades less than helpful. No, he had heard nothing about the weather. His TV on a cable link had gone on the blink. I switched on my little machine. The same crackle. He smiled, conducted me to the door and pointed upwards to where three power cables looped towards the restaurant and the chalets at the foot of the gorge. He walked out into the back garden and told me to switch on my set again where, as I understand it, the air-waves were filled by someone describing in Greek how Athens were in danger of losing their match against Italy. The manager shrugged his shoulders. Kyr'Zolotas would know all about the weather, he assured me.

But that good fellow wasn't in his usual haunts in Litohoro, neither the café in the square nor the tavern next door. He had left in a hurry. Why? Nobody knew. Where could I find out? From the taxi-drivers, they told me.

Of the four cabs parked in the square only one was manned by its owner, listening avidly to that damned match in Athens. Reluctantly he turned it down. Kyr'Zolotas? He had drived up to Prionia two hours ago, he said. Why? Perhaps he intended to rejoin his wife at the *refuge* the next day. After all, everyone had the right to . . . I left it at that.

A discouraging evening. Sitting on the balcony of the almost empty youth hostel in my overcoat, I sipped cup after cup of coffee, twiddling all the short-wave bands of my radio. Nothing but incomprehensible Russian and other Slavic tongues until, faintly, interspersed with static I heard the last few bars of 'Lillibullero', the nostalgic, thrice-blessed signature tune of the BBC World Service, and fragments of an announcement in English. It faded before I had learnt anything of importance but I had located the wavelength and managed to recapture the end of the news loud and clear. It would be repeated in half an hour, and announcer said.

Bad news. As Katie had foretold, a narrow but intense belt of low pressure was sweeping south-west across Central Europe. There followed reports from local correspondents in Belgrade and Bucharest. Deep snow. Main road and rail traffic had come to a standstill. But which way was the storm heading? No hints from London. I switched off the set and tramped down to the Aphrodite.

No encouragement there. The manager said he'd had a telephone call from my three friends at Katerini on the coast: they were sorry, but they'd seen TV pictures of the snow to the north and had decided to go up to Thessaloniki for a few days.

I felt gloomy, a mood shared by the whole village. They were talking about it in the tavern and the cafés, small groups around tables discussing what they'd seen on the box. They felt disgraced. A local lad had been chosen for the national team and Athens had lost by one goal. If it hadn't been for a penalty kick in the last three minutes it might at least have ended in a draw.

The weather? What weather? Oh, that *snow*! Yes, at least a fortnight before they'd expected it up there, but that sort of stuff wasn't any good for skiing. Too wet. It'd probably melt within a week. Anyhow, it might not reach them. *Real snow*, now, that wouldn't start until the end of October.

This from Christos Kakkalos, the young master of the house, namesake but as far as I could make out not otherwise related to the famous man who had guided the Swiss to the top of Mytikas nearly eighty years earlier. A not uncommon name thereabouts.

I asked him if I had time to get to the top of the ridge and back the next day. He wasn't sure, thought it might be dodgy. 'Who would know?' I asked him. He named someone in the village whose son kept an eye on his small flock above Prionia and operated under a special dispensation. It was an *Ethnikos Drimos*, a national park. Christos phoned him.

Answer: ambiguous. It depended on the wind. If it stayed south-east as it was at present, I could rely on at least a couple of days of snow-free weather. But if it backed – as he thought it might – I should turn round at once.

'Why not take a taxi to Prionia?' asked Christos.

The next morning I asked myself that more than once after scrambling up the scree I'd sampled two days earlier, and slid down to a torrent I didn't much like the look of. Deepish, I reckoned. For stepping-stones the gushing water was bridged with boulders touched on narrow ledges by red paint I'd been told about by my friend the guide. Would he had been there with a helping hand.

The alternatives were to risk chucking my rucksack on to the opposite bank with a mighty swing and then jump after it from ledge to ledge unhampered. The track on the far side looked tempting, since it followed the stream without an overhang in sight. But I felt dizzy and funked it. Then maybe I could wade across? Sounded with a stick, the water proved crotch-deep and flowing fast. Not worth a thorough wetting. Upstream on my side a cliff towered over the torrent. Nothing for it but to outflank the monster on a scree similar to the one I had scrambled down.

It took me more than an hour to advance what would

have been no more than perhaps a couple of hundred yards alongside the water. This roller-coastering on loose shale, precarious on the ridges on the top, had to be undergone twice. Since downright discomfort is as unpleasant to relate as it is to endure there will be only one mention of tobogganing on my bottom in a place where I couldn't trust leaning backwards on my feet.

Immediately overhead came comfort from the Gatherer of Clouds which were still scurrying resolutely from the south-west – but not long after midday when, rounding an arête near the top of the gorge, I found they were united in a classical anvil-shaped thunderhead. To hell with Zeus!

I knew the bolts of lightning would zip open swirling masses of water-vapour already tortured in their search for equilibrium. That's what happened: a few flickers like a faulty fluorescent tube and then, almost simultaneously, ferocious forks of light, a helluva crash, and a shower of hail. No place to be in a cyclonic storm. That's when I took to tobogganing – anything to get down quick.

At a height of maybe a couple of hundred feet above the torrent it's difficult to say whether I was more invigorated by the sight of an anchor-shaped peregrine plunging down on some sort of grouse-like bird in mid-air, or a young fellow approaching the stream where it was narrow enough to be jumped across from boulder to boulder in full kit.

'Sling your pack over,' he shouted.

I jumped, twice. Easy enough once you've done it and landed, physically, in the outstretched arms of a friendly young fellow, a mountain goat, Nick Smith from Lichfield in Staffordshire, who did me capital service that day. We went on upstream together.

Had he heard about the threat of blizzards throughout the Balkans? No! Did he know that we had about twenty-four hours before it was likely to beat about us? No! He looked up. The sky looked bruised, bilious, but he reckoned if we hurried we could make it.

Nick was less than a third of my age, and scuttled up and down impressive slopes at least twice as fast as I could but he was patient and irrepressibly curious. He kept disappearing down cracks in cliffs to see if corners couldn't be cut off, and emerging apologetically to say that we'd better keep on where we were or climb a bit higher. He was obliged to hurry. With limited resources he'd bought a return railway ticket to Stamboul, which meant being back in Thessaloniki early the next morning to board the ongoing train. In that time he hoped to reach the *refuge* above Prionia and then get back down in time to get a lift to the bus station.

He jumped the next crossing in one impressive bound and waited whilst I laboriously waded upstream in search of shallow water. Only one crossing defeated him. The boulders were almost under water some three or four feet in depth. He sighed and looked up to the crest of the highest scree we had yet seen. The track, marked only by the ruins of railings round tricky corners, had disappeared.

'Better make ourselves some ski-sticks,' he said, selecting four useful lengths of birch poles, and up we went to the knife-edge of the ridge of incoherent shale. I wondered wryly how I should have got on on my own. It took us the better part of an hour.

Half-way down the far side we saw the roofs of two monasteries a mile or more away further up the gorge. Nick, practical as ever, reckoned it a waste of time to throw away altitude by scrambling down to the stream again. As we could rely on our stout staffs why not try a traverse? he suggested. We made it, easily. At no time that day had I felt more confident. With those poles in our hands – and hindsight – we might have ignored the torrent from the start and saved a great deal of time and energy.

Another shower of hail. We ignored it. Clouds were closing in, but they were still sweeping up from the south-west. The monasteries were clinging like limpets to the walls of a cliff. The first one, St Spilio seemed deserted. I looked up. In a patch of Tiepolo-blue sky behind the great ridge, the one that housed the peaks of the gods on either side of Mytikas, I could just make out wisps of high cirrus. They were being driven in from the north-east, from the Balkans. Stratified clouds blowing in opposite directions are, meteorologically speaking, about as comforting as a thumb pointing downwards in an arena, but as I might have been mistaken I decided to say nothing.

After a great deal of bawling at the foot of the second monastery, St Dionysios, a young but heavily bearded brother appeared on the balcony high above us. In Greek I asked him whether we should turn to the left or the right to reach Prionia. He pointed to a short-cut through their vegetable garden. When we clambered up to their level and heard the murmur of chanting we felt rather bad about the noise we'd made.

More hail. Within a quarter of an hour we reached that small hamlet where the Black pines looked fit for Christmas cards. Except for those in the restaurant everyone seemed to be getting out in a hurry. Cars, cabs and coach-drivers were herding their passengers back for the run down to Litohoro. Any chance of a drink? Yes. A meal? No, not for at least another hour. It was five o'clock and they were over-full.

How long would it take us to reach the *refuge*? A waiter anxious to retain potential customers said, 'Many hours.' Untrue. A schematic map outside the stables made it clear that with any luck we should find shelter within two and a half hours at the most, but as Nick kept glancing at his watch we set off again after two tins of beer and a meat roll each. My good friend had no taste for it, but I managed to sneak in a double ouzo.

If the screes in the gorge might be compared to roller-coasters interspersed with two or three Big Dippers, the serpentine tracks through the trees above Prionia were merely undulatory 'in their discriminatory proportions', as they were described by an eighteenth-century botanist.* In a way which would have delighted Arthur Rackham the Black pines and Greek firs had been twisted and gnarled into weird shapes by the winds and snow of many winters. At their feet were the rusty-brown remains of seed-bearing plants which had survived the heat of the summer. Only a few tuberous species, such as the Autumn crocus with its drifts of purple flowers, managed to put on a fine show.

Although Nick was usually about a hundred yards ahead in his role of path-finder, I noticed that he was less of a mountain goat than he had been amongst those screes of accursed memory. He carried more weight than I did and although neither of us admitted the fact, we were both pretty tired. When I stopped for a few moments under pretext of admiring a plant or listening to a bird – a trick he saw through from the first – among those trees he sometimes stopped too.

What was that sharp indignant whistle from the ledge below us, he asked. I'd heard it myself but couldn't be sure. Through glasses I made out creatures which popped their heads out of rounded burrows in the manner of a jack-in-the-box. Although smaller they were much like Alpine marmots. We were in the company of European susliks which in late September normally gorge themselves near the snowline and begin deep hibernation. Our small colony had been rudely awakened. We soon knew why.

---

* John Sibthorpe, 1758–96.

Mytikas and his fellows on the skyline were grumbling. In lurid light could be made out clouds – not wisps of cirrus but damned great banks of cumulo-nimbus – rolling in directly from the north-east. Outlook: ominous. The snows were upon us. A ripple of light like children's sparklers seen in the dark ran the whole length of the ridge. Subconsciously I started to count: one second, two seconds, three seconds. The storm was still probably about three miles away, but the godly – or, as I thought at the time, god-awful – grumble became a whiplash-like crack of thunder. A ear-tingler. The time: half-past six. For the first time that day Nick looked apprehensive. 'How far do you think is the *refuge*?' he asked.

'Half an hour, if we scuttle,' I said, optimistically.

We scuttled. Nick mounted a bank, cutting off a corner. He looked round and waved me towards him. The hail had passed over. We could see it below, wavering like veils in a breeze. The trees were thinning out. We were above the main track. We saw riders on mules and small parties. Everyone seemed to be getting out except us.

We rejoined the main track. A young Scotsman with a *piolet*, a snow-pick, in his hand approached us. How far away was the *refuge*, we asked. 'Ten minutes,' he said. We should see it around the next bend.

'Anybody there?'

'Yes, an elderly German couple and a Swiss mountaineer.' When he left, he told us, they hadn't made their minds up whether to come down or risk spending the night there. He wasn't taking any chances: there could be a white-out before the morning, in his opinion.

He told us Costas Zolotas, the guide from Litohoro had gone off early to rescue a climber on Mytikas, or maybe Stefani. Either Zolotas had slipped – which he thought almost impossible – or he'd been hit by falling debris, and his arm had been badly broken. He'd limped down to another hut under the Ilias peak. His wife, normally in charge of *Refuge A*, had gone off to join him to make sure he was in one piece and comfortable. 'A *grreat* lassie,' he said. 'Everybody's favourite aunt.' We'd find everything in order.

We relaxed. There stood our objective, as handsome as an Alpine chalet, stout built, weather-boarded and as warm as toast. An open fire, light and a cooker from a generator.

Two scientific names were logged on my pocket recorder as I wrote the foregoing. *Cyclamen*, probably *neapolitanum*, and *Neophron*. The first the shy native species of that overblown horticulturalist's plant rarely seen native in Herefordshire. Alongside the chalet their flowers, the colour of petals of wild roses had just managed to stand above a light drift of hail.

Neophron is a fearsome-looking bald vulture, the so-called Egyptian species. Three rose like lifts from some refuse bins. I called to Nick but he was already inside asking if there were any tea available.

He stayed only to eat and drink something. He didn't much like local herb tea. We swapped addresses, promised to write, and off he went. From the balcony I watched him jog-trotting down towards the trees; a final wave and he had gone. I couldn't have had a better companion.

To my surprise and mild disappointment the elderly German couple and the man from Lausanne who had come to pay homage to Messrs Boissonas and Baud-Bovy left soon afterwards. There wasn't much I could do except ration out half a bottle of ouzo. I had the edge of the great range and the gods to myself.

Towards eleven o'clock I went out and looked up at the sky. A fine night. Had the north-easterlies blown across to

Italy? I glanced towards the bear. For what reason, I wondered, had that group of seven stars, the Septriones, been known by a variety of names, the Plough, the Wain and the Unwearied Ones, but throughout the world most commonly the Bear, *Ursa Major*? When the first white men landed on the American continent and learned to speak the language of the Indians, they pointed up north one evening and said: 'Those are the stars we call the Bear.' Yet a bear with a long tail, anatomically unlike any bear ever seen on earth. The Indians, delighted to hear their own opinions confirmed, said, 'Yes, we also call them the Bear. Like your own God – we also call him our father.'

Back in my room it felt too warm. I switched the heat down by a notch. The machine began to whirr like a bee. I flicked through my pocket diary of dates and places that began before the *Flying Tortoise* came to pieces to the west of Belgrade.

What had happened to our fellow-passenger Nacu Zdru from Kedrona in Macedonia? The last we had heard from him in London was a brief note and a front-page newspaper cutting from *The Greek American* headlined 'The Silencing of John Zdru'. This veteran of the Greek army with dual citizenship had been 'summarily expelled from Greece' – where he owned a house – 'without the benefit of even so much as a piece of paper showing the charges against him or grounds for those charges.' Zdru had provided us with our Vlach vocabulary and phrase sheets which had been as passports among the last of those itinerant pastoralists.

Tired but still tense, I turned off the light and, dressed only in my underpants, went to bed.

I woke up shivering. The time: half-past four. The hum continued. I had turned up some sort of air-conditioner, a cold one. I turned it off and burrowed into the blankets. In terms of Fahrenheit or any other thermometry it had been a two-dog night. That intriguing phrase came back from a tale told by my friend John Mitchell of the Massachusetts Audubon Society.

It concerned Richard Porter of East Charleston, Vermont, aged seventy-five or thereabouts. He had never heard of an electric blanket. He didn't have central heating in his three-roomed cabin, nor a modern airtight wood stove, nor a kerosene heater, and he regularly allowed the fire in his wood stove to burn itself out each night. He wasn't averse to cold draughts, and for that reason never insulated the pine-board walls of his cabin even though the temperature commonly dipped below zero for weeks at a time. And yet in spite of his apparent lack of conveniences, Porter said, he never felt cold at night. He had devised a system of living blankets which automatically piled themselves on his bed in response to the temperature.

Porter kept a number of dogs as companions. Townspeople regularly saw him walking along back roads surrounded by his pack, a mixed crew of all shapes and sizes, some large, some small, some friendly, 'and the rest too lazy to be unfriendly'. He became known as the Dog King. Not surprisingly it was his subjects who kept him warm at night.

About the time when the box stove began to cool in winter, the first of Porter's alternative heating systems, a black-and-tan named Spike began to stir from his spot alongside the stove and climb on to his bed. Louise, an old bitch, joined Spike when the temperature fell still further and the other four dogs began to come in through a dog-door which he had cut into one of the panels. On really bad nights he had five intimate companions, but he could make do with only two when he felt rather chilly.

Apprehensively I got up and wiped a small port-hole in the misted window with my forefinger. It was snowing heavily. Nothing furious. The flakes floated down thickly, as can be seen in the overturned sphere of a Victorian paperweight. From outside came a shrill explosive whistle.

Might have been those Balkan marmots, or some bird I couldn't put a name to.

At first light I inspected the platform where conical drifts of snow against the gauge measured three-quarters of a metre, say two and a half feet. The wind gusty, the snow fitful. During weirdly bright light somewhere between bright orange and pale purple I could see the spume blowing between occasional glimpses of the peaks. Must be mighty windy up there. Better wait an hour to see how it developed. The chances were that Costas's assistants would lead the mules up from Prionia. I had told Nick that, if it came to a pinch, two or three of us would probably stay put until midday.

Time passed, slowly. I have no gift for doing next to nothing. The generators weren't working, but with bunk made up and floors swept I set about the fire with cut blocks of fir, and soon had bits of mutton fished out of a stew and braised them nicely in a skillet with chopped onions.

By nine o'clock I set off with a staff as stout as any used by Friar John to discountenance the Devil.

The enormity of the whiteness wrinkled my eyes. Branches of a few conifers were hung about with icicles a foot or more in length, as if on a commercial Christmas tree. Between them, an encouraging sight: a raised track of solid rock, steep in places but wind-honed of all but streaks of snow. Snowscapes are notably deceptive. Small objects appear twice their natural size. As far as could be judged from its ever-narrowing perspective the track extended for about a mile, maybe more or less, before disappearing behind a hummock, probably an extensive scree of snow at the foot of ledge. And beyond that? We should discover when we got there.

We? Yes, my companion, my staff and I. It probed with

resolution where I trod gingerly. Bully for the lad from Lichfield.

How long, I wondered, had it taken him to jog down to Prionia in the almost dark? I re-enacted some of the high spots of our previous day. With thoughts on something he had told me about a winter scramble down his native hills – perhaps the Lickeys or The Roaches – I took my eyes off the track and stumbled. Better to keep to the job in hand.

From a depression a dozen or more yards to the left I again heard that shrill explosive whistle. Those marmot-like susliks? They should have been snugly underground hours ago. Walking cautiously, I left the safety of the track and made towards them. Each step probed knee-deep snow and made flatulent noises. I peered down into a long concavity in the lee of several boulders. A flock of birds like jackdaws with lemon-yellow bills was feeding amongst the exposed tops of bushes. Alpine choughs. At my appearance those masters of aerial acrobatics whirled up into the air whistling and chirruping excitedly before floating down towards the chalet.

The hummock above, which looked inconsiderable at the start, had grown immeasurably as if some mythical animal several times the size of Melville's Moby Dick had been laid low for impiety and shrouded as an afterthought at the foot of Zeus.

Because of the elusive qualities of objects seen in snow-scapes I'd have taken no bets on how long it would take me to reach the Great White Whale. A backwards glance showed I was on what good master Costas called a *zeek-sack* interesting for at least one piece of lore unrecorded – as far as I know – in the writ of Proc Zoo Soc Lond,* the stepping stones of doctorates. From one of those mounting transects I looked down to the one below to see a scurry of curious

* *Proceedings of the Zoological Society of London.*

325

nose-to-tail lemming-like animals, perhaps susliks, marmots or stoats. Had they included those giant Sumatran rats to which Sherlock Holmes attributed the desertion of the *Marie Celeste* – a story 'for which the world is not yet prepared' – I wouldn't have been surprised. Everything seemed to be going down when I was still trying to scramble up.

It took, perhaps, half an hour to reach the outermost flippers of the White Whale and there beyond them, stretching out into white nothingness and shown only by a slight depression, stretched the remains of the track.

It had to be faced: there was nothing of comfort above Moby Dick. More hail, lateral hail. I could scarcely see. I turned round. My own footprints were disappearing. I started to walk down, fast. The time, near eleven o'clock. That raised track up which I had clambered was becoming distinguishable only by its eminence.

Who had made it? Probably Klephts, certainly ELAS. Olympos had remained impregnable throughout the Occupation. Comforting to recognize what I had seen before: the sanctuary of the choughs, the skeletal remains of an ancient pine, perhaps the last in that snowscape without trees.

I looked behind. There was nothing except a *grisaille* of swirling hail and wet snow. Mytikas? I never saw Mytikas nor his subjects again. I had done with them.

Curious word, that: Mytikas. Until I talked to the graceful lady in the Information Bureau in Litohoro I thought it stemmed from *muthos* defined as: 'A purely fictitious narrative usually involving supernatural persons, actions or events and embodying some popular ideas concerning natural or historical phenomena.'*

'Not at all,' she said. 'It means nose-shaped, or pointed.' This pleased me since many months ago, that is before we

---

* *The Complete Oxford English Dictionary.*

set off on this walk, I had read Geoffrey Kirk, that considerable scholar who states plainly in one of the best-known of his works: 'It is sometimes hard to resist the temptation of viewing the "Homeric world" as a real one, possessing a simple historical value of its own. The truth is, of course, that the epic is to an important extent *fictitious* – more than that, it is a fiction that contains contributions from different periods over a span of half a millennium or more. Yet the historian need not altogether despair. In its total complexity the world of the poems bears no exact resemblance to any historical setting in any historical period; yet many of its elements are based on fact and can be assessed in comparison with objective evidence disclosed by archaeology.'

Heinrich Schliemann, that rich German archaeologist, imagined he had gazed on the face of Agamemnon, but the gold mask was later identified as being some small local chief. Schliemann (1822–90) paid a small army of excavators to burrow like moles into a *tell*, an enormous mound, bigger even than my Moby Dick, at Hissarlik near the coast of Turkey and discovered what he believed to be Ilium or Troy in the Troad. Nine 'cities', stratified like a Neapolitan ice were buried one above the other, the seventh of which is now reckoned to be a post-Mycenaean fortress, the basis of *The Iliad*, 3,000 years of mythology and scholarly speculation.

Who was Homer? Nobody knows. I cling to Geoffrey Kirk* who suggests in a quiet way that the greatest, the first, the prince of story-tellers, the most skilled in the quiet world of mythology, started to sing in the eighth century BC about Greece, already through her 'dark age', a loose confederation which had re-emerged 'as a strong and individual force in the eastern and central Mediterranean'. He was probably an

---

* *Homer and the Oral Tradition*, Cambridge University Press, 1976.

Ionian, probably too a-literate – meaning he couldn't read – but he had an imagination that rivalled that of Shakespeare about whom there is no known fellow.

In those deep thoughts I stumbled and at least twice failed to sound the track with my fine staff. I fell crotch-deep into a pit of snow, scrambled out, and laughed as ever Rabelais did in the face of the bishops, men whom he called those Sorbangraes and Sorbionnes, 'Oddipols, Joltheads, who in their disputes do not search for truth but for contradictions only and debate.'

The chalet appeared not far below, and beyond it a well-worn track. I heard the whinny of mules, the finest mules you have ever heard. They had come up from Prionia.

'Are you all right?' cried Madame Costas Zolotas from the doorway.

'No!' I said, 'repeat no. I am suffering from a-Mytikasia.'

Index

INSIGHT ● GUIDES

ITALIAN LAKES

POCKET GUIDE

⊙ Walking Eye App

YOUR FREE EBOOK AVAILABLE THROUGH THE WALKING EYE APP

Your guide now includes a free eBook to your chosen destination,
for the same great price as before. Simply download the Walking Eye
App from the App Store or Google Play to access your free eBook.

HOW THE WALKING EYE APP WORKS

Through the Walking Eye App, you can purchase a range of eBooks and destination
content. However, when you buy this book, you can download the corresponding
eBook for free. Just see below in the grey panel where to find your free content and
then scan the QR code at the bottom of this page.

Destinations: Download essential destination
content featuring recommended sights and
attractions, restaurants, hotels and an A–Z of
practical information, all available for purchase.

Ships: Interested in ship reviews? Find independent reviews of river and ocean ships in this
section, all available for purchase.

eBooks: You can download your free accom-
panying digital version of this guide here. You
will also find a whole range of other eBooks,
all available for purchase.

Free access to travel-related blog articles
about different destinations, updated on a
daily basis.

HOW THE EBOOKS WORK

The eBooks are provided in EPUB file format. Please note that you will need an eBook reader installed on your device to open the file. Many devices come with this as standard, but you may still need to install one manually from Google Play.

The eBook content is identical to the content in the printed guide.

HOW TO DOWNLOAD THE WALKING EYE APP

1. Download the Walking Eye App from the App Store or Google Play.
2. Open the app and select the scanning function from the main menu.
3. Scan the QR code on this page – you will then be asked a security question to verify ownership of the book.
4. Once this has been verified, you will see your eBook in the purchased ebook section, where you will be able to download it.

Other destination apps and eBooks are available for purchase separately or are free with the purchase of the Insight Guide book.

TOP **10** ATTRACTIONS

MALCESINE
The picturesque fishing village lies at the foot of Monte Baldo. See page 56.

SANTA CATERINA DEL SASSO
This enchanting church convent clings to a cliff face above Lake Maggiore. See page 34.

VILLA DEL BALBIANELLO
Built in 1787 for an eccentric cardinal, it embodies the effortless style and beauty of the region. See page 42.

VILLA CARLOTTA
Famed for its sumptuous gardens, it sits on Lake Como's western shore. See page 44.

SIRMIONE
With a dramatic 13th-century castle, it is one of Lake Garda's most visited resorts. See page 49.

VERONA'S ROMAN ARENA
Once the scene of gladiatorial combat, it now stages operatic extravaganzas. See page 75.

THE BORROMEO ISLANDS
A suitably grandiose home for a flock of peacocks. See page 28.

VILLA TARANTO
Its botanical gardens are planted with around 20,000 different species of trees, shrubs and flowers. See page 32.

BERGAMO'S CITTÀ ALTA
Packed with magnificent medieval and Renaissance monuments. See page 65.

BELLAGIO
The 'pearl of Lake Como' enjoys unrivalled panoramic mountain views. See page 45.

8.00am

Breakfast

Take breakfast in your hotel or join the locals with a cappuccino and *cornetto* (croissant) in a lakeview café.

10.00am

Baroque extravaganza

Head for Stresa's ferry station at Piazza Marconi, buy a ticket that includes admission to the island sights and hop on one of the regular ferries going north to Ancona. Alight at the first stop, Isola Bella, the Borromean princes' summer residence. Explore the sumptuously decorated Palazzo Borromeo, and the beguiling, ship-shaped terraces of gardens, complete with statues and peacocks.

1.45pm

Isola Madre

Most boats en route to Isola Madre call at Baveno, a quieter version of Stresa, set below a pink granite mountain. Stay on the boat for the ten-minute crossing from here to Isola Madre, the largest, and once the wildest, of the Borromean islands. Stroll through gently landscaped gardens, with their profusion of exotic trees and shrubs, then make a brief visit to the villa, which is noticeably subdued after Palazzo Borromeo.

11.30am

Fisherman's Island

Catch the next ferry for a five-minute hop across to the tiny Isola dei Pescatori (also called Isola Superiore) with its pretty fishing village. Stroll through its tiny alleys, strung with fishing nets, then lunch on fish fresh from the lake at one of the hotel restaurants, soaking up the views from a lakeside terrace. Alternatively, enjoy a picnic on the pebble beach.

THE **ITALIAN LAKES**

3.00pm

Monte Mottarone

Catch the ferry across to Carciano and take a cable car ride to the Monte Mottarone peak (20 minutes), a natural balcony commanding magnificent views over the Alps and lakes. For the very finest views, which on a clear day encompass seven lakes, climb from the upper cable-car station for about 20 minutes to the summit, or take the chairlift.

5.00pm

Down the mountain

Descend to Stresa on the cable car or, for an adrenalin-fuelled ride, try the Alpyland Coaster with 2-seater bobs speeding down at up to 40kph (25mph). If time permits, alight halfway down at the Giardino Botanico Alpinia, the rock gardens with over 1,000 species of Alpine and medicinal plants.

8.00pm

Wining and dining

Dine at Il Vicoletto (see page 106) or opt for one of the alfresco pizzerias, preferably with an open-fired oven, in the centre of the resort. After a leisurely dinner, end the evening with a lakeside stroll and a liqueur in a local bar.

6.30pm

Belle Époque grandeur

Follow in the footsteps of Ernest Hemingway and take an *aperitivo* in the palatial Grand Hotel des Iles Borromées overlooking the lake.

INTRODUCTION

Set among the southern foothills of the Alps, the Italian lakes extend over four different regions of northwest Italy: Piedmont, Lombardy, Trentino and the Veneto. The famous trio are Maggiore, Como and Garda, but there are also a number of smaller, peaceful lakes scattered among the valleys.

Each lake has its own character, whether it is tiny, jewel-like Orta, with its perfectly preserved medieval village and islet; beguiling Como where mountains plunge into the deep waters and picture-postcard villages cling to the slopes; vast and varied Garda – fjord-like in the north, sea-like in the south; or stately Maggiore, where snowcapped mountains form a dramatic backdrop to the enchanting Borromeo Islands. What they all have in common is a fertile shoreline, with a varied

⊙ GETTING ROUND THE LAKES

The main lakes see large numbers of holidaymakers from late spring to early autumn. Long stretches of the lakeside, including Como's eastern shore and much of Lake Maggiore's western one, are spoilt by heavy traffic on narrow and tortuous roads. While a car is clearly useful for touring, it is far more relaxing to base yourself in one lake resort and hop around by boat.

Ferries, hydrofoils and excursion cruisers provide excellent services linking almost all the towns and villages. Get up early and you can tour an entire lake, even one as big as Maggiore or Como, and have lunch on board the ferry. Cable cars, which climb to vantage points on the hillsides above the lakes, also offer some sensational views.

and exotic array of flora that thrives in the benign spring-to-autumn climate.

VILLAS, GARDENS AND CASTLES

Sumptuous lakeside villas and their gardens, created originally for northern European nobility or well-heeled Milanese, are a major draw of the larger lakes. Como in particular has drawn the rich and famous, from Pliny the

Toscalano-Maderno

Younger who built villas at Bellagio to George Clooney who has a lakeside villa at Laglio. Palatial residences such as Como's Villa d'Este and Villa Serbelloni have been converted to luxury hotels, other villas and gardens throw their gates open to the public, and those in private hands can be admired from the lake as you chug past on a ferryboat.

Incongruous with the mountain settings, the lake shores are Riviera-like, studded with olive groves, palms and citrus trees; lakeside promenades are lined by palms and oleanders while throughout the spring a proliferation of azaleas, rhododendrons and camellias create a blaze of colour on the gently sloping banks.

Rising above the lakeshore villages are the lofty belltowers of Romanesque churches and the battlements of medieval castles. On Lake Garda the crenellated castles were the work of the power-hungry Scaligeri from Verona. Maggiore's fortifications and island palazzi were built by the Borromeo family of Milan

Latin lake names

The lakes are often referred to by their old Roman names: Verbano for Maggiore (after the verbena plant that flourished and still flourishes on its shores), Lario for Como, Benaco ('Beneficent') for Garda, Cusio for Lake Orta and Sebino for Lake Iseo.

– who to this very day own the islands and the lake's main castle at Angera.

A PLAYGROUND FOR THE RICH AND FAMOUS

As with every beautiful corner of Italy, the region is steeped in association with famous figures. In Roman times the poet Catullus owned a villa at Sirmione, Virgil was born near Mantua and the writer/historians Pliny the Elder and Pliny the Younger came from Como. Shelley, Wordsworth and other romantic poets were bewitched by the dramatic natural beauty of the deep-blue waters and mountain peaks. Shelley sung the praises of Lake Como: 'it surpasses in beauty everything I have ever seen hitherto'.

In the late-19th century the lakes became a pleasure ground for the rich, royal and famous. Queen Victoria stayed in Villa Cara at Baveno near Stresa in 1879; later the Grand Hotel in Gardone Riviera on Lake Garda hosted Somerset Maugham, Vladimir Nabokov and Winston Churchill. D.H. Lawrence, in describing Limone on Lake Garda, wrote of 'a lake as beautiful as the beginning of creation'. Hemingway, who was recuperating at Stresa's Grand Hotel des Iles Borromées after a WWI battle wound in 1918, used the resort as a backdrop in *A Farewell to Arms*.

Today's big names are soccer stars, Hollywood celebrities and Russian tycoons. The 'Clooney effect' (ie George's 25-room holiday home at Laglio) has sent property prices rocketing on the southwestern shores of Lake Como.

HISTORIC CITIES

The southern stretches of the region, typified by the flatlands of the Po and great swathes of industry, are also home to artistically rich cities such as Bergamo, Brescia, Mantua and Verona. In the heart of the cities (or in the case of Bergamo on top of the hill) there are fine historic centres bearing the marks of centuries of history. While Bergamo and Verona are immediately appealing, Mantua and Brescia are more of an acquired taste. Verona apart, these historic cities are comparatively free of crowds and commercialism, being bypassed by tourists making a beeline for Italy's more famous cities. Easily accessed from the lakes, they make ideal destinations for day trips.

Just an hour's train ride or drive from lakes Maggiore and Como, Milan is Italy's economic and cultural capital. Though famous for fashion, it has artistic riches too, among them the vast Gothic Duomo, Leonardo's *Last Supper* and the Brera art gallery.

Passenger ferry on Lake Como

WHICH LAKE?

The main resorts on Maggiore and Como have a comfortable genteel charm, attracting large numbers of older visitors (mainly British and German) who are content to enjoy the scenery from the lakeside promenade, take boat trips around the lakes, visit islands, gardens and lakeside villas, and take funicular rides to admire the views. On Lake Maggiore the grande dame resort of Stresa is the main place to stay, just a ferry hop from the Borromeo Islands. Upper Maggiore lies in Switzerland and although the resorts are Italian in feel, with their sunny piazzas and alfresco eateries, there is a marked Swiss efficiency about them. Lake Como, particularly popular with the British and Americans, is the most romantic of the lakes, offering dramatic scenery, picturesque villages, belle époque resorts and the beautiful village of Bellagio at the heart of the lake.

German-orientated Lake Garda generally attracts a younger crowd and is more suitable for families. There are sports, beaches and theme parks galore, and sufficient nightlife to keep the energetic entertained until the early hours. The lakes in general are a sporting paradise, offering water sports, hiking, mountain biking, skiing (in winter) and adventure sports. Lake Garda, with all those and more, is one big fitness centre. The *pelèr* (or *suer*) wind from the north, and the *ora* from the south, ensure superb sailing and windsurfing conditions, especially at the northern end of the lake. The mountains and ridges above the lakes offer endless opportunities for hikers and rock climbers; and for the less actively inclined there are cable cars up the slopes where you can enjoy some breathtaking views.

Then there is little Lake Orta, the only Italian lake lying entirely in Piedmont. The village of Orta San Giulio, overlooking the tiny Isola San Giulio, is arguably the most picturesque of any in the lakes and is certainly worthy of a detour from Lake Maggiore. Lake Iseo, between lakes Como and Garda, is more tranquil and less self-consciously quaint than the larger lakes.

A BRIEF HISTORY

This region's remarkable landscape was formed at the end of the last Ice Age when the Alpine glaciers retreated, leaving deep lake-filled valleys. For over 10,000 years people have also been leaving their mark here, from the prehistoric rock carvings at Val Camonica to the magnificent 17th- and 18th-century villas that surround Lake Como. The region's location on trade routes between Rome and central Europe played a crucial role in its history, ensuring prosperity, but also luring a succession of foreign invaders.

EARLY SETTLERS

Lombardy and the lakes lie within a larger area that the Romans called Gallia Cisalpina ('Gaul this side of the Alps'), a vast wild tract of land and lakes. Gallic tribes, pushing south from the Rhine Valley, were inhabiting the fertile plains of the Po Valley by the 4th century BC, creating their settlements at what are now Milan, Brescia, Verona, Mantua, Bergamo and Como. In 224 BC the Romans put an end to these Celtic forays by conquering the area south of

Pope Leo I

Roman relics

The most conspicuous legacies of Roman rule are Brescia's Capitoline Temple and Roman theatre and Verona's superbly preserved arena, the third largest surviving from ancient times.

the Po, and just a year later Flaminius crossed the river, dismantled its bridges and defeated all of the Celtic tribes, including the powerful Insubres.

However, during the Second Punic War and its aftermath, when the Romans were more concerned with defeating Hannibal, the Gauls rose up again, attacking the Roman fortresses on the River Po. Consular armies were despatched north, defeating the tribes at the River Mincio near Mantua. A further victory near Lake Como finally obliged the Gauls to sue for peace. With the final reduction of Cisalpine Gaul, the Celtic tribes were progressively merged with the Romans.

HUNS, GOTHS AND LOMBARDS

By the 3rd century AD Cisalpine Gaul had become a commercially prosperous region of the Roman Empire and an important gateway to northern Europe. Attila the Hun, invading his way through Italy, plundered and pillaged Milan, Verona, Bergamo and Brescia in AD 452, but after the mediation of Pope Leo I, the infamous barbarian warrior halted at the Po and promised never to return.

Following the breakdown of the Western Roman Empire in 476 the region was subject to further waves of invaders. The German Odoacer crowned himself king at Pavia but was later vanquished by Theodoric the Ostrogoth. During his 40-year reign Theodoric ruled through surviving Roman institutions, welding together Goths and Romans, administering justice, and creating fine buildings, including a palace for himself in Verona on the site of the present-day Castelvecchio.

The Lombards, a warfaring Germanic tribe, descended on the region, putting an end to any vestige of political unity that may have survived the Roman era. They crossed the Alps in the spring of 568, and two years later they had conquered all the main cities north of the Po, with the exception of Pavia, seat of the royal palace. Their kingdom in Italy lasted a couple of centuries and was in the main ruled by the king and his royal officials who kept a check on the power of the dukes and counts. The Lombards were eventually absorbed into the Italian population, adopting Roman life and customs, freely intermarrying and, in many cases, converting to Christianity. Ethnically and socially they left an indelible mark on the people of northern Italy.

Invasion of papal territories by the Lombards forced the pope to appeal for support from Pepin, the Christian king of the Franks. In 774 Pepin's son Charlemagne and his army conquered much of Italy, including the north, and took the Lombard crown. On Christmas Day 800 Pope Leo III revived the Roman imperial title when he crowned Charlemagne Holy Roman Emperor. However, the Franks failed to establish a durable state in Italy and in 1024 the royal palace

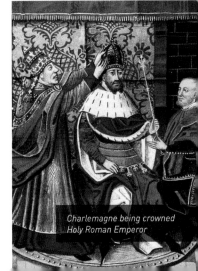

Charlemagne being crowned Holy Roman Emperor

at Pavia, symbol of the power of the Holy Roman Empire, was destroyed by the local people.

ERA OF THE COMMUNES

The early 11th century saw the emergence of the commune, or free city-state, the quintessential institution of medieval northern Italy. Prior to this, local aristocrats and the emerging commercial classes had been prepared to play second fiddle to the state in exchange for a degree of patronage from the emperor or king. As the rulers' power and influence waned, the strength and independence of the aristocrats and tradesmen increased.

As a consequence, economic and de facto governmental power passed to the localities, giving birth to the communes. These were self-governing municipal institutions with their origins in rebellion, treaty or charter. Typical rights included the control of justice, personal liberty of the townsmen and powers to regulate trade and levy local taxes and tolls. Milan acquired communal status in 1045, followed later by Brescia, Como, Bergamo, Verona and Mantua.

These communes were vulnerable to factional feuds, with powerful families often grouping together and gobbling up rival city-states. The great ideological conflict

Castello Scaligero

between the papacy and the Holy Roman Empire gave further impetus to conflict when these 'superpowers' vied for support in the northern cities. Within each city-state rival families adopted the labels 'Guelph' for the papacy and 'Ghibelline' for the empire. The famous vendetta in Verona between Montagues (Ghibellines) and Capulets (Guelphs) is just one example.

> ## The Scaligeri
>
> The ruthless and tyrannical Scaligeri dynasty ruled Verona from 1260 to 1387. A number of their castles, all with characteristic fishtail battlements, can be seen around Lake Garda (Castello Scaligero at Malcesine is a good example) and their elaborate Gothic mausoleums still stand in central Verona (see page 75).

THE GREAT DYNASTIES

The 13th century saw a shift in territorial and city-state power. The main cities fell to despotic rulers: Milan to the Visconti, Mantua to the Bonacolsi, Verona to the della Scalas (or Scaligeri). By the mid-14th century the smaller cities had lost their independent communal status. Milan had swallowed up great swathes of northern Italy and by 1402 had even extended its territories south to Tuscany.

As well as able administrators, the family dynasties were dynamic patrons of the arts. Milan and Mantua, which was by now under the civilizing rule of the Gonzagas, were great centres of art, drawing the leading artists, poets and scholars of the time. Under the mighty Visconti dynasty, cathedrals, fortresses and palazzi were constructed across the region, among them the cathedrals of Milan and Como and the Certosa (Charterhouse) of Pavia. Ludovico il Moro of the Sforza family, who inherited Milan from the Visconti, attracted Bramante, the great High

Renaissance architect and decorative painter; and Leonardo da Vinci, who produced most of his ground-breaking artistic, scientific and medical studies here. The Mantuan court drew the great Florentine architect, Alberti, and the painter, Mantegna, who glorified the Gonzaga family in his brilliant fresco decorations. Verona produced the great Renaissance artist, Veronese, and celebrated architects such as Sanmicheli; Brescia produced its own school of painters; Bergamo played host to a whole range of painters from the workshops of Milan and Venice, and saw

⊘ SAINT CARLO BORROMEO (1538–84)

Born into the Borromeo dynasty (who to this day own Lake Maggiore's Borromeo islands, the castle at Angera and the fishing rights of the entire lake), the ascetic Carlo became a leading light in the Catholic Counter-Reformation. He was born in the (now ruined) castle of Arona on the southern shores of Lake Maggiore and devoted his life to the reform and welfare of the church.

Appointed cardinal and Archbishop of Milan by his uncle, Pope Pius IV, Carlo founded seminaries and colleges for the education of clerical and lay members, rid Milan's Duomo of all its ornamentation, paid regular visits to hundreds of parishes and worked ceaselessly during the plague of 1576–8 to accommodate the sick and bury the dead.

However, political turmoil beset him as he became embroiled in disputes with the governor and senate, and faced rebellion from various religious orders. In 1569 members of the order of the Humiliati (Brothers of Humility) hatched an unsuccessful conspiracy to take his life. Carlo was canonised posthumously by Pope Paul V in 1610.

the creation of the Colleoni Chapel, a masterpiece of the Lombard Renaissance.

From the early 1400s the republic of Venice, until then an exclusively maritime power, with naval bases from the lagoon to Constantinople, had begun to extend her net into the hinterland. Starting with Verona in 1405, huge swathes of territory were taken by military conquest from Milan, including Brescia and Bergamo,

Saint Carlo Borromeo tending to plague victims

to extend the Venetian Empire to the River Adda. In 1454 the war was ended by the Peace of Lodi and an Italian league was formed, made up of the two dominant powers in the area, Milan and Venice, plus Florence.

FOREIGN INTERVENTION

In the late 15th and early 16th centuries, the small duchies that made up Italy became a battleground in the struggle between France and Habsburg Spain, the two great powers of the age. In the aftermath of the 1525 Battle of Pavia, when the French were expelled from the Duchy of Milan, treaties with the pope settled the future of Italy for the next two centuries. The state of Milan was restored to the Sforza dynasty, but on the death of Francesco II in 1535 it fell under the domination of the Spanish Habsburg Emperor, Charles V, who later granted the duchy to his son, the future Philip II of Spain. Spanish rule

Battle of Solferino, 1859

was to endure until 1706. Venice on the other hand, with its increased territorial domains, maintained its independence. The Gonzaga rule of Mantua survived the territorial aggrandisements of both Milan and Venice, and the ruling family continued as masters of Mantua until the early 18th century.

In Spanish northern Italy the kaleidoscope of dynastic and interstate struggle gave way to a period of economic stagnation and political decline. Executive power was in the hands of a governor, assisted by a senate, but important directives came from Madrid. The Italian aristocratic and bourgeois classes lost their political and commercial vigour and the effects were compounded by military levies and requisitions in support of Spanish wars, inflation, famine and plague.

During the War of Spanish Succession (1702–13) Austria seized control of most of northern Italy, including the Lakes. In 1796, following his victories in Piedmont, Napoleon swept into Lombardy, and the northern cities became part of the short-lived Cisalpine Republic, allied with France. At the close of the Napoleonic wars Lombardy was restored to Austria, under the Congress of Vienna.

Austrian rule, which if anything was disliked even more than that of Spain, finally came to an end when Camillo Cavour, the architect of Italian unification, decided that the only way of defeating Austria was with the support of France. In 1859 two thousand French troops were moved by rail into northern Italy under the command of Napoleon III. The Austrians were defeated first at Magenta, west of Milan, and then at Solferino, close to Lake Garda, this time with the help of Italian troops who either fought with the French or deserted the Austrian side. Some 40,000 men perished in the battle, inspiring the Swiss humanitarian, Henri Durant, who witnessed the carnage, to found the International Red Cross. The battles of Magenta and Solferino can be seen as a watershed in the military campaign for the unification of Italy – which was finally achieved in 1871.

20TH CENTURY AND BEYOND

Rapid growth and industrialisation characterised the post-unification period. Milan became the economic and cultural capital of Italy and over 50 years the population trebled in size. It was in Milan that Mussolini created the Fasci di Combattimento in 1919, the nucleus of the National Fascist Party. Following the fall of the socialist regime, Mussolini put Lake Garda on the political map by setting up his puppet republic in Salò in 1943, under the protection of a German army. In April 1945, just before the Allies reached Milan, Il Duce was finally captured at Dongo on Lake Como as he tried to flee to Switzerland. The following day he was executed along with 15 Nazi officials and his mistress, Clara Petacci. Their bodies were strung by their feet from the girders of a petrol station in Milan's Piazzale Loreto.

Following widespread destruction in World War II, Milan and the Lombard cities saw major reconstruction and rapid economic recovery. Milan became an industrial powerhouse, forming, with Genoa and Turin, the 'industrial triangle' of Italy.

The city has emerged as Italy's leading centre for commerce, finance and fashion. But alongside the economic boom came political scandal, organised crime and terrorism. In the early 1990s Milan was the focus of the great political scandal dubbed *Tangentopoli* (Bribesville). Extensive investigations, known as the *Mani Pulite* (Clean Hands), exposed political corruption on a massive scale.

BERLUSCONI'S RISE, FALL AND RISE AGAIN?

Among the accused in the *Mani Pulite* was Italy's media magnate, Silvio Berlusconi. The controversial and colourful billionaire was elected to his second spell as Prime Minister in 2001 on a tide of populism and nationalism, with a pledge to reform the economy. The country's longest serving post-war Prime Minister, he continues to dominate Italian politics, serving three terms so far. But his career has been dogged by sex and corruption scandals and his government led Italy to the brink of financial disaster. The 75-year old resigned in November 2011, after losing his parliamentary majority in a vote on austerity measures to cut the country's spiralling debt of €1.9 trillion.

Berlusconi's successors Mario Monti, Enrico Letta and the Democratic Party's young and energetic leader Matteo Renzi all failed to pass significant changes. Renzi's ambitious constitutional reforms package was rejected in a 2016 referendum, leading to his resignation and a new period of political uncertainty.

The 2018 elections led to a hung parliament, which at the time of writing remains unresolved. Berlusconi's Forza Italia party (reformed in 2013) came fourth with 14% of the vote. With his six-year ban from office following a conviction for tax fraud being overturned in May 2018, the way is paved for Berlusconi to run for a fourth term as Italy's Prime Minister.

HISTORICAL LANDMARKS

c.8000 BC–3rd century BC Inhabitants of the Val Camonica, north of Lake Iseo, leave thousands of carvings on the rocks, illustrating prehistoric life.

202–191 BC Romans start to establish colonies in Milan, Como, Brescia, Verona and other settlements.

222 BC Romans conquer Milan (Mediolaum).

AD 286 Milan becomes capital of the Western Roman Empire.

313 Constantine grants religious freedom to Christians in Milan.

568 Lombards invade Po Valley and lakes.

774 Charlemagne brings Lombard rule to an end.

11th century Emergence of the communes or city-states.

1118–27 Como defeated by Milan in the Ten Years War.

12th–15th century Milan ruled by the Viscontis and Sforzas; Lake Garda and Verona by the Scaligeri (della Scala) dynasty.

16th century Milan and the western lakes controlled by Spanish, the eastern lakes by the Venetian Empire.

1714 Spain cedes Lombardy to Austria.

1796 Napoleon invades. Milan becomes capital of the Cisalpine Republic.

1814–70 The Risorgimento – liberation and political unification of Italy.

1859 French defeat Austrians in the battles of Magenta and Solferino.

1870 Italy is unified under King Vittorio Emanuele II.

1921 Mussolini founds the National Fascist Party in Milan.

1943–5 Mussolini is installed as head of a puppet republic at Salò, Lake Garda. In 1945 he and his mistress, Claretta Petacci, are executed.

2001 Silvio Berlusconi is elected Prime Minister.

2002 The euro replaces the lira as the official Italian currency.

2011 The 150th anniversary of Italian Unification. Silvio Berlusconi steps down as Prime Minister. Mario Monti heads a new national unity government.

2014 Democratic Party's Matteo Renzi forms a new government.

2017 People vote for greater autonomy in non-binding referendums in Veneto and Lombardy.

2018 Elections lead to a hung parliament. Matteo Salvini, a right-wing Populist, becomes Deputy Prime Minister after receiving most votes.

Picturesque street in Bellagio, Lake Como

 WHERE TO GO

It is worth devoting a couple of weeks in order to experience the lakes region and the historic Lombard cities fully. The A4 autostrada provides a quick way of getting across the region by car, but the roads around the lakes can be very slow going. If you are without a car or your time is limited to a week or less, make your base at one of the larger lake resorts and take one or two relaxing ferry trips around the lakeshore. The Roman and Renaissance delights of Verona warrant an overnight stay.

LAKE MAGGIORE

Famed for its jewel-like islands and mountain-girt northern shores, Maggiore is the second largest of the Italian lakes. Long and narrow, it snakes 65km (40 miles) from the Swiss canton of **Ticino** in the north to **Lombardy** in the south. The western shore, where most of the main resorts are located, lies in **Piedmont**. The most scenic section of the lake is the **Gulf of Borromeo**, named after the family who have had a monopoly on Maggiore's star attractions for four and a half centuries.

STRESA AND THE GOLFO BORROMEO

Stresa, 'Queen of the Lake', lies at the foot of the majestic **Mottarone peak** and boasts glorious views to the islands. Following the opening of the **Simplon Pass** in 1906, the town became a highly fashionable resort, with splendid belle-époque villas and gardens, sports clubs and a casino. Today, huge old-fashioned hotels line its immaculate, garden-lined promenade. Foremost amongst these is the sumptuous **Grand Hotel des Iles Borromées**, whose star-studded guest list has included

For love of the lake

According to Stendhal, 'when a man has a heart and a shirt he should sell the shirt in order to see Lake Maggiore'. Byron, Shelley, Flaubert, Ruskin and Dickens were among other literati who have sung the praises of the lake.

Queen Victoria, Churchill and Ernest Hemingway.

The resort may have lost the cachet it once enjoyed (today's visitors are more likely to be package tourists or conference delegates than royalty or celebrities) but as a base on the lake it still can't be beaten for views, excursions and easy access to the **Borromeo Islands ①** (Isole Borromee). It also has an appealing older quarter behind the waterfront where the narrow cobbled streets are lined by little shops and eateries, and the central, plane-shaded piazza buzzes with café life after dark.

From Stresa it's a quick ferry hop to **Isola Bella**, the first of the Borromeo Islands (www.borromeoturismo.it; late-Mar–late-Oct daily 9am–5.30pm; cumulative ticket available with Isola Madre). It was in the mid-16th century that Count Carlo III decided to transform the rocky islet (then known as Isola Inferiore) into a monumental baroque palace and gardens. He named it Isola Isabella after his wife, later shortened to Isola Bella (Beautiful Island). In the 17th century Carlo's son, Vitaliano, took over the project, commissioning leading architects and artists. It was not until 1959 however, that the scheme was finally complete.

Designed to give the impression of the prow of a grandiose vessel, the island creates a dramatic impact as you approach by boat. The palace, terraces and gardens occupy almost the entire island, leaving just a cluster of houses near the harbour and a few souvenir shops. The stern facade belies a lavish interior, full of gilt and stuccowork, marble statues and Murano chandeliers. A tour takes in the Sala di Napoleone (Napoleon's Room) where he and Josephine slept in 1797. At lake level there are six mosaic grottoes, built by the Borromeans to avoid the stifling summer heat.

The garden is a baroque extravaganza of statuary, exotic plants and flowers. The ten ornate terraces culminate in a huge statue of a unicorn – one of the Borromeo symbols. Even if you find the grounds unbearably pompous you can't fail to admire the remarkable variety of exotic flora, planned to create colour and scent from early spring to late autumn – not to mention the sublime views across to the Mottarone peak.

A five-minute ferry ride from Isola Bella brings you to **Isola dei Pescatori**, or – as you hear the ferry men announce it – 'Isola Superiore dei Pescatori'. The full name derives from the Latin

The garden terrace on Isola Bella

Visiting the islands

To see the Borromeo Islands at a leisurely pace, you should allow a whole day – though a longish morning or afternoon may suffice. Bear in mind that in season the islands are inundated with crowds – the earlier you set off the better – and beware of boat touts near the main ferry landing stage charging far higher prices than the ferries.

superior, indicating that it is further north than Isola Bella ('Isola Inferiore'). The quaint, picturesque and laidback Fishermen's Island couldn't be more of a contrast to formal Isola Bella. Heralded by the spire of its church, it is no more than a cluster of simple fishermen's houses and narrow alleys. At the end of the 19th century the population was around 200 and visitors were a rarity. Today there are 50 permanent residents. Despite the summer influx of tourists the island manages to preserve fishing traditions and is a lovely spot to stop for lunch and try the fish fresh from the lake.

The ferry stops at **Baveno** before arriving at the second of the Borromeo islands: **Isola Madre** (same opening hours as Isola Bella, see page 28). Different again, this one is a thickly wooded island, where English-style gardens dominate. The island has belonged to the Borromeo family since the 1500s and the glorious gardens were designed in the 19th century on what was formerly hunting ground. Peacocks and pheasants roam freely among the rare plants and exotic flora. Renowned for azaleas, rhododendrons and camellias, the gardens also nurture banana plants and sugar cane, lemon trees, magnolia, a Ginkgo biloba and a 200-year old Kashmir cypress tree, reputedly the largest in Europe. The palace is far less grandiose than its sister on Isola Bella. The rooms have been reconstructed and the interior has a mixed collection of Borromeo portraits, baroque allegorical paintings, tapestries, porcelain and a puppet theatre.

MONTE MOTTARONE

Between lakes Maggiore and Orta, the **Mottarone peak ❷** is a natural balcony commanding a wonderful panorama of the lakes and the Alps; on one of those rare clear days you are said to be able to see seven lakes. Access is either by car (the last section is a toll road owned by the Borromeo family), foot (four hours along marked trails) or via the Mottarone cable car on the north side of Stresa (www.stresa-mottarone.it; daily 9.30am–5.30pm). Half way up, the cable car stops at the **Giardino Botanico Alpinia** (Apr–early Oct daily 9.30am–6pm), an Alpine garden with over 1,000 species and fine lake views.

The garden can also be reached by a minibus from Stresa. The Mottarone is also popular with hang gliders and mountain bikers (bikes and helmets can be rented). The latest attraction is the adjustable speed **Alpyland Coaster** (www.alpyland.com; Apr–Oct Mon–Fri 10am–5pm, Sat–Sun 10am–6pm, Nov–Mar weekends only) which enables you to bobsleigh down the mountain at speeds of up to 40kph (25 mph) come snow or sunshine.

Peacocks roam the gardens on Isola Madre

Monte Mottarone

On the southern edge of Stresa the **Villa Pallavicino** (www.parcopallavicino.it; mid-Mar–Sept daily 9am–7pm, last entry at 5.30pm, Oct–early Nov 9am–6pm, last entry at 4.30pm) has a 20-hectare (50-acre) park with botanical gardens and a collection of animals, some of which roam freely through the grounds. Only the gardens are open to the public.

Baveno is a smaller version of Stresa which became prosperous from the pink granite quarried from its slopes. This was used in Milan's Galleria Vittorio Emanuele II and St Paul's in Rome. Like Stresa, Baveno became fashionable in the 19th century, and in 1879 was visited by Queen Victoria. Rising above the village is the spire of the Church of Santi Gervasio e Protasio, which retains its Romanesque facade and an enchanting baptistery with frescoed vault and cupola.

VERBANIA

Facing Stresa across the Gulf of Borromeo, suburban **Verbania** was created by Mussolini in 1939 to unite several communities, including **Intra** and **Pallanza**. By far the prettiest of these is **Pallanza**, where magnolias and oleanders line the quaysides and colourful cafés flank the piazzas. The resort has some fine villas and gardens, such as the famous **Villa Taranto ❸** (www.villataranto.it; Mar daily 8.30am–5.30pm, Apr–Sept until 6.30pm, Oct

9am–4.30pm) on the outskirts of town. In 1931 Neil McEacharn, a retired Scottish captain and passionate horticulturist, purchased the property and converted what was an unruly wooded headland into one of Europe's leading botanical gardens.

Twenty hectares (50 acres) are planted with around 20,000 different species of trees, shrubs and flowers, collected by McEacharn from five different continents, and notably Asia. A hundred gardeners were employed and the lake waters were used for irrigation. In 1952 the gardens were opened to the public and a new ferry stop, Villa Taranto, was created. McEacharn donated the complex to the state in 1938; he died here in 1964 and is buried in a mausoleum in the gardens. Eighty thousand tulips, 300 varieties of rhododendrons and a similar number of dahlias ensure colour from spring to autumn. Magnificent species of trees include cypress, sequoia, horse chestnuts from India and a splendid *Davidia Involucrata* (called the 'handkerchief tree' because of the white hanging squares it produces in spring). In the Victoria Amazonica Greenhouse the giant water lilies measure up to 2m (6.5ft) and resemble huge green trays. The flowers, which are nocturnal, only live for around 48 hours and gradually change colour from creamy white to pink and purplish red.

Gignese umbrellas

In the hills above Stresa, the village of Gignese is best known for the Museo dell'Ombrello e del Parasole (tel: 0323 89622; www.gignese.it/museo; Tue–Sun 10am–noon, 3–6pm). The museum displays 19th- and 20th-century umbrellas and parasols, and documents the life of the local umbrella-makers, some of whose descendants still make and repair umbrellas. Gignese is 8km (5 miles) from Stresa, on a road linking lakes Maggiore and Orta.

Villa Taranto, Verbania

SOUTHERN LAKE MAGGIORE

South of Laveno on the east side of the lake, the enchanting little church of **Santa Caterina del Sasso** ❹ clings to a steep cliff
face above the lake (www.santacaterinadelsasso.com; Mar daily
9am–noon, 2–5pm, Apr–Oct 9am–noon, 2–6pm, Nov–Feb weekends only 9am–noon, 2–5pm). You can reach the church by taking
a ferry or local boat, then climbing up 80 steps from the landing stage; alternatively, park on the square above, which is linked
by a new elevator dug into the rock, or the 268-step pathway. It
was thanks to a local merchant and usurer (or so it is said) that
the church was founded in the 12th century. Alberto Besozzi was
saved from a shipwreck in 1170 and in thanksgiving spent the rest
of his life praying in a cave by the rocks where he was washed
ashore. His prayers were said to have saved the area from the
plague and the locals built a votive chapel to Santa Caterina.
This was enlarged to a monastery in the 14th century. Beautiful

14th–19th-century fresco cycles decorate the church and the Gothic chapterhouse.

In the 11th century the twin fortresses of **Arona** and **Angera** were built to safeguard the strategic southern part of the lake. Arona's is in ruins, but the **Rocca Borromeo** (www.borromeo-turismo.it; daily late-Mar–late-Oct 9am–5.30pm) still dominates Angera. The castle became the property of the Visconti dynasty in the late 13th century and was then purchased by the Borromeo family. The oldest wing features the Sala della Giustizia (Hall of Justice), decorated with 14th-century frescoes depicting the 1277 Visconti victory over the della Torres, which brought their dynasty to power. The fortress is also home to the **Museo della Bambola**, an outstanding doll and toy museum.

The Rocca Borromeo looks across the lake to the ruined castle of **Arona**, on a rocky outcrop above the town. This was the birthplace of Saint Carlo Borromeo (1538–84), who was archbishop and cardinal of Milan and a key figure of the Counter-Reformation. Towering above the town is his huge copper statue, familiarly known as **San Carlone** (the big St Charles; www.statuasancarlo.it; mid-Mar–mid-Oct daily 9am–12.20pm, 2–6.15pm, early Mar and mid-Oct–Nov weekends only, Dec Sun only 9am–12.30pm, 2–4.30pm). You can climb right up inside the statue, and look through his eyes, though this is not to be recommended on a hot summer's day. Arona itself has a few pleasant older parts, museums and lake-view cafés, but the town gets very crowded in the summer.

NORTHERN LAKE MAGGIORE

The main resorts of the northern lake all lie on the sunny western shores. **Cannero Riviera** occupies a charming site amid subtropical flora, looking over to the picturesque ruins of the Malpaga castles. Lovely little **Cannobio**, last town before the Swiss border, has a long promenade and a delightful old quarter preserving its medieval character. In the nearby Val Cannobina, Orrido di Sant'Anna is a deep and dramatic gorge, carved out by the River Cannobino – a lovely spot for a picnic, or lunch perhaps at the restaurant Sant'Anna.

Locarno, the main resort of Swiss Lake Maggiore, is a sunny, southwest-facing town with a mild climate and flourishing parks and lakeside gardens. The heart of the town is the porticoed **Piazza Grande**, flanked by lively cafés and pizzerias where you can sit and watch the fashionable crowds go by. In summer this is the venue for open-air concerts, and in August an outdoor screen is set up for the International Film Festival (www.pardolive.ch). Southwest of the piazza, the 14th-century but much-restored Castello Visconteo is home to the Museo Archeologico, noted for its Roman remains. Up from Piazza Grande, the old town has some handsome villas, churches and the Casa Rusca art museum, with work by the French artist Jean Arp and his contemporaries.

For wonderful views of the lake and Alps take the funicular or walk up to the **Santuario della Madonna del Sasso** (daily 7.30am–noon, 3–6pm) above the resort. You can go on up from here via a glass and steel cable car to the panoramic plateau of Cardada (1,350m/4,430ft; www.cardada.ch). A 10-minute walk and a chairlift will take you higher still to Cimetta (1,671m/5,482ft), with even more staggering views.

Across the Maggia River from Locarno lies the smaller town of **Ascona**. This is another fashionable resort, and traditionally a magnet for writers and artists. Paul Klee, Hermann Hesse, Isadora Duncan and Carl Jung were among those who were lured by its charms. Klee was one of several artists in the 1920s who donated works to the **Museo di Comunale d'Arte Moderna** (Museum of Modern Art, Via Borgo 34; www.museoascona.ch; Tue–Sat 10am–noon, 2–5pm, Sun 10.30am–12.30pm). Ascona's

The main room of Rocca Borromeo di Angera

natural magnet is the lakefront promenade, with views across the water to the **Isole di Brissago**, the tiny twin islands which you can visit by boat either from Ascona or Locarno.

LAKE COMO

Celebrated since ancient times for its great natural location, Como is the most dramatic and romantic of the three great lakes. Shaped like an inverted Y, it has three branches which meet at the Punta Spartivento ('the Point that divides the Wind'), the seductive setting of the enchanting resort of Bellagio. Of the lower two branches the Ramo di Como or western branch is the most scenic, its shores studded with villas, gardens and picturesque harbours and villages. The eastern branch, known as the Lago di Lecco, is more stark and rugged and has at its southern tip the large industrial centre of Lecco.

Cannobio on Lake Maggiore

Although the lake is smaller than Maggiore and Garda, it has the longest perimeter at 170km (106 miles). It is also the deepest lake in Italy and one of the deepest in Europe (410m/1,360ft at its deepest point). In the centre, useful car-ferry services link the resorts of Menaggio, Bellagio and Cadenabbia, saving a lot of mileage and some hair-raising driving. (The road from Bellagio to Como is very narrow and precipitous.)

COMO TOWN

A large industrial centre and transport hub, **Como 5** may not be the obvious choice for a lakeside base. But it has a fine lakeshore setting, an historic quarter with cobbled, traffic-free streets, and some lively cafés and shops selling the famous Como silk, as well as jewellery and leather. The Piazza del Duomo in the centre is a natural magnet. The square is dominated by the lavishly sculpted facade of the **Duomo** (http://cattedrale.diocesidi como.it; Mon–Fri 9.30am–5.30pm, Sat 10.45am–4.30pm, Sun and holidays 1–4.30pm). A fusion of Gothic and Renaissance, with a dome added in 1744, the church took some 350 years to complete. The portal is flanked by niche statues of Pliny the Elder (on the left) and Pliny the Younger (on the right) – surprising since both Plinys were pagans. The interior is full of works of art, including Renaissance tapestries hanging in the nave and paintings by Gaudenzio Ferrari (c.1471/81–1546) and Bernardino Luini (1480–1532), two Lombard painters influenced by Leonardo da Vinci.

Next to the Duomo is the lovely arcaded **Broletto**, the former Court of Justice, built in 1251, at the same time as the adjacent Torre del Comune (clock tower). The **Basilica di San Fedele** (daily 8am–noon, 3.30–7pm) stands on the nearby Piazza Fedele, an attractive medieval square with porticoed houses. The Lombard-Romanesque church has been much altered over the centuries and was given a new facade in the early 20th century. Originally Como's cathedral, the church was the work of the *Maestri Comacini*, medieval stonemasons of Como renowned throughout Europe for their craftsmanship. Another example

◎ SONS OF COMO

Como's most famous sons were **Pliny the Elder** (AD 23–79), the Roman scholar who wrote the 37-volume *Historia Naturalis* (Natural History) and died during the eruption of Vesuvius in AD 79, and his nephew and adopted son, **Pliny the Younger** (AD 61–113), an author and lawyer who left a large collection of private letters offering a fascinating insight into public and private life of the times. The same Pliny is said to have owned at least two villas at Bellagio, one on the hilltop for study and reflection (possibly on the site of the current Villa Serbelloni), and another on the lakeshore for hunting and fishing.

Como's most famous scientist was **Alessandro Volta** (1745–1827), who invented the battery and after whom the volt is named. The neoclassical Volta Temple on Como's waterfront houses a collection of his instruments and inventions.

of their work is the Romanesque gem of **Sant'Abbondio** (Via Sant'Abbondio, out of the centre; daily 8am–6pm, winter 8am–4.30pm), with a remarkable cycle of mid-14th century frescoes in the apse, depicting scenes from the *Life of Christ*.

The Comaschi (citizens of Como) have been producing silk and other textiles since the 15th century and the town is the centre of Italy's silk industry. Silkworms are no longer bred here, but Chinese fibres are imported to be woven, dyed and printed. Armani, Hermès and Versace are just three of the famous designers who depend on Como for their silk. The small **Museo Didattico della Seta** (Silk Museum, Via Castelnuovo 9; www. museosetacomo.com; Tue–Fri 10am–6pm, Sat 10am–1pm) on the edge of town documents the story of Como's silk, with sections on silkworm breeding and the silk-making processes.

Locarno is in the Swiss part of Lake Maggiore

For a bird's-eye view of the town take the **Brunate funicular ❻** which rises up the hillside east of the centre. In seven minutes you are at the hilltop village of Brunate from which there are expansive views across the lake to the Alps. Brunate can also be reached on foot from Como and makes a good starting point for hikes in the hills.

Como's highlights

Guided tours of Como's most important monuments take place every first and third Saturday of the month whatever the weather (www.visitcomo. eu; May–Sept) at the information point at Via Maestri Cumacini, flanking the Duomo.

RAMO DI COMO

The Como branch of the lake, known as the **Ramo di Como**, is best seen by boat. You can travel either by *Battello*, the regular ferry boat which stops at all the landing stages; by *Aliscafo*, the faster hydrofoil which makes fewer stops; or by excursion cruiser. Boats depart from Piazza Cavour in central Como and tickets can be purchased from kiosks on the lakefront. From Como to Bellagio the boats afford splendid views of the villages tumbling down the steep wooded hillsides and the neoclassical villas and gardens overlooking the lake.

The first main stop is **Cernobbio**, famous for the grandiose villas built here in the 16th to 18th centuries. Best known among them is the **Villa d'Este**, which since 1873 has been the most luxurious hotel on the lake (see page 137). It was built in the 16th century for Cardinal Tolomeo Gallio, Secretary of State to Pope Gregory XIII and at one time was home of Caroline of Brunswick (1768–1821), the disgraced and estranged wife of George Frederick, who later became King George IV of England.

Since becoming a hotel the villa has hosted royalty, politicians and film stars. Some of Cernobbio's splendid villas have been converted to conference or exhibition centres, such as the 19th-century Villa Erba; others are owned by wealthy businessmen or celebrities: George Clooney has a huge waterfront mansion at Laglio, a pretty lakeside village which has been used as a back-drop for his Fiat ads, and Richard Branson has a lakeside villa at Lenno. At the romantic little village of Moltrasio, 3km (2 miles) north of Cernobbio, **Villa Le Fontanelle** was the favourite haunt of the late designer Gianni Versace. The villa, whose invitees included Madonna, Elton John and a string of other celebrities, was sold to a Russian multi-millionaire after Versace's death.

Villa del Balbianello ❼ (mid-Mar–mid-Nov, Tue and Thu–Sun 10am–6pm, last entry 4.30pm) also attained celebrity status when its grounds were used for big Hollywood hits such as *Star Wars* and the Bond movie *Casino Royale*. It stands in an enchanting setting on the wooded headland south of Lenno. A private shuttle boat service runs from Lenno jetty or you can take a boat service from Como. Alternatively, on a Tuesday, Saturday or Sunday you can go by foot from Lenno (about 1km), following signs from the church square. You can wander in the gardens independently, but if you

Como Town

want to visit the villa you must take an hour-long tour.

Built as a retreat in 1787 by Cardinal Angelo Maria Durini, the villa incorporates the remains of a Franciscan convent, which you can still see at the lower level. The eccentric cardinal led a life of study and contemplation, sleeping between black sheets in a black bedroom with a coffin beside his bed

Ferry trips

A ferry trip is the best way to see the lake. Coastal roads that plunge you into dimly lit tunnels and are often traffic-clogged in season do not make for relaxing driving; what's more, many of the lake's loveliest features are only visible from the water.

to remind him of his fate. One of Durini's descendants, Count Guido Monzino, acquired the property in 1954. On his death he left the villa and contents to the FAI, the Fondo Ambiente Italiano, Italy's equivalent of the National Trust. Monzino, who led a North Pole expedition in 1971 and the first successful Italian ascent of Everest in 1973, used the villa as an international centre for the study of explorations. As well as some fine English antiques, ceramics, paintings and *objets d'art*, there is a library with hundreds of books devoted to mountaineering and polar expeditions, a map-reading room used to plan the expeditions, and a museum full of Monzino's mountaineering memorabilia. The gardens, climbing up the headland, combine magnificent oak, cypress and plane trees with immaculate lawns, romantic paths and pergolas. The climax is the open loggia at the top with glorious vistas of the lake.

In the lee of the promontory the **Isola Comacina** is the only island of the lake. Tiny though it is, the settlement was fortified by the Romans and became a political and military centre in the Middle Ages, acquiring the name of Crispoli, City of Gold.

Villa d'Este in Cernobbio

The islanders supported Milan in its destruction of Como in 1128 and in retaliation Como ravaged the island in 1169, forcing them to take refuge in Varenna. The baroque Oratorio di San Giovanni and the ruins of medieval churches are all that remain. The island was bequeathed to the King of Belgium in 1914, later donated to the state and today is under the supervision of the Brera Academy of Fine Arts in Milan. A handful of artists live in cottages here. The Locanda dell'Isola Comacina dishes out an expensive lunch to tourists. Alternatively, there are plenty of peaceful spots for a picnic.

CENTRO LAGO

Grand old villas and luxuriant gardens line the lakeshores at Tremezzo. The most famous among them is **Villa Carlotta** ❽ (www.villacarlotta.it; daily late Mar–Sept 9am–6.30pm, Oct 9.30am–5pm), a vast neoclassical pile graced by over 5.6

hectares (14 acres) of gardens, and famous for its numerous varieties and huge species of azaleas and rhododendrons. The villa was built from 1690–1743 by the Clerici, a wealthy Milanese family of merchants. Most of the contents you see today were acquired by the following owner, Giambattista Sommariva. Meanwhile, his political arch rival, Duke Francesco Melzi d'Eril, constructed a beautiful villa in Bellagio, right opposite Villa Carlotta. Competition between them led to continual embellishment of both residences and gardens. In 1843 Villa Carlotta was acquired by Princess Marianna of the Netherlands, wife of Prince Albert of Prussia, who gave the villa to her daughter, Carlotta, as a wedding present – hence its present name.

The villa has a magnificent entrance with a grand stairway, gardens, balustrades and fountains. The interior, a bit of an anti-climax after the gardens, is decorated with Empire furniture and neoclassical and romantic sculpture and painting. There are works by Canova, though the much-vaunted *Cupid and Psyche* is a copy of the original which is in the Louvre.

Bellagio ❾, 'pearl of the lake', enjoys an unrivalled setting on the wooded promontory that divides the Lecco and Como arms of the lake. Walks around the cape afford sublime views of mountains in all directions, and notably north to the often snow-capped mountains along the Swiss border. The impossibly picturesque old town (or *borgo*) retains its medieval layout with porticos, cobbled alleys and stepped streets leading up from the waterside. Enticing cafés, where you can sip a cocktail and watch the ferries plying across the lake, stretch out along the waterfront. All of this of course draws boatloads of tourists throughout the season, but it is enchanting nonetheless. Ideally stay a night or two and enjoy the village after dusk when the day-trippers have departed.

On the hill behind the village are the gardens of the **Villa Serbelloni** (guided tours only, starting from the medieval tower in Piazza della Chiesa; mid-Mar–Oct Tue–Sun at 11am and 3.30pm). The villa, not to be confused with the exclusive hotel of the same name on the lakeside, belongs to the Rockefeller Foundation and is not open to the public. The steep path takes you well above the villa for sublime lake and mountain panoramas. On the south side of the village are the exotic gardens of **Villa Melzi** (www.giardinidivillamelzi.it; late Mar–Oct 9.30am–6.30pm), which spill down to the lake. The fine, if faded, neo-classical palace (closed to the public) was built for Francesco Melzi d'Eril, vice-president of Napoleon's Cisalpine Republic.

Setting off from Bellagio, passenger boats, hydrofoils and car ferries ply across the lake to Menaggio and Varenna. On the western side of the lake, **Menaggio** is larger than Bellagio and not quite as picturesque, but it has its charms and makes

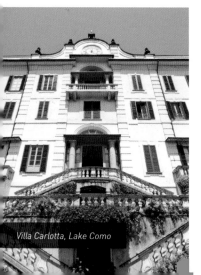

Villa Carlotta, Lake Como

an excellent base for boat trips, bike tours and trekking in the hills. Large, belle-époque hotels are peacefully set along the lakeside promenade, restaurant terraces make the most of the views and there's a lively little centre with bars, small shops and a well-stocked tourist office. Golf, rock-climbing, riding, tennis, cycling, water-skiing, windsurfing and canoeing are just a few of the activities on offer – and there's a good beach and large pool at the Lido.

Serious trekkers might consider the Alta Via del Lario, the route that winds from Menaggio to Gera Lario, following high ground along the Swiss border.

Varenna ⑩, across the lake, is a perfectly preserved medieval village where narrow stepped alleys lead down to a romantic lakeside walkway, shaded by porticos and arbours. In many ways this little gem is just as charming as Bellagio, but far less crowded and commercialised. Moreover, it has a handful of excellent hotels and restaurants, and two lakeside villas with gardens open to the public. **Villa Monastero** (www.villamonastero.eu; opening hours vary) is a former Cistercian convent founded in 1208 by nuns who escaped from Isola Comacina when the island was sacked by Como. Transformed into an aristocratic residence in the 17th century, the villa is now an international cultural and scientific centre, with beautiful terraced gardens spilling down to the lake, and a house museum with 14 antiques-filled rooms open to the public. Neighbouring **Villa Cipressi** (Apr–Oct 9am–6.30pm), named after its lofty cypress trees and now a hotel, also has terraced lakeside gardens open to the public. For a bird's eye view of the Bellagio peninsula, climb up steep steps or drive to the semi-ruined medieval **Castello di Vezio** (www.castellodivezio.it; early Mar–Oct, hours vary), a venue for regular falconry displays at around 3pm.

Manzoni's town

The commercial city of Lecco, on the southern tip of Lago di Lecco, is famous as the centrepiece of Alessandro Manzoni's masterpiece *I Promessi Sposi* (The Betrothed), published in 1827. Manzoni memorabilia can be seen at his childhood home, and locations from his novel can be identified in the town and surrounding landscape.

Bellagio

RAMO DI COLICO

The northern branch of the lake, called the **Ramo di Colico** or Alto Lario, has no resorts of great charm but you may like to visit the **Abbazia di Piona** (daily in season 9am–noon, 2.30–5pm). This 11th-century abbey has a pretty setting on the tip of the Olgiasca promontory enclosing the small bay of Lake Piona. The abbey was founded by Cluniac monks but is now home to Cistercians. The ruins of the Lombard Romanesque church retain early frescoes and there are beautiful Gothic/Renaissance cloisters (1252). The monks are famous for their home-made strong brews which are sold in the shop here. The abbey can be accessed by ferry in summer.

LAKE GARDA

The largest and easternmost of the lakes, Garda is bordered by three different regions: Lombardy, Trentino and the Veneto. The scenery is enormously diverse, from the fjord-like north, where the Brenta Dolomites drop sheer into the water, to the gentle hills of vineyards and olive groves, and the sea-like southern basin, fringed by beaches. Sheltered by the mountains, it enjoys an equable climate and luxuriant vegetation along its shores. Garda is the cleanest lake and the most popular for swimming, windsurfing and sailing. The lake is a favourite playground of German and Austrian tourists and in season you can expect crowded campsites and coachloads of day-trippers, particularly in the south.

THE SOUTHERN SHORES

Sirmione ⑪, Lake Garda's most famous resort, has an enticing setting on a narrow peninsula that juts 4km (2.5 miles) into the lake. The old town is heralded by the photogenic **Rocca Scaligera** (Scaligera Castle; Tue–Sat 8.30am–7.30pm, Sun 9.15am–5.45pm), accessed via a drawbridge over the fish-filled moat. The castle was built in 1259 by Mastino I della Scala, the fishtail battlements being the trademark of the della Scala family.

The narrow alleys around the castle teem with tourists throughout the season – Sirmione is just minutes away from the Milan–Venice motorway and popular with day-trippers. But beyond the castle you can escape the worst of the crowds and find pleasant lakeside terraces, beaches and a headland of olive and cypress trees. At the tip of the peninsula lies the famous **Grotte de Catullo** (www.grottedicatullo.beniculturali.it; Mar–mid-Oct Tue–Fri 8.30am–7.30pm, Sat–Sun 9.30am–6.30pm, mid-Oct–Feb Tue–Fri 8.30am–5pm, Sat–Sun 8.30am–2pm), the ruins of a vast Roman villa. The site was named after the Roman poet Catullus, but although his poems make reference to a home in Sirmione there is no evidence this was his villa. The archaeological remains – some of the most important of their kind in Italy – cover over 2 hectares (5 acres) of the promontory and are set high above the lake amid olive and cypress trees. Deciphering the various rooms on the various levels is not easy, but it is lovely just to wander around.

West of Sirmione, **Desenzano del Garda** is the largest town on the lake, and one of the most colourful and lively. An important Roman port, it retains a 3rd-century **Villa Romana** (Mar–mid-Oct

Tue–Sun 8.30am–7pm, mid-Oct–Feb Tue–Sun 8.30am–5pm and the antiquarium 9am–7pm) with remarkable floor mosaics depicting scenes of hunting and local life. The heart of the town is the picturesque **Porto Vecchio** (Old Port) flanked by cafés and the venue of a large and popular Tuesday market. Behind the port, narrow lanes lead up to the medieval castle, while along the front, the promenade is pleasant for strolling.

East of Sirmione, **Peschiera del Garda** was a medieval strong-hold of the Venetian empire. The town is still dominated by the mighty bastions of its fortress, but there is not a great deal to detain you here. Nowadays, Peschiera is associated more with amusement parks than history. **Gardaland** (see page 93) is Italy's number one theme park, with 46-hectares (113 acres) of Disneyland-styled attractions (www.gardaland.it), and **Movieland Studios** (see page 93) offers film-themed attractions, shows and aquatic slides and rides (www.canevaworld.it).

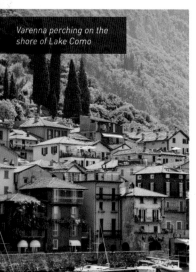

Varenna perching on the shore of Lake Como

THE WESTERN SHORE

North of Desenzano the town of **Salò** ⑫ has a long history dating back to Roman times. In 1337 it became the capital of the Magnifica Patria, a community of 42 towns; during a less-fortunate episode in the town's history, it became the seat of Mussolini's puppet republic in 1943 – his last desperate attempt to reorganise

Fascism in Italy. The Art Nouveau-style Villa Simonini (now the Hotel Laurin) was the headquarters of the Italian Foreign Ministry, presided over by *Il Duce*. On a beautiful deep bay, and backed by the Monte San Bartolomeo, Salò is an appealing combination of bustling local town and elegant resort – with no

> ### Roman spa town
>
> Sirmione has been a spa since Roman times. Large numbers of visitors come to its thermal establishment for treatment using the sulphurous water that emerges from a spring in the lake (www.termedisirmione.com).

hint of its ignominious past. The narrow streets and squares of the historic quarter lie behind a long lakeside promenade. The late-Gothic **Duomo** (daily 8.30am–noon, 3–6.30pm) along the waterfront, spied from afar by its distinctive bell tower, has an unfinished brick facade, with a Renaissance portal. The piazza here is the setting for summer performances of the Gasparo da Salò Festival of Music, celebrating the inventor (or perfecter) of the violin, born here in 1540.

Off the headland south of Salò lies the little, cypress-studded island of **Isola di Garda**. In private hands for several centuries, the island was inherited by Camillo Cavazza and the current residents are his English wife and her seven children. From April to October boats leave from Salò once a week, from Gardone Riviera twice weekly; the island can also be visited from other resorts in the lower lakes. Two-hour guided tours (occasionally given by one of the family) include the neo-Gothic villa and fine gardens, with tastings of local products such as wine and olive oil.

Just along the coast, **Gardone Riviera** ⓭ maintains much of the elegance that drew royalty and wealthy international visitors in the late 19th and early 20th centuries. The

Scaliger castle in Sirmione

Austrian Emperor and other European elite built palatial villas here and Gardone became the most fashionable resort on the lake. Among the eminent guests at the belle-époque Grand Hotel, which still stands on the waterfront, were Somerset Maugham, Nabokov and Churchill. Further along, at the Villa Fiordaliso, Mussolini stayed with his mistress Clara Petacci during the Salò Republic. This lovely Art Nouveau lakeside villa is now a hotel and restaurant where you can enjoy fine cuisine on the lake.

The biggest draw of Gardone, particularly for Italian day-trippers, is **Il Vittoriale** (www.vittoriale.it; park and gardens: daily late Mar–mid-Oct 8.30am–8pm, mid-Oct–late Mar 9am–5pm; guided tours of house Tue–Sun and War Museum Thu–Tue). This eccentric residence, set in 9 hectares (22 acres) of gardens with lake views, was home to the flamboyant poet, dramatist, soldier and socialite, Gabriele d'Annunzio (1863–1938). The memorabilia from his wartime, literary, artistic and womanising pursuits – not to mention the vast wedding cake mausoleum – are all a celebration of the man himself. Among the eccentricities are the coffin in the spare bedroom, the dark or painted windows (D'Annunzio hated daylight), an embalmed tortoise which died of overeating and the prow of the battle-ship, *Puglia*, wedged into the hillside.

In the early 20th century Arturo Hruska, a botanist and dentist to the last Tsar of Russia, transformed the sloping site above the town into an oasis of flora. The **Heller Garden** (www.hellergarden. com; Mar–Oct daily 9am–7pm) contains flourishing Alpine, sub-tropical and Mediterranean species. It's a wonderfully peaceful spot where you can wander among pretty rockeries, lush lawns, Japanese-style gardens, streams and waterfalls.

Toscalano-Maderno north of Gardone is the main embarkation point for the car ferry to Torri del Benaco. Going north, **Gargnano** is one of the main sailing centres on the lake and it is hard to find a more pleasant lakeside place to stay. Remarkably unspoilt, it has a lively little port, a promenade of orange trees, a couple of very enticing hotels (see page 139) and a gourmet restaurant serving some of the best cuisine on the lake.

The picturesque little town of **Limone sul Garda** is bypassed by the main coast road, but heaves with tourists all through the season. The rows of white stone pillars of the now-defunct lemon terraces or *limonaie* are testimony to the citrus-fruit industry

---

⊙ TIGNALE AND TREMÓSINE

Well worth a diversion from the shore is the panoramic route climbing up to Tignale and Tremósine, scenic plateaux of alpine meadows. (Note, though, that the narrow roads and hairpin bends are not for the faint-hearted). The 43km (27-mile) detour from the lake starts on the road 4km (2.5 miles) north of Gargnano. This snakes its way up to Tignale (555m/1,821ft), then descends before climbing up again to the Tremósine plateau – an even higher balcony commanding views of the entire lake basin. From here the main road comes down to join the lake at Limone sul Garda.

Salò at night

which made Limone rich. Trade declined in the 20th century with competition from cheaper citrus fruits grown in the hotter climate of the south. Fruit trees still flourish and market stalls brim with bottles of lemon liqueur, lemon-shaped ceramics and the freshly picked fruits. You might assume the village is named after the citrus fruit but it is more likely that it derives from the Latin *limen* or border, referring to the former frontier here between Austria and Italy.

GARDA TRENTINO

The northern tip of the lake lies in Trentino, which was under Austrian rule from 1815–1918. Set against the dramatic backdrop of Monte Brione, the main resort of **Riva del Garda**  has been luring visitors from the north since the 19th century. Today it is a thriving holiday resort, attracting a large number of German and British tourists, but managing to retain much of its former character and elegance. Strategically located between Verona and the Alps, the town was a major trading port, coveted by rival factions and variously acquired by the Veronese Scaligeri (1349), the Viscontis of Milan (1380) and the Venetian Republic (1440).

The moated **La Rocca**, dominating the waterfront and accessed over a drawbridge, is testimony to the Scaligera era. Since it was built in 1124 the castle has been remodelled several times, and under the Austrians the tower was truncated, turning the castle into a garrison. Today it is home to the Museo Alto Garda (www.museoaltogarda.it), with displays of art and archaeology and varied temporary exhibitions. Overlooking the harbour, **Piazza III Novembre** is the appealing main square, flanked by medieval Renaissance palazzi and the lofty **Torre Apponale**. The tower has variously served as a prison, a store for salt and grain, and as a look-out point during World War I.

Cafés and pizzerias along the waterfront make the most of the views, and there are parks, gardens and pebbly beaches. The waters are dotted with windsurfers and dinghies all year round – you can rent equipment and have lessons, or just take a leisurely stroll along the waterfront to admire the views. You

⊙ LIMONE'S ELIXIR OF LIFE

In the late 1980s scientists discovered that many of Limone's inhabitants had a mystery protein in their blood that declogs their arteries of fat and gives them virtual immunity to heart attacks and strokes. The chemical, called Apolipoprotein A-1 Milano (shortened to Apo A-1 Milano) has been identified in around three dozen Limonesi. The mutant gene has been passed from generation to generation – Limone was an isolated village pre-1932, only accessible by boat or by crossing the mountains, and intermarriage was common. All the carriers are descendants from the same couple who lived in Limone in the 18th century. Human trials based on Apo A-1 Milano have demonstrated proof of efficacy against cardiovascular disease in animals and humans but as yet, no drugs are commercially available; and in case you're wondering, no link has (yet) been established between the protein and Limone lemons.

can walk all the way to **Torbole** (4km/2.5miles), described by Goethe as 'a wonder of nature, an enchanting sight'. Its setting below sheer rocks and beside the River Sarca is as alluring as ever, but the village is spoilt by the main road cutting off the centre from the lake, and unless you're into rock climbing, windsurfing or sailing there is little to detain you.

THE EASTERN SHORE

Stretching 50km (31 miles) along the eastern bank of the lake, the so-called **Riviera degli Olivi** is typified by tourist development as well as olive groves and vine-clad hills. The main road, known as the **Gardesana Orientale**, hugs the shoreline and is frequently traffic-clogged in summer. The northern section, between Torbole and Malcesine, has a series of dimly lit tunnels, plunging you from dazzling bright sunlight into blackness. This tunnelled stretch is the setting of a dramatic opening car chase in the Bond film *Quantum of Solace*, climaxing in a spectacular crash.

Gargnano on Lake Garda

The resort of **Malcesine** ⓰ lies at the foot of Monte Baldo, and clusters beneath the striking Castello Scaligero. This fishing village-turned-tourist magnet is a picturesque maze of cobbled alleys, with medieval porticoes and a small port which buzzes with activity throughout the season. The **castle** (Apr–Oct daily 9.30am–7.30pm, Nov–Mar Sat–Sun and holidays 11am–4pm) has fine views of the lake from the battlements and tower, and is home to the Natural History Museum of Monte Baldo and Lake Garda.

Behind the resort the panoramic rotating cabins of a funicular whisk you up **Monte Baldo** (2,220m/7,275ft) in 10 minutes (www.funiviedelbaldo.com; late Mar–mid-Nov daily 8am–6pm). The cabins

> ### Goethe at Garda
>
> The Sala Goethe in Malcesine's castle is devoted to the German writer's drawings, notes and views on Lake Garda and the castle. While compiling his *Travels in Italy* he visited the lake in 1786 when it was under Austrian rule. The writer was sketching the castle at Malcesine when he was arrested as an Austrian spy. He was imprisoned here but soon released after convincing the authorities of his innocence.

can also accommodate mountain bikes and hang gliders so you can freewheel or float back. The ridge offers some ravishing **views** and scenic walking trails. In winter the funicular takes you to the ski slopes. Malcesine is a popular hub for all sports enthusiasts: in addition to hiking, mountain biking and winter sports, there is windsurfing, kitesurfing, sailing and scuba diving on the lake, and tennis and horse riding on the shores.

Yet another Scaligeri castle heralds the town of **Torri del Benaco**. Views from the tower encompass almost the entire lake, from Sirmione to Limone. The castle museum is devoted to Torri's ancient way of life: boat building, fishing and olive cultivation. Modern Torri is busy with car ferries that ply across the waters to Toscolano-Maderno, but the old port has maintained its original character, and the Hotel Gardesana's café terrace, which overlooks it, is a delightful spot to watch the world go by.

Riva del Garda

In ancient times Lake Garda was called 'Benacus' (beneficent) – and it is occasionally still referred to by the Latin name. The lake took its current name from the town of **Garda** which lies below a huge rocky outcrop on the south-eastern shore. The town today is a bustling holiday resort where life focuses on a long, spacious prom-enade, lined by tourist cafés. Behind the water-front the narrow alleys of the old quarter are packed with small shops, souvenirs and trat-torias. **Punta San Vigilio** to the west is a delightful spot, where an ancient lane of cypress trees leads to the tip of a peaceful promontory with a little church and a 16th-century villa. On a tiny harbour the luxury hotel Locanda San Vigilio, with just 7 rooms and a lakeside restaurant, has been welcoming guests since the early 16th century. On the other side of the promontory the Baia delle Sirene (Bay of the Sirens) has a good but crowded beach and is a pretty spot to take a picnic in the shade of olive trees.

South of Garda, **Bardolino** offers plenty of opportunities for tasting the eponymous wine. Head for the excellent little **Museo del Vino** above the town (www.museodelvino.it; mid-Mar–Oct daily 9am–12.30pm, 2.30–7pm, Nov–mid-Mar 8.30am–12.30pm, 2.30–6.30pm). In the adjoining Zeni Winery (www.zeni.it) you can try the local reds, whites and rosés, and purchase bottles at very reasonable prices. In late September and early October Bardolino hosts the Festa dell'Uva (Grape Festival) where corks pop non-stop. Wines aside, Bardolino is a pleasant lakeside resort with a tree-lined promenade and a profusion of small bars and cafés and two ancient churches. At Cisano di Bardolino the **Museo dell'Olio di Oliva** (Olive Oil Museum; www.museum.it; Mon–Sat 9am–12.30pm, 2.30–7pm, Sun 9am–12.30pm) offers free tasting of local olive oil and has a little shop selling vinegars, olives, honey, pasta and pesto, as well as olive oil.

LESSER LAKES

LAKE ORTA

The westernmost of the lakes and the only one entirely in Piedmont territory, **Lake Orta** is just 14km (9 miles) long and 3km (2 miles) at its widest point. It may not sound that small but it's minute in comparison to neighbouring Maggiore, and a lot more peaceful. The highlight is **Orta San Giulio** ⑯, a perfectly preserved medieval village with mesmerising views

---

◎ MONTE BALDO

The 35km (22-mile) mountain chain of Monte Baldo is famous for its profusion and variety of flora. Way back in the 16th century it became known for its rare botanical species and was visited by scholars of botany and herbalists working for European royal courts. Specialists have been exploring ever since, and now there are around 20 species which have *Baldense* as part of their official name. Among the species unique to the high ridge are *Anemone baldensis* (known as the Mount Baldo windrose) and *Veronica bonarota*.

over **Isola San Giulio**. This little island in the centre of the lake seems to float on the morning mist, and by night it's illuminated and every bit as magical.

Orta San Giulio positively oozes charm, with its cobbled, car-free alleys, ancient houses and enticing lakeside **Piazza Motta**. Nicknamed the *salotto* or drawing room, the square is overlooked by the lovely Palazzotto, the old town hall, with its loggia and faded frescoes. The little harbour is a scene of constant activity with rowing boats and water taxis plying back and forth to the island. Legend has it that San Giulio, a missionary from the Greek island of Aegina, rid the island of dragons and snakes in the 4th century and founded the basilica here. It was rebuilt in the 10th century and became a centre of pilgrimage. Though much remodelled since, the church retains its richly carved, 11th-century black-marble pulpit, frescoes from four centuries and the remains of the saint. From the basilica a peaceful cobbled path, called the Way of Silence *(Via del Silenzio)* going in one direction and the Way of Meditation *(Via della Meditazione)* in the other, circuits the island, passing a Benedictine monastery (no public access) and private villas overlooking the lake.

On a hill above Orta San Giulio are the 21 chapels of the **Sacro Monte** (Holy Mount; daily 9.30am–6.30pm, off season 9am–4.30pm),

Malcesine

decorated with 17th- and 18th-century frescoes and life-size terracotta figures illustrating scenes from the life of St Francis. Even if you don't make it to all the chapels, this is a lovely location with lake views and a welcoming little restaurant (the Sacro Monte).

VARESE AND ITS LAKE

Prosperous **Varese** is essentially a modern city and manufacturing centre which, given all the attractions of nearby lakes Como and Maggiore, is largely ignored by tourists. In its favour are the Art Nouveau villas, parks and gardens (it is styled *Città Giardino* or City of Gardens), sophisticated shopping and small historic centre. The Bernascone belltower rises 77m (253ft) above the centre; beside it the Basilica of San Vittore (1580–1615) was later given a neoclassical facade; and behind it the Baptistery of San Giovanni, with some remarkable 14th century frescoes, is one of the few surviving buildings from the medieval town. North of the town don't miss **Villa Panza** (Tue–Sun 10am–6pm), a beautiful 18th-century villa and gardens, which houses a major collection of modern American art that belonged to the last owner of the villa, Giuseppe Panza.

The **Sacro Monte** is a major pilgrimage site 8km (5 miles) northwest of Varese on the wooded slopes of Monte Campo dei Fiori. Along the steep Via Sacra are 14 devotional chapels with life-size terracotta figures and frescoes. From the Sanctuary of Santa Maria del Monte and its village at the top there are fine

Traffic-free town

During the holiday season the village of Orta San Giulio is closed to traffic and, unless you are unloading at a hotel, cars must be left in the paying car park outside the centre. From here you descend to the central piazza on foot. Avoid visiting the lake on Sundays when coach-loads of tourists pour into the village.

Monte Baldo cable car

views – and even better ones if you were to carry on 5km (3 miles) to the Parco Regionale di Campo dei Fiori.

Shaped like a battered boot, **Lake Varese** is a tiny lake west of the city. This is a gentle, undramatic lake framed in rolling hills. Isolino Virginia, the tiny wooded island off the west shore, has a restaurant and the little Museum of Prehistory.

South of Varese, sitting among the industries of the Olona valley (and very poorly sign-posted), is the Renaissance gem of **Castiglione Olona** ⓱. Cardinal Branda Castiglioni (1350–1443) created this beautiful complex by bringing the new Renaissance style from Tuscany to his native village. The leading Florentine artist, Masolino, was commissioned to decorate the buildings and there are stunning frescoes depicting the *Life of the Virgin* (1428) in the collegiate church above the old quarter and the *Life of John the Baptist* (1435) in the nearby baptistery.

LAKE ISEO

Between the provinces of Bergamo and Brescia, **Lake Iseo** is comparatively tranquil and unknown. It lacks the picturesque villages of the larger lakes but has a fine setting within a ring of wooded mountains. Taking centre stage is **Monte Isola** ⓲, a large, car-free island with chestnut woods, vineyards, olive groves and a population of around 200, living in sleepy mountain and lakeside villages. A haven for day-trippers, the island offers pleasant walks, bike rides and restaurants serving fish straight out of the surrounding waters. The lake's speciality is *tinca* (tench) served with polenta, or you could be offered crayfish, trout, pike or perch, washed down perhaps with one of the local Franciacorta sparkling white wines.

Iseo is the lake's main town, and though very tourist-focused, retains a certain charm with its fine promenade and maze of narrow lanes. **Sarnico** is a popular sports centre and has an attractive old quarter of narrow streets, small squares and arcaded houses. **Lovere**, a steel-making centre with Celtic origins, dominates the northern lake. The town has a well-preserved historic quarter, an art gallery (Accademia di Belle Arti Tadini Gallery; www.accademiatadini.it) and a café-lined lakefront where the first steamer was launched on the lake in 1841. At picturesque **Pisogne**, across the water, the church of Santa Maria delle Neve is known as La Cappella Sistina dei Poveri (the Poor Man's Sistine Chapel) on account of the beautiful fresco cycle (1534) by Romanino.

From Pisogne you can drive north through the **Camonica Valley**,

Lake Lugano

Known also by the Italians as Lake Ceresio, its ancient name, the many-fingered Lake Lugano lies deep in the mountains between lakes Como and Maggiore. Just over a third of the shore belongs to Italy, the rest to the Swiss canton of Ticino. The steep wooded hills rising sheer from the water preclude development along most of its shores and lively, stylish Lugano is the only large town, with sunny lakeside promenades, café-lined piazzas, luxury shops and galleries.

Orto San Giulio

named after the Bronze-Age Camuni tribe who recorded scenes of everyday life by carving on the rocks of the valley floor. The valley is nowadays marred by industry but the rock engravings, which span several thousand years from the Ice Age to the Roman era, constitute one of the largest and finest collections of prehistoric art in Europe. The engravings are scattered all along the valley but the best examples are contained within Capo di Ponte's **Parco Nazionale delle Incisioni Rupestri** 🔞 (National Park of Rock Engravings; www.parcoincisioni.capo diponte.beniculturali.it). In this Unesco World Heritage Site, over 300,000 rock carvings are etched onto glacier-seared sandstone in an area covering 8km (5 miles). Big Rock 1, for example, is engraved with over 1,000 drawings (warriors, women, shamen and deer-hunters amongst them), which run from the Neolithic era to the Iron Age.

South of Lake Iseo lies the hilly, wine-producing region of **Franciacorta** 🔟. The **Strada del Vino Franciacorta** (www.stradadelfranciacorta.it) is an 80km (50-mile) wine route from Brescia to Lake Iseo, featuring vineyard tours and tastings. Franciacorta produces red and white wines but is best known for *spumante*, made according to Champagne methods. This is the best fizz you'll find in Italy.

LOMBARD CITIES

BERGAMO

Following the Napoleonic army on horseback in 1800, Stendhal arrived in **Bergamo** ㉑ from Milan having crossed 'the loveliest country in the world'. Today the *autostrada* and a great swathe of industry separate the cities, but Bergamo itself has seen remarkably little change over the two centuries. The modern city was constructed on the plain in the late 19th and early 20th centuries, but the **Città Alta**, the hilltop city where Stendhal stayed, is one of Italy's most alluring medieval centres.

From the **Città Bassa**, the pleasant enough but traffic-filled Lower City, a cable car takes you 100m (330ft) up the hill – and 500 years back in time. In 1428 Bergamo was swallowed up by the Venetian Republic; the great walls encircling the upper city, the fortress and the lions of St Mark all bear witness to over three and a half centuries under the sway of the Serenissima.

Piazza Vecchia

Via Gombito and Via Colleoni, lively medieval streets lined by delectable little food shops and eateries, lead from the upper cable-car terminal to the heart of old Bergamo. The enchanting **Piazza Vecchia** is a showpiece of medieval and Renaissance buildings, surrounding the beautiful Contarini fountain.

On the southern side of the square, the magnificent Venetian-Gothic **Palazzo della Ragione** (Mar daily 10am–noon, 2–6pm, Apr–Sept daily 9am–noon, 2–8pm, Sat until 11pm, Oct Sat–Sun 10am–noon, 2–6pm, Nov–Feb 10am–noon, 2–4pm) is the oldest communal palace in Italy, built in the 12th century though much remodelled. The elegant external stairway leads up to the main hall which houses a collection of fresco

Sacro Monte church fresco

panels taken from nearby churches and convents.

The glass lift in the city's bell tower, known more familiarly as the **Campanone** (www.museodellestorie.bergamo.it; Apr–Oct Tue–Fri 10am–6pm, Sat and Sun until 8pm, Nov–Mar Tue–Fri 9.30am–1pm, 2.30–6pm, Sat and Sun 9.30am–6pm), affords fine views of the town. The bell still chimes 100 times every evening at 10pm, in memory of the curfew under the Venetians. On the far side of the piazza the imposing white building is the Palazzo Nuovo, which today serves as the civic library.

Piazza del Duomo

Beyond Piazza Vecchia's loggia lies the smaller **Piazza del Duomo**, which is crammed with three major monuments. The **Cappella Colleoni** (Mar–Oct Tue–Sun 9am–12.30pm, 2–6.30pm, Nov–Feb 9am–12.30pm, 2–4.30pm) was built in 1472–6 as a mausoleum for the Venetian *condottiere* (mercenary), Bartolomeo Colleoni, who had the old sacristy of the neighbouring Santa Maria Maggiore demolished to create the space. A masterpiece of the early Lombard Renaissance, it has a multicoloured marble facade enriched by medallions, columns, sculpture and reliefs. The interior is no less opulent, decorated by Tiepolo frescoes and containing the intricately carved tomb of Colleoni, surmounted by a gold equestrian statue of the *condottiere*. The chapel also contains the tomb of his daughter, Medea, who predeceased him.

The adjoining church of **Santa Maria Maggiore** (Apr–Oct Mon–Sat 9am–12.30pm, 2.30–6pm, Sun 9am–1pm, 3–6pm, Nov–Mar Mon–Sat 9am–12.30pm, 2.30–5pm, Sun 9am–1pm, 3–6pm) has a beautiful Gothic porch adorned with statues and reliefs. The interior was reconstructed in the 16th century and has a profusion of gilt, stuccowork and paintings as well as some fine Florentine and Flemish tapestries and exquisite inlaid panels on the (roped-off) choir stalls, designed by Lorenzo Lotto. Back in the piazza, the charming octagonal **Baptistery** is a copy of the 14th-century original which used to be inside the basilica. The **Duomo** (7.30am–noon, 3–6.30pm) is the poor relation in a remarkable group of buildings, its late 19th-century facade looking somewhat sober beside that of Santa Maria Maggiore and the Cappella Colleoni.

Off Via Gombito, the Via Solata leads up to **La Rocca** (www.museodellestorie.bergamo.it; June–Sept Tue–Fri 10am–1pm, 2.30–6pm, Sat 10am–7pm, Oct–May Tue–Sun 9.30am–1pm, 2.30pm–6pm), a 14th-century fortress that was reconstructed by the Venetians. This commands fine views across the city and is home to the History Museum, dedicated to the Risorgimento. The Natural History Museum and the Archaeological Museum can be found at the **Cittadella** to the west, built as a fortress by Bernabò Visconti though much altered and restored over the centuries.

The cultural highlight of the Città Bassa is the restored **Galleria Accademia Carrara** (Piazza Giacomo Carrara 82; www.lacarrara.it; Wed–Mon 9.30am–5.30pm, times vary, see website for latest schedule), a rich collection of 15th–18th-century art, and particularly strong on the Venetian and Lombard schools. Opposite, and housed in a former convent, the GAMeC gallery of modern

Gaetano Donizetti

The composer Gaetano Donizetti, one of the great masters of bel-canto opera, was born in Bergamo in 1797. He is commemorated in the city by a street, a theatre, a memorial, a monument and the Museo Donizettiano. He was a highly successful musician but endured great tragedy in his personal life. All three of his children died at a young age and his wife succumbed to the plague. Donizetti suffered from syphilis, was institutionalised, and died in Bergamo in 1848.

and contemporary art (www.gamec.it; permanent collection Tue–Sun 10am–1pm, 3–5pm; temporary exhibitions, times vary) features some first-class temporary exhibitions.

BRESCIA

Lombardy's second city after Milan, industrial **Brescia** 22 lacks the charm (and the tourists) of Bergamo or Verona. You are unlikely to choose it as a base, but for those interested in art and architecture, there is an outstanding museum complex and some fine monuments reflecting the various eras of its long history. The town flourished under the Romans, who left their mark in the grid layout of the city and the Capitoline Temple. In medieval times the town became a wealthy independent commune, supplying arms and armour to Europe; but like Bergamo, it came under Venetian rule from 1426–1797.

Piazza della Loggia

Life centres on three very different squares at the centre of the city. The most appealing is the Venetian-style **Piazza della Loggia**, the loggia being the richly decorated palazzo dominating the square – today the town hall. The upper level was designed by the leading Venetian architects Palladio and Sansovino. On the south side the piazza is flanked by the Monte Vecchio di Pietà (1489) and the Monte Nuovo di Pietà (late-16th century), the old and the new pawnbrokers; on the opposite side of the square, the Torre dell'Orologio echoes St Mark's Torre dell'Orologio in Venice, with a splendid astronomical clock (1544) and two clockwork figures that strike the hour. Neighbouring **Piazza della Vittoria**, accessed via an archway, was built during the Mussolini era and couldn't be more of a contrast.

Piazza Paolo VI

The religious core of the city is **Piazza Paolo VI**, formerly the Piazza del Duomo. The square changed its name in honour of Pope Paul VI (1897–1978) who was born in Brescia. The massive **Duomo Nuovo** (New Cathedral; Mon–Sat 7.30am–noon, 4–7pm), whose huge green cupola can be seen from afar, stunts the lovely **Rotonda** (Tue–Fri 9am–noon, 3–7pm), the Duomo Vecchio or Old Cathedral. This is an unusual round Romanesque building constructed on the site of an 8th-century basilica which was destroyed by fire in 1097. The interior contains the beautifully decorated sarcophagus of Bishop Berardo Maggi (1308) in red Verona marble. The austere building with a tower to the left of the Duomo Nuovo is

Piazza Vecchia, Bergamo

Santa Maria Maggiore, Bergamo

the Broletto, the medieval town hall, today the city council offices.

Roman ruins and Santa Giulia Museo della Città

The Via dei Musei beside the Broletto takes you to the **Piazza del Foro**, the old Roman forum. Towering above it are the mighty columns of the Capitoline Temple erected in AD 73 by Emperor Vespasian. Beside the temple the **Roman Theatre** has recently been excavated (Parco Archeologico di Brescia Romana; www.bresciamusei.com; Tue–Fri 9am–5pm, Sat–Sun 10am–6pm; combined ticket for the temple and theatre). Archaeological finds from the site are housed in the nearby Santa Giulia **Museo della Città** (City Museum; Tue–Fri 9am–5pm, Sat 10am–9pm, Sun 10am–6pm), laid out in the monastery of Santa Giulia. Founded in AD 753 by the Lombard king, Desiderius, the complex was continually extended up until the Renaissance and features the Romanesque church of Santa Maria in Solario, rich in frescoes and home to the rare, bejewelled 9th-century Cross of Desiderius, and the medieval Basilica of San Salvatore whose Nun's Choir is decorated with striking early 15th-century frescoes. The museum explores some 2,000 years of the city's history (from prehistory to the Venetian era), through statuary, frescoes, mosaics, medieval graves and other works of art. From the Roman era, the highlight is the bronze life-sized statue of *The Winged Victory*, discovered in the Capitoline Temple in 1826. The Santa Giulia monastic complex was awarded Unesco World Heritage status in 2011, forming one of seven key sites chosen to represent Italy's Longobard (Lombard) civilisation from AD 568–774.

Rising above the forum is the vast 14th-century Visconti **Castello** (Tue–Fri 9am–5pm, Sat–Sun 10am–6pm), incorporating the Museum of the Risorgimento and the Museum of Ancient Arms. Due south of the Piazza del Foro, on Piazza Moretto, the **Pinacoteca Tosio-Martinengo** has a fine collection of works by Brescian Renaissance and baroque masters. The gallery is currently closed for restoration, so these are temporarily on display at the Santa Giulia Museo della Città.

CREMONA

Synonymous with Stradivarius, **Cremona** has been the centre of the violin-making industry since the 16th century. Andrea Amati created the first modern violin here in 1566 and his more famous pupil, Antonio Stradivarius, was born here in 1644. The International School of Violin Making ensures the continuation of the tradition and concerts often take place in the town. The International Festival of Stringed Instruments takes place every third October (2018, 2021 etc).

Music apart, Cremona is a provincial market town on the River Po, with a fine medieval square but not a great deal else to detain you. The city's main monuments are all grouped on the **Piazza del Comune**. The magnificent **Duomo** (Mon–Sat 8am–noon, 3.30–7pm) facade incorporates elements of the Romanesque, Gothic and Renaissance styles; inside, the nave and chancel are decorated with frescoes. The **Torrazzo**, at 113m (370ft), is the tallest bell tower in Italy – the energetic can climb 487 steps to the top for fine views over the city.

Palazzo della Loggia, Brescia

To the right of the Duomo the octagonal baptistery was built at the same time and remodelled in Renaissance style. Across from the Duomo, the red-brick Loggia dei Militii was the former headquarters of the local militia. The Palazzo dell'Arte on Piazza Marconi is home to the **Museo del Violino** (Violin Museum; www.museodelviolino. org; Tue–Sun 10am–6pm) showcasing the origins of the violin and the violin-making industry. Also on display are exquisite pieces owned by Cremona's Town Hall and the Fondazione Stauffer, including Stradivarius' Cremonese 1715. More Stradivarian memorabilia can be seen at the Museo Stradivariano within the Museu Civico Ala Ponzone (Via Ugolani Dati 4), 10 minutes' walk north of the Piazza del Comune.

MANTUA

Formerly one of the great Renaissance courts in Europe, **Mantua** (or Mantova) is nowadays a provincial town with unprepossessing outskirts and a diminished population. But it has a lovely unspoilt medieval centre concentrated around three interlinked piazzas. The vast Palazzo Ducale, the Palazzo Tè and other great architectural monuments of Mantua are testimony to the power and artistic patronage of the Gonzaga family who lorded it over the town for nearly four centuries.

Palazzo Ducale

The huge cobbled **Piazza Sordello** is dominated by the **Palazzo Ducale** (tel: 041 2411897; www.mantovaducale.beniculturali. it; Tue–Sun 8.15am–7.15pm; reservations must be made in advance to see the Camera degli Sposi, only 1,500 visitors permitted daily). The palazzo was originally built by the despotic Bonacolsi, lords of Mantua from 1272–1328. When the Gonzagas took control of the town in 1328, the palace became their fortress and home, and was extended over the centuries to become a colossal complex of over 450 rooms, with courtyards, piazzas and gardens. Although much altered, the palace still gives a vivid idea of the brilliance of the Gonzaga Court.

Among the artistic highlights are Pisanello's unfinished series of 15th-century frescoes of the *Knights of the Round Table*, 16th-century Flemish tapestries modelled on Raphael's cartoons of the *Acts of the Apostles*, Rubens' huge portrait of *The Gonzagas Adoring the Holy Trinity*, and most famous of all, the *Camera degli Sposi* (Bridal Chamber) in the Castello di San Giorgio, decorated by Mantegna's frescoes (1465–74), glorifying the Gonzaga family. A spectacular experiment of perspectival illusionism, the frescoes cover the entire room, including the architectural features. Most innovative of all is the trompel'oeil ceiling, with putti and ladies in waiting peering down over the foreshortened balustrade.

Piazza Broletto and Piazza delle Erbe

From Piazza Sordello an archway leads to **Piazza Broletto**, the centre of medieval public life. The red-brick Broletto is the old town hall which separates the square from Piazza delle Erbe. On the Piazza Sordello side the Torre della Gabbia was converted to a prison and has an iron cage where prisoners were put on public display.

Named after the fruit and vegetable market, the **Piazza delle Erbe** is the loveliest of Mantua's squares. It is framed on three sides by porticoes and shops, and at night you can dine out by candlelight in front of the arcades of the Palazzo della Ragione. This large 13th-century, crenellated palace hosts major art exhibitions. Below piazza level is the beautiful Romanesque (though remodelled) **Rotonda di San Lorenzo** (Mon–Fri summer 10am–1pm, 3–7pm, winter 10am–1pm, 2–6pm, Sat–Sun 10am–6pm), the oldest of Mantua's churches. The interior walls and vaults still preserve traces of Byzantine-influenced frescoes.

Basilica di Sant'Andrea

Situated on the neighbouring Piazza Mantegna, the **Basilica di Sant'Andrea** (daily 8am–noon, 3–7pm) was a major landmark in Renaissance architecture. Replacing a Romanesque church, it was designed by the great Florentine architect and theorist Leon Battista Alberti for Lodovico Il Gonzaga. Inspired by classical architecture and evoking the grandeur of ancient Rome, the basilica combines a temple front and triumphal arch. The imposing interior is laid out on a Roman basilica plan and profusely decorated. The first chapel on the left houses the tomb of the painter, Andrea Mantegna, who died in Mantua in 1506.

Palazzo Tè

A bus ride or 20-minute walk from the centre will bring you to **Palazzo Tè** (www.palazzote.it; Tue–Sun 9am–6.30pm, Mon 1–6.30pm). This exuberant villa was

Sons of Mantua

Mantua's most famous sons are the poet Virgil, whose statue you can see in a niche on Palazzo Broletto, and Andrea Mantegna, who was court painter to the Gonzagas and produced the famous Camera degli Sposi in the Palazzo Ducale.

built and decorated in the mannerist style by the architect and painter Giulio Romano (1499–1546) for the pleasure-loving Federico II Gonzaga and his mistress, Isabella Boschetti. Fantastic frescoes adorn the rooms, ranging from the life-size horses of the Gonzagas to the erotic murals of the Sala di Amore e Psyche (Cupid and Psyche Room). The tour de force is the Sala dei Giganti (Room of the Giants) depicting the victory of Jupiter over the rebellious Titans. The entire room, including the vaulted ceiling, is frescoed to give an illusionistic effect, with rocks tumbling down onto the Titans (and seemingly the spectators too).

The Capitoline Temple, Brescia

VERONA

Verona ㉓ is a city of superlatives: the largest and most enticing city in the Veneto after Venice, boasting the world's third-largest Roman amphitheatre, some of the finest piazzas and monuments in northern Italy, along with the grandest open-air opera. Above all, however, Verona is celebrated for Shakespearean tales of young love. Crowds from all corners of the world come to pay respects to the so-called Casa di Giulietta (Juliet's House) and the famous marble balcony.

Strategically placed on the River Adige at a crossing of major trade routes, the town flourished under Roman rule, but it was

Mantua reflections

under the hugely powerful and frequently tyrannical Scaligeri (or della Scala) dynasty (1260–1387) that the city reached its zenith. The Visconti from Milan had a brief spell as lords of Verona; but from 1405 the city came under the sway of the Venetians, who ruled here until the French invasion of 1796.

PIAZZA BRÀ AND THE ARENA

The natural tourist magnet is the spacious **Piazza Brà** , dominated by the **Arena** (Tue–Sun 8.30am–7.30pm, Mon 1.30–7.30pm, off season until 5pm, during opera festival until 4pm). Built in the 1st century AD, this is the world's third-largest Roman amphitheatre after the Colosseum in Rome and the Campano Amphitheatre at Capua in Campania. Elliptical in form, it measures 73m x 44m and has 44 marble tiers, seating 20,000. The outer wall was damaged by a series of earthquakes in the 12th century; otherwise it is remarkably well-preserved. In Roman times it was the scene of gladiatorial combat, mock battles and games; today it is the stage for the world-famous Verona opera performances. On the west side of the square, the gently curving Listone is lined by open-air cafés, pizzerias and restaurants, a popular rendezvous and favourite spot to watch the leisurely *passeggiata* (evening stroll) and street-theatre performers.

PIAZZA DELLE ERBE

From the Listone, the elegant, shop-lined Via Mazzini brings you into bustling **Piazza delle Erbe** , the heart of Verona and formerly the Roman forum. The market nowadays is more a source of snacks and souvenirs than herbs or fresh produce, but it is still an appealing piazza with its white canopies, handsome palazzi, marble fountain and monuments. Finest of the palaces is the baroque Palazzo Maffei, surmounted by six statues of Roman gods and flanked by the Gardello Tower (1370). On the west side is the over-restored crenellated Casa dei Mercanti (14th century); across the square the much-restored Casa Mazzanti was built for the Scaligeri family and decorated with 16th-century frescoes. On the same side is the Domus Nova (1659) and the Palazzo della Ragione (Palace of Justice).

PIAZZA DEI SIGNORI AND ARCHE SCALIGERE

Linking Piazza dei Signori with Piazza delle Erbe is the Arco della Costa, 'arch of the rib' – the rib referring to the whalebone hanging below the arch, which – according to legend – will fall on the first honest person to pass underneath. Centre of civic life until the 16th century, the **Piazza dei Signori** is a far more formal square than Piazza delle Erbe, reminiscent of a stage set from a Shakespeare play. The trio of civic buildings are the **Palazzo della Ragione**, the Palazzo del Governo, and – most elegant of all – the Venetian Renaissance **Loggia del Consiglio**, topped by five statues of famous Romans. The Palazzo della Ragione, with a pretty courtyard and Gothic stairway, underwent major restoration and has opened as a centre for exhibitions of art. For panoramic views take the elevator or steps up the Torre dei Lamberti (http://torredeilamberti.it; Mon–Fri 10am–6pm, Sat–Sun 11am–7pm, last entry 45 minutes before, ticket includes Modern Art Gallery entry), the watchtower of the medieval palace.

Piazza Broletto, Mantua

Beyond the arch at the north end of the square lies the little Romanesque church of Santa Maria Antica and the **Arche Scaligere**, the extraordinary Gothic mausoleums of the Scaligeri family. These are so lofty it is difficult to see any detail – though you can spot the Scaligeri symbol of the five-rung ladder *(scala)* on the palisade that surrounds them. The most conspicuous is the equestrian tomb of Cangrande ('The Big Dog') which is a copy of the original, now in Verona's Castelvecchio.

LA CASA DI GIULIETTA

There is no evidence that the **Casa di Giulietta F** was Juliet's house – or even that Romeo and Juliet existed. The medieval dwelling was acquired by the city of Verona in 1907 and the famous balcony (which is far too high anyway for Romeo to have climbed) was added in 1935. Nevertheless, Shakespeare fans and romantics flock here to gaze at the tiny courtyard and marble balcony. The walls have been cleaned of graffiti and Juliet pilgrims are now requested to leave their love messages on the board inside the entrance arcade, in the mailbox or on the Juliet website.

The bronze statue of Juliet is a focus of attention, particularly the gleaming right breast (rubbing it is said to bring you luck in love). The house interior (Tue–Sun 8.30am–7.30pm, Mon 1.30–7.30pm, last admission daily 6.45pm) feels far from medieval but enables visitors to pose on the balcony. Romeo and Juliet Verona tours also include 'Juliet's Tomb' in a Franciscan monastery 800m (775 yards) south of Piazza Brà. Fans from around the world get married here in civil ceremonies.

CHURCHES AND ROMAN THEATRE

South of the Casa di Giulietta is **San Fermo Maggiore** G (www. chieseverona.it; Mar–Oct Mon–Sat 10am–6pm, Sun 1–6pm, Nov–Feb Mon–Sat 10am–1pm, 1.30–5pm, Sun 1–5pm), a beautiful Romanesque church which was reconstructed in the 14th century.

⦿ VISITING VERONA

Verona may be steeped in history, but the heart of the city is very much alive, especially during the opera season. Tourists mainly visit on fleeting half-day tours, but this is a city which merits at least a one-night stay to take in the wealth of sights – and ideally the opera too. Nearly all of the city's attractions are found in the historic quarter, and can easily be covered on foot. The streets of the centre are largely traffic-free and the city lends itself to strolling. Sightseers can take advantage of the VeronaCard, valid for one or two days which allows unlimited travel on city buses and admissions to museums, monuments and churches.

You don't have to be an opera buff to enjoy a performance in Verona's arena. The open-air experience in one of the world's great Roman amphitheatres is an unforgettable one – even if you can't understand a word. The mood is festive and fun rather than formal. You can take your own food (alcohol is not allowed but there are vendors selling wine). The programme features favourite operas, typically *Aida*, *Carmen* and *Tosca*, and the performances are lavish affairs (see page 86).

The interior has a wealth of frescoes and a magnificent Gothic ship's-keel roof. Don't miss the Romanesque Chiesa Inferiore (Lower Church) over which the main church was built and which today serves as a crypt.

Northeast of Piazza dei Signori is **Sant'Anastasia** (same hours as San Fermo), the largest church in Verona, with a soaring Gothic interior and vast red marble pillars dividing the aisles. Among the many frescoes is Pisanello's *St George and the Princess* (1433–8) above the arch of the Pellegrini Chapel to the right of the altar. To the northwest, near the river, is the Romanesque/Gothic **Duomo** (Mar–Oct Mon–Sat 10am–5.30pm, Sun 1.30–5.30pm, Nov–Feb Mon–Sat 10am–1pm, 1.30–5pm; Sun 1.30–5pm), which has a finely carved portal and, inside, an *Assumption* (1530) by Titian (first chapel to the left of the main entrance). More charming than the actual Duomo is the ancient little San Giovanni in Fonte, originally the baptistery, and the Church of St Elena, both accessed through the door below the Duomo's organ.

Across the river lie the ruins of the **Roman Theatre** (Tue–Sun 8.30am–7.30pm, Mon 1.30–7.30pm). With beautiful views of the city, this provides a fine setting in summer for the Shakespeare Festival, concerts, ballet and jazz (see page 87). From here you can take a lift up to the monastery where exhibits from the small Archaeological Museum are displayed.

Letters to Juliet

Juliet's Club was set up to sustain the myth of Romeo and Juliet and the romantic image of Verona. Thousands of unsolicited letters arrive each year, from all over the world, addressed to the Shakespearean heroine. These are all read and each one is answered by one of the many volunteer Juliet secretaries. If you want to add to the fan mail, visit www.julietclub.com.

CASTELVECCHIO AND SAN ZENO MAGGIORE

In the 1350s, Cangrande II della Scala built the **Castelvecchio**  beside the Adige River as a fortress and residence. The triple-arched Ponte Scaligeri (rebuilt after destruction in World War II) was constructed across the river here as a private bridge and an escape route in the event of enemy attacks or local rebellions. The building has been beautifully converted to the **Museo di Castelvecchio** (Tue–Sun 8.30am–7.30pm, Mon 1.30–7.30pm). The collection includes some fine examples of medieval sculpture as well as paintings by Carpaccio, the Bellinis, Mantegna, Tiepolo and other Venetian masters.

Verona's Arena

A walk westwards along the river bank from Castelvecchio will take you in the direction of **Basilica di San Zeno Maggiore** (Mar–Oct Mon–Sat 8.30am–6pm, Sun 12.30–6pm, Nov–Feb Mon–Sat 10am–1pm, 1.30–5pm, Sun 12.30–5pm), arguably the finest Romanesque church in northern Italy. San Zeno, a 4th-century saint, built the original church on this site, and his tomb lies in the crypt along with those of other saints and bishops. The facade is beautifully proportioned and features a rose window representing the wheel of fortune, a main portal with marble bas-reliefs and wooden doors with 48 superb bronze panels of biblical scenes. The interior is spacious and simple, with Andrea Mantegna's exquisite triptych, *Madonna and Saints* (1459) on the high altar.

Windsurfing on Lake Garda

 # WHAT TO DO

SPORTS AND OUTDOOR ACTIVITIES

The lakes are a sporting paradise. You can choose from a huge range of aquatic sports, trekking in the hinterland, mountain biking, horse riding, golf or – for the more adventurous – paragliding, hang-gliding and canyoning.

WATERSPORTS

Lake Garda is a haven for sailors and windsurfers, particularly in the north where the lake narrows and the winds create ideal conditions all year round; Sirmione in the south is another good spot for windsurfing. The resorts of Riva del Garda and Torbole have numerous watersports schools with gear to rent and tuition for all levels. Gargnano hosts the annual Centomiglia sailing regatta in early September, with over 300 boats racing around the lake. Lake Como has sailing, windsurfing and water-skiing; you can hire motorboats from Como, and some main resorts such as Menaggio on Lake Como have beaches, pools and water sports. Bellagio has a lido, complete with beach, bathing area, sunbeds, cocktail bar, restaurant and a taxi shuttle service to and from Cadenabbia.

Swimming. There are a number of great places to swim in the lakes, particularly Lake Garda, which has the cleanest and warmest waters of the three main lakes. Some resorts provide lidos with beaches, pools, water sports and activities for children; others have just a narrow strip of shingle. The waters around the town of Como are polluted but as you go further north the lake becomes much cleaner.

HIKING, CLIMBING AND CABLE CARS

Trekkers are increasingly attracted by the quiet routes and breath-taking views above the lakes. The ridges and Alpine foothills offer some wonderful walking, from easy lake or woodland trails to strenuous climbs in the mountains. The Club Alpino Italiano (www.cai.it) organises guided tours and runs refuges along the mountain itineraries. The best months for walks in the Alps are May to October.

For those who want the views without the hike, there are some spectacular cable-car/funicular trips including Malcesine to Monte Baldo, Stresa to Monte Mottarone and Como to Brunate. Beware however, that the summer haze frequently restricts what should be amazing views.

As well as the views, the Monte Baldo ridge on Lake Garda, accessed from Malcesine by funicular, offers opportunities for mountaineering, hang-gliding, free climbing and canyoning, from amateur to competitive level. Further north around Torbole and Riva del Garda free climbers hang above the lake and further north the town of Arco hosted the IFSC climbing and paraclimbing world championships in 2011 and climbing youth championships in 2015. Above Lake Como the peaks of the Grigna and Resogone are for serious hikers, and there is free climbing at Lecco.

CYCLING AND MOUNTAIN BIKING

Cycling is a serious pursuit in the region and there is even a museum devoted to it on the Madonna del Ghisallo hilltop south of Bellagio (www.museodelghisallo.it). Mountain biking is particularly popular, especially on Monte Baldo and the northern end of Lake Garda, the hills and mountains around Lake Como and Mottarone above Stresa on Lake Maggiore. In summer the ski slopes make natural trails for mountain biking, cycling and hiking. Mountain-biking itineraries are supplied by local tourist offices, bikes and helmets can be hired and guides are also available.

GOLF

Golf courses are dotted around the region, many of them with wonderful views of the lakes and Alps. Among the most prestigious courses are the Villa d'Este Golf Club (www.golfvilladeste.com) near Montorfano, southeast of Como, and the Franciacorta Golf Club.

Mountain biking

SPECTATOR SPORTS

The Italian Grand Prix takes place in September at Monza, 15km (9 miles) northeast of Milan. Soccer, as in the rest of Italy, is hugely popular: the rival Milan clubs, AC Milan and Inter play at the San Siro Stadium, Via Piccolomini 5, 5.5km (3.5 miles) from the centre of Milan. Tickets can be booked through the AC and Inter websites on www.acmilan.com and www.inter.it.

OTHER SPORTS

Lombardy has 110 peaks exceeding 3,000m (9,840ft) and 600km (373 miles) of ski slopes. In the winter months it's possible to ski and snowboard at Monte Baldo (Lake Garda), Mottarone (Lake Maggiore), the Grigna mountains above Lecco (Lake Como) and the resorts above Bergamo and Brescia, but you can't always guarantee the snow. For information on ski resorts, consult www.skiinfo.it. There are plenty of opportunities for horse

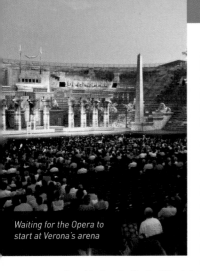

Waiting for the Opera to start at Verona's arena

riding in the hills and valleys and along the ridges. Equestrian centres offer lessons for all standards, as well as one- or two-day horse-riding tours.

ENTERTAINMENT

Most of the towns and villages on the lakes are peaceful places where visitors are content with a stroll and a drink or two in a lakeside bar or café. Lake Garda generally attracts a younger crowd and is the liveliest of the lakes, particularly Desenzano in the south, with bars, live music and around half a dozen nightclubs in and around the resort. Bardolino, on the other side of the lake, is quite a lively spot with plenty of bars open late as well as a couple of discos.

The larger towns in the region have bars with occasional live music, a jazz club or two, wine bars and discos which are often on the town outskirts. **Brescia**, a university city, is lively after dark especially on weekends. You can wine and dine at one of the many restaurants and wine bars in the piazzas and streets of the old town, enjoy concerts and opera at the Teatro Grande, live it up at late-night bars or just wander up to the castle to enjoy the views and an *aperitivo* on a café terrace.

Verona is famous for its Arena where opera extravaganzas are staged from late June to the end of August. Performances alternate, so that during one month you have a choice of at least four operas. Book well in advance – you can do so online at www. arena.it or by telephoning the call centre on (+39) 045 8005151. The Arena's website gives the full programme and a detailed seating plan. Seats range from the most expensive stalls (€200) to the unreserved stone steps up in the gods (€20–25). Hotels in the city get booked up well in advance for this period, so it is well worth checking that accommodation is available before reserving seats (www.veronabooking.com). An alternative is to stay on the Verona side of Lake Garda and either drive or take a late public bus back from Verona to the lake.

At the same time as the operas, Verona's Roman Theatre stages the open-air **Shakespeare Festival** (with occasional performances in English), as well as concerts, ballet and jazz performances. For details and to book online, visit www.estatete atraleveronese.it. Last-minute tickets are sold shortly before the performances. Free concerts are held regularly in the Piazza dei Signori during the summer months. Verona is also a great place for eating out, with numerous restaurants ranging from simple little trattorias to temples of gastronomy. The Listone on Piazza Bra, overlooking the Arena, is a lovely spot either for a pre- or post-prandial drink, *gelato* or full meal.

Stresa's **Settimane Musicali di Stresa** (www.stresafestival. eu) is an annual festival of classical concerts, performed by internationally renowned artists. The venues are churches, castles and villas located around Lake Maggiore and Lake Orta, and on the Borromeo Islands.

APERITIVI

In Italian towns the pre-prandial *aperitivo*, from around 6–9pm, is a way of life. The price of the drink may seem steep, but snacks, canapés and sometimes a whole buffet is included in the price and can provide a cheap alternative to dinner in a restaurant.

Aperitifs at The Brothers Cafe

Happy hour (two drinks for the price of one) is usually 7–9pm or 8–10pm. Cafés and bars offer a remarkable range of beverages: Prosecco or *spumante* (Italian sparkling wine, which you can have by the glass), *pirlo* (white wine with Campari or Aperol), Negroni (Campari with vermouth and gin) and a long list of liqueurs and other cocktails. An *enoteca* or wine bar will have a huge list of vintage and non-vintage bottles, with snacks or sometimes main courses to go with them.

SHOPPING

Northern Italians demand style and elegance and this is reflected in the shops in cities such as Brescia, Bergamo and Verona. Lakeside villages and resorts are more limited but the larger among them have some stylish fashions, and plenty of shops selling silk and leather, gourmet food, olive oil and wine.

FASHIONS

Serious fashion followers will head for nearby **Milan**, trend-setting capital of Italy (for details see *Berlitz Pocket Guide Milan*). But there are other cities in the region offering a stylish selection of fashions, leather and jewellery. **Verona** is an appealing place to shop, especially the traffic-free Via Mazzini in the centre with its designer (and other) boutiques and **Bellagio** and **Menaggio** have some stylish shoe and gift shops. **Brescia** is another good shopping city, with well-known designer stores, jewellery shops, antiques and art galleries. The streets of **Bergamo**'s Città Bassa (Lower Town), especially Il Sentierone and Via XX Settembre, offer a wide choice of fashions, leather goods, especially high quality shoes and jewellery.

Como is famous for high-quality silk, with shops offering dazzling displays of silk scarves, ties and shawls. The tourist office has a list of silk factory outlets in the area where you can get 40–70 percent discounts on silk prints, scarves, ties, and shirts which are produced for the top fashion designers.

SHOPPING OUTLETS

For elegant silk-lined jackets, hand-painted square scarves, cushions, silk stoles and blouses at 30–50 percent discount head to the outlet of Frey Emporio della Seta (www.frey.it) at Via Risorgimento 49 in Fino Mornasco south of Como. Close to Brescia the functional but well-designed **Franciacorta Outlet Village** in Rodengo Saiano (7km/4.5 miles west of Brescia, Ospitaletto exit off the A4 motorway; www.franciacortaoutlet.it) has 150 stores selling clothing, shoes, accessories, cosmetics, household items, linens and electrical goods. At the **Foxtown Outlet** (www.foxtown.ch) in the Swiss village of Mendrisio, 15km (6 miles) northeast of Como, you can snap up bargains from top brands such as Gucci, Versace, D&G and Prada. Armani fans should head for its outlet at Via Provinciale per Bregnano 13, Vertemate (south of Como) which has some great bargains in its three-storeyed warehouse.

MARKETS

Watch out for the local weekly or fortnightly markets in the larger towns where you can pick up anything from fashions

Flowers for sale in Garda's Saturday market

and handbags to whole hams and cheeses. The largest market in the region is at **Luino** on Lake Maggiore's eastern shore, which claims to be the biggest weekly market in Europe. There are some 350 stalls, attracting bargain hunters from Switzerland, Austria and Germany – as well as Italy. Some of the main towns host monthly antiques markets where you can browse among handicrafts, worthless junk or genuine antiques. **Brescia**'s Mercatino dell'Antiquariato, held in the Piazza della Vittoria on the second weekend of the month, is one of the best. Look out for the work of goldsmiths, engravers and wrought-iron artisans in Bergamo and Brescia, and ceramicists around Mantua. Local tourist offices can supply you with details of markets and any food and wine fairs that are coming to the region. Bargaining at any of the markets is always worth a try, however limited your Italian.

FOOD AND WINE

Lakeside villages and resorts teem with tiny delis selling everything from home-cured hams, speciality risotto rice, herbs and honey to local wines, grappa and liqueurs. The best olive oil in the region is made around Lake Garda, a pale aromatic oil. The panettone Christmas cake, made with raisins and candied orange and lemon zest, is a Milanese speciality; nowadays it's sold all year round throughout Italy and abroad.

Cremona is known for *torrone*, Italy's version of nougat, and *mostardo di Cremona*, which is pickled fruits in mustard oil. Local wines are often a good buy, whether it's the reds from Bardolino (Lake Garda) or Valtellina (near Lake Como), the sparkling whites from Franciacorta (Lake Iseo) or the Valcalepio wines from the province of Bergamo. Tourist offices can supply details of wine tours, estates and cellars.

Bergamo's medieval Città Alta (Upper City) has delis to die for, with counters along the Via Gombito laden with wonderful arrays of prosciutto, pasta and regional wines. Try the Salumeria Angelo Mangili at Via Gombito 8, a long-established little deli packed with fresh pasta, whole hams and cheeses. In the Città Bassa (Lower Town) Agripromo (Via Borgo Palazzo 128) specialises in authentic local produce such as salami, polenta della Bergamasca, olive oil and Valcalepio wines. A

⊙ TORRONE FROM CREMONA

Legend has it that at their sumptuous wedding feast in 1441 Bianca Maria Visconti and Francesco Sforza were presented with a magnificent dessert in the shape of Cremona's belltower (known as the Torrione). Made of egg whites, honey and nuts, it was named after the tower and presented to courts throughout Europe. Modern *torrone* is a popular confectionary like nougat, usually made industrially and sold throughout Italy and beyond. A few artisans do however remain faithful to the old recipes. Cremona still clings to the *torrone* culture – and every October hosts a *torrone* festival.

Torrone, a local speciality

regular bus service links both the upper and lower town of Bergamo with Orio del Serio airport just 5km (3 miles) away, making it ideal for last-minute shopping. If you don't make it to the town you can always stock up at the **OrioCenter** across the road from the airport, which is one of Europe's largest shopping centres (www.oriocenter.it).

CHILDREN'S LAKES

Although the lakes cater more for adults than children, there is no shortage of activities for youngsters. Along with ferry and cable-car rides there are pedaloes, rowing boats and kayaks to hire, parks and medieval castles to visit, and on Lake Garda, the largest theme park in Italy. All the lakes have watersports tuition available and some resorts have sandy or pebble beaches or lidos equipped with pools. Theme parks apart, the most exciting rides are the **Monte Baldo cable car** (www.funi viedelbaldo.com), where the rotating panoramic pods ascend Monte Baldo from Malcesine on Lake Garda, and the **Alpyland Coaster** (www.alpyland.com), above Lake Maggiore, which enables you to control a two-man bob sleigh down Monte Mottarone at speeds of up to 40kmph (25mph).

Peschiera on Lake Garda is a children's paradise – not the town itself, but the stretch of shoreline to the north which has no fewer than three theme parks. Italy's number-one theme park, **Gardaland** (at Castelnuovo 5km/3 miles north of Peschiera; tel: 045 6449777; www.gardaland.it; daily 10am–6pm, with exceptions). The theme park boasts 40 attractions and 40 shows, plus the Sea Life aquarium (www.sealifeeurope.com). Laser shows and fireworks add to the attractions on summer evenings. Be prepared for very long queues in summer. Tickets can be booked online. Just to the north, **Movieland** (www.movieland.it) offers more thrilling rides, film-themed shows with stage sets and special effects, and a fun-filled Acqua water park with a variety of rides and slides, a white-sand beach and an adventure island. **Acquasplash Franciacorta** (at Corte Franca, near Lake Iseo) offers plenty of aquatic activity with swimming pools, slides and chutes.

⊙ LAKE TRIPS BY BOAT

Hopping on a ferry is a great way of seeing the lakes. The first steamboats were launched in 1826; nowadays you can travel on hydrofoils *(aliscafi)*, excursion cruisers, car ferries *(traghetti)* as well as the reasonably priced *battelli* (passenger ferryboats) which link up the towns and villages. Timetables are widely available from ticket offices and tourist information offices. Ferries run throughout the year, though services are less frequent off-season.

Drinks and snacks are usually available on board, and some ferries operating longer routes offer a three-course set lunch. On lakes Maggiore, Como and Garda, ferries are operated by Navigazione Laghi (visit www.navlaghi.it for maps and timetables). On the larger lakes, no single pass covers the entire lake, but the area is divided into zones for which you can purchase a 24-hour pass.

Parco della Villa Pallavicino at Stresa on Lake Maggiore is a popular spot for youngsters, with 40 different species of animals and birds, many of them roaming free in the park, and a well-equipped playground. In summer a little electric train links the park with central Stresa. On the other side of the lake **Rocca Borromeo** is one of the region's best-preserved castles, and home to a doll museum. Lake Garda has several medieval castles.

Budding gladiators can let their imaginations run wild in Verona's beautifully preserved **Roman Arena**, and older children might enjoy one of the opera extravaganzas (this is not formal opera – you can sit on the steps up in the gods and take a picnic). For other ideas to keep kids amused in Verona visit www.veronaforkids.it.

Teacups at Gardaland

CALENDAR OF EVENTS

There are numerous annual events around the lakes, from Verona's world-famous operas and Milan's fashion fairs to low-key food and wine festivals and local village events. Information is available from local tourist offices. The following is a selection of the highlights:

February/March: Carnival in Verona, Lecco and other towns and villages; parades, floats, music and dancing.

March: Stresa's spring to autumn *Settimane Musicali* begins.

Early April: Celebrations at Pontida, Bergamo, to mark the 1176 defeat of Barbarossa by the Lombard League.

Easter: Parade of symbolic floats at Bormio near Sondrio and costumed parade at Schivenoglia, Mantova.

Last Sunday of May: Legnano's *Sagra del Carroccio*: medieval pageant and *palio* contest commemorating the Lombard League's 1176 victory.

June: International piano festival, Bergamo. Festival of San Giovanni Battista, 24 June, Isola Comacina, Lake Como; mass in the ruins of the basilica, candlelit boat procession and fireworks.

Late June–August: Verona's opera season at the Arena (www.arena.it) and the Shakespeare Festival at the Teatro Romano, Verona, with English-language performances by the Royal Shakespeare Company; also jazz, ballet and modern-dance performances (www.estateteatraleveronese.it).

July: International Sailing Regatta at Gargnano, Lake Garda. Third week: Lago Maggiore Jazz, performances at Stresa, Angera and other towns on Lake Maggiore, attracting big names in the world of jazz.

August: Illuminated boat race followed by fireworks at Laveno Mombello, near Varese. Ten-day Film Festival at Locarno, Lake Maggiore.

August–September: *Palio Baradello* at Como, celebrating the victory of Barbarossa over Milan.

September: Italian Grand Prix at Monza (first week). Music Festival in Ascona, Lake Maggiore. Como's international music festival (Sept–Nov). *Mostro Autunno Pavese*, gastronomic festival in Pavia. *Festa dell'Uva* (Grape Festival) on the last weekend of the month, Bardolino, Lake Garda. Franciacorta wine and food festival. Firework display, Sirmione, Lake Garda.

EATING OUT

Eating out is one of the great pleasures of a holiday in the lakes. Many of the restaurants enjoy seductive lakeside settings, and offer a wide choice of appetising dishes from smoked cured hams and seasoned sausages to creamy risottos, flavoursome pastas and fish fresh from the lake. Each region has its specialities: from Brescia comes *casonsèi*, giant ravioli stuffed with parmesan, spinach and eggs; from Lake Iseo the highly prized baked *tinca* or tench, served with polenta; from Mantua, *tortelli di zucca*, delicate egg pasta enveloping pureed pumpkin; from Milan the famous *risotto alla milanese*, coloured and flavoured with saffron.

Rice, rather than pasta, is the mainstay of the local diet, grown on the vast paddy fields around the Po and in the Veneto. Meat and dairy products are abundant, with butter, rather than olive oil, used in Lombard cuisine. Cheeses, from the Parmesan-like *grana* to the creamy cows' milk cheeses, appear on every menu, either enriching pastas and risottos or served on a platter with fresh bread and olive oil. Fresh herbs and vegetables, such as *porcini* mushrooms, artichokes, red chicory and asparagus, are key ingredients, grown in abundance and used with fish, meat, risotto and pasta.

WHERE TO EAT

There are dozens of casual, family-run trattorias serving authentic local dishes, as well as more classy and elegant places catering for gourmets. Although traditionally a **ristorante** is smarter, more professional and expensive than a **trattoria**, the difference between the two nowadays is negligible. An **osteria**, traditionally a tavern or inn serving wine

Alfresco dining overlooking Lake Como

and pasta, can be any type of restaurant, from traditional to hip. The ubiquitous **pizzeria** usually offers a wide-ranging menu including many types of pasta, meat dishes and even fish, as well as pizzas. The best pizzas come bubbling hot from a wood-fired brick oven (in small towns only available in the evening), the worst are thick-based squares with a thin layer of tomato and cheese topping, served in cafés during the day. *Pizza al taglio*, sold by the slice with a variety of toppings, is the most popular Italian takeaway food item.

An **enoteca** or wine bar will have a wide selection of fine wines with a platter of cheese or cold meats to accompany them. A **tavola calda** is a self-service or takeaway with hot meals such as pasta, risottos, meat and vegetable dishes. For a quick bite, go to a **bar** or **café** where you can find a selection of rolls with savoury fillings and *tramezzini* (crustless, generously filled sandwiches). Standing at the bar *(al banco)* is always a lot cheaper than sitting at a table with waiter service.

In the larger resorts a whole string of waterside cafés and pizzerias will be vying for your trade, some advertising a *menu turistico* in several languages. Often the better-value places are in side streets, away from the waterfront or on the edge of town, though it's hard to resist the lakefront views.

WHAT TO EAT

As in the rest of Italy, restaurants (as opposed to pizzerias) offer four courses: *antipasto* (the hors d'oeuvre), *primo* (the first course, which is pasta, risotto or soup), *secondo* (the second course, i.e. fish or meat) and finally the *dolce* (dessert). Traditionally you were expected to have at least three courses; now, in most establishments, it's quite acceptable to opt, say, for an *antipasto* followed by a pasta dish, or perhaps a pasta dish followed by a dessert.

Antipasti

The selection of hors d'oeuvres will typically include *antipasto di pesce*, which is likely to be marinated freshwater fish such as *persico* (perch), *tinca* (tench) or *lavarello* (a lake white fish) and an

Fresh gilt-head prepared with citrus fruits and herbs

antipasto di carne, a selection of cold meats such as thinly sliced *prosciutto crudo* (cured ham), mountain hams, salami, seasoned sausages, smoked beef, *bresaola* (dried salted beef) or, in Trentino, *Speck* (cured smoked ham).

The cold cuts will come with bread, extra-virgin olive oil (Lake Garda produces the best) and perhaps with *mostarda de Cremona*, which is fruit pickled in a mustard sauce. Around Lake Como, restaurant menus may feature *missoltini* or *missul-titt*, sun-dried salted shad which is lightly grilled and served with oil and vinegar.

Il Primo

Rice is prepared in dozens of different ways, enriched with fish, seafood, meat and vegetables. The ingredients will vary according to the seasons. The most famous rice dish of the region is *risotto alla milanese*, made with short-grain Arborio rice, stock, beef marrow, onions, saffron and Parmesan cheese.

> ### Set menus
>
> Set menus vary from a basic two- or three-course meal, usually with a choice of meat or fish, to a seven-course blow-out *menu degustazione*, giving you the chance to try several house specialities. All set menus include service and cover charge; some also throw in house wine, mineral water and coffee.

Other popular combinations are *risotto ai funghi*, with mushrooms (often *porcini* or wild mushrooms); *risotto alla pescatora* with prawns, squid, mussels and clams; *risotto al nero di seppie* from the Veneto, coloured and flavoured with the ink of cuttlefish.

Pasta comes in all shapes and sizes, is often home-made and, like risottos, is served with a remarkable range of sauces. *Caoncelli* from Bergamo and Brescia is made with spinach, eggs, cheese, amaretti biscuits and breadcrumbs; *strangolapreti* ('priest stranglers') are elongated dumplings made of spinach, bread, eggs and cheese. In addition to regional sauces you are likely to find the *popular al pomodoro*, tomato sauce flavoured with onion, garlic or basil; *alla carbonara*, with eggs, bacon, Parmesan and pecorino cheeses, and *al ragu*, the Neapolitan meat sauce.

Soups can be a meal in themselves, especially the delicious *zuppa di pesce*, more of a fish stew than a soup. *Minestrone alla milanese* is vegetable soup with rice and bacon; *zuppa pavese* is a clear broth with egg and bread.

Il Secondo

Try and choose seasonal **fish** from local waters, such as *lavarello*, which may come either stuffed with vegetables and herbs, cooked in a sauce such as garlic and almond or capers and tomatoes, simply served on a spit or perhaps puréed and served with bread. Look out also for *luccio mantecato*, cream of pike, accompanied by polenta; *filetto di pesce persico alle erbe aromatiche,* fillet of perch with aromatic herbs; lake trout *(trota)* stuffed with herbs or perhaps baked with olives, capers and anchovies, or simply grilled; and *carpione*, a kind of carp found only in Lake Garda.

Most menus also feature fish from the Italian seas (and beyond), such as *branzino* (bass), *orata* (bream), *sogliola* (sole) *gamberoni* (giant prawns), *calamari* (squid) and *vongole* (clams). Non-lake fish may well be frozen – and some of the more upfront restaurants will indicate this with a star against the item. Smaller fish are served whole at a fixed price, the larger species will be charged by the *etto* (100g) and it's wise to check out the price before ordering.

Salted dried cod is used in dozens of recipes. From the Veneto, for example, comes *baccalà mantecato*, dried salted cod made into a creamy paste with garlic and olive oil and served with polenta – something of an acquired taste. Also from the Veneto and not to everyone's taste is *sarde in saor*,

Practicalities

Normal opening times of restaurants are lunch from 12/12.30–2/3pm, dinner 7.30/8–10pm or even later in main resorts. Expect to pay €1.50–€5 cover charge and in some restaurants a service charge of 10–15 percent.

sardines in a sweet-and-sour sauce.

The main Milanese **meat** specialities are *osso buco*, veal-shank stew; and *costoletta alla milanese*, veal cutlet fried in breadcrumbs (called *wienerschnitzel* in northern Lake Garda). Most menus will feature simply cooked steak, pork, chicken, veal, lamb, duck and often more humble fare such as braised donkey, rabbit casserole, jugged hare or stewed tripe. The choice will vary accord-

Spaghetti alle vongole

ing to the season. Around Brescia you may come across *lumache alla bresciana*, snails cooked with spinach and served with Parmesan. Polenta often accompanies meat dishes, especially in Trentino and around Bergamo, Brescia and Lake Garda. *Peara* sauce is a Veronese speciality, a blend of breadcrumbs, bone marrow, beef stock, black pepper and Parmesan. The Milanese *cassoeula*, a pork and Savoy cabbage casserole, is served with polenta and traditionally eaten in winter.

Main courses often come with **vegetables** *(contorni);* salads are ordered and served separately and are almost invariably *verde* (green) or *mista* (mixed). Vegetarian restaurants are a rarity though meat- and fish-free dishes are increasingly available on menus. You might try grilled vegetables as an *antipasto*, then a risotto or pasta with fresh *porcini* or other vegetables.

Desserts don't play a major role on the menus. The usual choice is fruit salad, ice cream, sorbet and perhaps a home-made

Osso bucco with risotto

apple tart or tiramisu (literally 'pick-me-up'), the alcoholic chocolate and coffee gateau from the Veneto.

Cheeses are abundant, from the soft white ricotta from the mountains; the creamy robiolo from the pre-Alpine valleys of Lombardy; the tangy Taleggio from Valsassina (Lake Como); to the hard Parmesan-like grana from the Padua Plain. Panettone, the large cake containing raisins and candied fruit, is a speciality of Milan; *torrone* is a honey and almond nougat originating from Cremona.

WHAT TO DRINK

Lombardy produces some excellent red wines, best of which are the dry, smooth reds from Valtellina on the Swiss/Italian border near Lake Como. The Oltrepò Pavese zone, in the Po Valley south of Pavia, is Italy's third-largest wine producer, noted for good, full-bodied, dry reds; it also produces Pinot sparkling white wine and a large quantity of Riesling. The hilly Franciacorta region bordering Lake Iseo produces good red and white wine, but is best known for its sparkling *spumante*, which makes an excellent aperitif. Lake Garda's best wines are still white and sparkling Bianco di Custoza, and dry red Bardolino, which you can try at the Vinoteca adjoining the Museo del Vino in Bardolino (www.zeni.it) and buy very cheaply in and around the town. The Verona region produces the famous white Soave, red Valpolicella and the lesser-known but top-quality smooth red Recioto, best served with dessert.

A good meal is usually concluded with a *digestivo*, such as a brandy, *grappa* (the variable local firewater made from grape skins) or *limoncello*, made from lemons.

⊙ COFFEE BREAK

An Italian café almost invariably serves a decent cup of real coffee. A cappuccino (familiarly called a *cappuccio*), won't be a huge Starbucks-like mug of froth but a normal-sized cup with a generous amount of espresso and a frothy topping. Italians only drink cappuccino for breakfast but are used to foreigners drinking it all day. After around 11am and particularly after meals the locals get their injection of caffeine from a small black espresso.

Tourist hotels often have a DIY machine for 'American coffee' at breakfast time, but normally a waiter will be happy to make you an Italian cappuccino at no extra cost. In a region of people-watching piazzas and mesmerising lake views it's a great temptation to sit for hours over one cup of coffee (or cocktail if you wish), and no one minds if you do. The following is a list of just a few of the different types of coffee served in bars or cafés.

Espresso or *caffè* – small and black

Caffè lungo – weaker coffee

Caffe doppio – double espresso

Caffè latte – milky coffee

Caffè macchiato – small espresso with a dash of milk

Caffè corretto – with grappa, brandy or other liqueur

Caffè freddo – iced coffee

Decaffeinato or *decaff* – decaffeinated coffee

TO HELP YOU ORDER...

A table for one/two/three **Un tavolo per una persona/per due/per tre**

I would like... **Vorrei...**

The bill, please **Il conto, per favore**

aglio garlic
agnello lamb
aragosta lobster
baccalà salted cod
basilica basil
birra beer
bistecca beefsteak
branzino bass
bresaola cured beef
burro butter
capretto kid
cavallo horse
cipolle onions
coniglio rabbit
cozze mussels
fagioli beans
fagiolini green beans
finocchio fennel
formaggio cheese
frittata omelette
frutti di mare seafood
funghi mushrooms
gamberetti shrimps
gamberi prawns
gamberoni giant prawns
gelato ice cream
insalata salad

lumache snails
maiale pork
manzo beef
melanzane aubergine
olio oil
olive olives
orate bream
pane bread
panna cream
patate potatoes
peperoni peppers
pesce fish
piselli peas
pollo chicken
polpo/pólipo octopus
pomodori tomatoes
prosciutto ham
riso rice
salsiccie sausages
sogliola sole
spinaci spinach
trota trout
uova eggs
verdure vegetables
vitello veal
vino wine
zucchini courgettes

PLACES TO EAT

The prices indicated below are a basic guide for a three-course evening meal per person, including wine, cover charge and service.

€€€€	over 65 euros
€€€	45–65 euros
€€	30–45 euros
€	below 30 euros

LAKE MAGGIORE

Borromeo Islands

Belvedere €€€€ *Via di Mezzo, Isola dei Pescatori, tel: 0323 32292,* www.belvedere-isolapescatori.it. An idyllic waterside setting on the charming Isola dei Pescatori, with meals served in the garden, on the verandah or in the lakeview dining room. The restaurant specialises in fresh lake fish such as *laverello* grilled with butter and sage, trout, perch or mixed grill from the lake. By day you get here by ferry, by night the hotel boat will come and collect you from Stresa, Baveno or Pallanza. (Reservations essential for evening meals). If you're tempted to stay, the Belvedere is also a hotel, with attractive, simply furnished lakeview rooms. Open Mar–Nov. Closed Tue in March and Oct.

Cannobio

Grotto Sant'Anna €€ *Via Sant'Anna, 30 (on the road to Valle Cannobina), tel: 0323 70682.* Perched on the edge of the Orrido di Sant'Anna, a spectacular gorge, with a large garden and river-view terrace. The simple excellent value menu offers lake and sea fish, delicious pasta and risotto and desserts to die for. Closed Mon.

Lo Scalo €€€€ *Piazza Vittorio Emanuele III 32, tel: 0323 71480,* www. loscalo.com. Sophisticated restaurant right on the waterfront in a porticoed 14th-century palazzo which once sheltered local fishing boats. Delicious home-made pastas, fish from the lake and a serious wine list. Closed Mon, except evenings mid-summer, and Tue lunch.

Mergozzo

Piccolo Lago €€€€ *Via Filippo Turati 87, Fondotoce, Lake Mergozzo, tel: 0323 586792*, www.piccololago.it. The 'Little Lake' restaurant boasts two Michelin stars and a beautiful setting on the tiny Lago di Mergozzo, between Mergozzo and Fondotoce. Traditional Piedmontese dishes, rich risottos and trout, pike and perch from the lake are elegantly prepared and presented. This is also a hotel with 12 modern rooms and lakeside pool. Closed Mon–Tue and lunch on Wed.

Pallanza

Osteria del Riccio €€€ *Vicolo dell'Arco 1, tel: 0323 558842.* A cosy restaurant enjoying lovely lake views. Seafood is the speciality here but the rest of the menu is also definitely worth a try. Open for dinner Tue–Fri and for dinner and lunch Sat–Sun.

Ristorante Milano €€€€ *Corso Zannitello 2/4, tel: 0323 556816,* www.ristorantemilanolagomaggiore.it. Frighteningly pricey but worth splashing out for the great lakeside location by the old harbour, the exquisite fish dishes and the succulent meat from Piedmont. Everything here is freshly sourced, the setting is elegant and the service faultless. Closed Mon dinner and Tue.

Stresa

Il Vicoletto €€ *Vicolo del Poncivo 3, tel: 0323 932102;* www.ristorantevicoletto.com. Tucked away in an alley (*vicoletto*) off the main square, this tiny restaurant with its contemporary menu bucks the trend of Stresa's pizzeria and spaghetti-oriented restaurants. Emphasis here is very much on quality rather than quantity – the menu is small, and the helpings are not huge (you'll have room for the heavenly desserts). Expect simple pastas, and roast meat and fish, all using top quality ingredients. Space is limited inside and out, so reservations are recommended. Closed Thu and mid-Jan–Feb.

La Botte € *Via Mazzini 6/8, tel: 0323 30462*. 'The Barrel' is a simple little wood-panelled eatery serving good-value Piedmontese dishes, hearty steaks, pasta and pizzas. Inside tables only, very popular and often crowded. Closed Wed.

Osteria degli Amici €€ *Via A.M. Bolongaro 31, tel: 0323 30453*. Popular for pizzas cooked in a wood-fired oven, pastas and risottos, steak or grilled fish. For ambience opt for a table outside under the vines – there are outdoor heaters for cooler evenings. Closed Wed.

LAKE COMO

Bellagio

Barchetta €€€ *Salita Mella 18 13, tel: 031 951389*, www.ristorantebar chetta.com. A long-established and consistently good trattoria up a stepped alley from the waterfront. The menu features creative pastas, creamy risottos and delicious fresh fish. A heated terrace means you can enjoy the views even on cool days. For simpler fare, snacks and pizzas there is a separate area open at lunchtime.

Silvio €€ *Via Paolo Carcano 10–12, tel: 031 950322*, www.bellagiosilvio. com. Above the gardens of Villa Melzi, on the main Bellagio to Como road, this is worth the detour for the freshest of fish, caught by Silvio's family, and the peaceful setting above the lake. *Taglioni al lavarello* (pasta with lake fish) and *semifreddo di grappa e uvetta* (ice cream with grappa and raisins) are house specialities. This is also a hotel with modestly priced rooms. Closed winter.

Brunate

Trattoria del Cacciatore € *Via Manzoni 22, tel: 031 220012*, www.trattoria delcacciatore.it. Leave the bustle of Como and take the 7-minute cable car ride up to the hilltop village of Brunate. This is a delightful rustic, inconspicuous trattoria (follow signs or ask the way), with red tablecloths and a wisteria-clad pergola. Meals are simple affairs, with meat antipasti, pasta and meat casseroles with mushrooms and polenta. Closed Tue and Sun dinner. In winter only open by reservation.

Como

Er Più €€€ *35/56 Via Castellini 21, tel: 031 272154;* www.erpiucomo. it. One of the few good restaurants in Como, this is a haven for fish fans. You can have it smoked, salted, fried, oven-cooked, marinated, in a soup or in a stew. The fish comes from both lake and sea, and the menu typically features everything from lobster, scallops and clams to seabass and salmon. Desserts, created by the patisserie chef since 1974, are irresistible. To save on cost go at lunch time when the set menu is half the price of the evening meals. Closed Tue, occasionally in Aug, and one week in Jan.

La Colombetta €€€€ *Via Diaz 40, tel: 031 262703;* www.colombetta. it. A family-run restaurant housed in the very romantic setting of a former church in Como's historic centre. Excellent contemporary dishes and an extensive wine list. George Clooney is a regular there. Closed Sunday.

Isola Comancina

Locanda dell'Isola Comacina €€€€ *Isola Comacina, tel: 0344 55083,* www.comacina.it. You are ferried to the deserted island from Sala Comacina and served a rustic lunch of antipasti, grilled trout and salmon, chicken cooked in a wood oven and dessert. The meal ends with a rite-of-fire to exorcise the curse put on the island in the 12th century by the Bishop of Como. A rather gimmicky experience, but unique nonetheless. Closed winter and Tue off-season.

Varenna

Il Cavatappi €€ *Via XX Settembre, tel: 0341 815349,* www.cavatappi varenna.it. 'The Corkscrew' is a minute eatery on a little alleyway with just five tables. Simple but delicious cuisine, a well-stocked wine cellar and a very cosy atmosphere. Mon–Tue dinner only, closed Wed Sept–Apr.

Vecchia Varenna €€€ *Contrada Scoscesa 10, tel: 0341 830793,* www.vec chiavarenna.it. Irresistible waterside setting with lake and mountain views and an excellent choice of fish. You can have it stuffed with vegetables and herbs, on a spit, in fishcakes, baked with olives and capers or flavouring risottos. Carnivores are not ignored – there is braised donkey, stewed rabbit or – for more conventional tastes – steak and pork. Daily lunch and dinner, closed Jan.

LAKE GARDA
Desenzano del Garda

Caffè Italia €€€ *Piazza Malvezzi 19, tel: 030 9141243,* www.ristorantecaf feitalia.it. Historic café in the centre where you can grab a quick morning cappuccino and brioche at the bar with the locals, enjoy a light lunch on the terrace or a blow-out seven-course *menu degustazione* (tasting menu). The piles of prawns, oysters, scallops and other seafood sitting on ice are more than likely to tempt you.

Esplanade €€€€ *Via Lario 3, tel: 030 9143361;* www.ristorante-espla nade.com. One of Lake Garda's top restaurants where Chef Massimo Fezzardi's cuisine combines tradition with creativity. Enjoy a stunning lake setting and a menu typically featuring *millefeuille* of artichokes with roast scampi and purée of anchovy, salt-crusted Piedmont fillet of beef and duck ravioli with rosemary and goose liver. Closed Wed.

Gargnano

La Tortuga di Orietta €€€€ *Via XXIV Maggio 5, tel: 0365 71251,* www.ris torantelatortuga.it. Save this one for a special occasion and since it's very small make sure to book a table. In the charming fishing village of Gargnano this rustic restaurant serves exquisite dishes and great wines. Fish predominates but you can also find meat antipasti and main courses such as carpaccio of duck and lamb with rosemary and thyme or fillet of veal with truffles. Closed Tue.

Moniga del Garda

Agriturismo del Trenta €€ *Via Mazzane 2, Moniga del Garda (north of Desenzano del Garda), tel: 0365 503395,* www.agriturismo30.com. Enjoy great value set meals and lake views from the vine-clad terrace of this rural *agriturismo*. Many of the ingredients, including fruit, veg and wheat flour are produced on the farm. Delightful staff complete the picture. Booking is essential.

Riva del Garda

Ristorante Restel de Fer €€€ *Via Restel de Fer 10, tel: 0464 553481,* www. resteldefer.com. Delightful rustic trattoria and inn, run by the Meneghelli family since 1400. Many of the dishes are based on ancient Trentino recipes. Fish comes from Lake Garda and the Trentino rivers, meat is organic, vegetables are home-grown and the extra virgin oil is produced from the family olive grove. Try the Trentino wines from the well-stocked cellar and round off the meal with a grappa. Daily for dinner, lunch for small groups with a reservation. Closed Nov.

Sirmione

Risorgimento €€€ *Piazza Carducci 5–6, tel: 030 916325,* www.risorgimento-sirmione.com. Sirmione is packed with takeaway pizza places but for proper food and smart service the Risorgimento is the place to go. On a lively piazza near where the ferries come and go, it has a wide choice of fish, served with pasta and risotto, or simply grilled, as well as flambéed steaks and mouth-watering desserts. Closed Tue.

Torri del Benaco

Gardesana €€€ *Piazza Calderini 20, tel: 045 7225411,* http://gardesana. eu. This historic hotel's (see page 140) lakeside setting is as delightful as ever, overlooking the harbour and castle. The menu offers up fresh fish from the lake, along with sea fish, giant prawns, meat dishes and pizza. Open mid-Mar–mid-Oct. Closed Mon.

Lake Orta – Orta San Giulio

Al Boeuc € *Via Bersani 28, tel: 0332 915854*. Ancient, atmospheric tavern where you can sample good wines, *prosciutto*, *bruschetta* or *bagna cauda*, a warm garlic and anchovy dip served with crudités. There are some tables outside lining the pleasant cobbled alley. Closed Thu.

Taverna Antico Agnello €€ *Via Solari 5, Miasino, tel: 0322 980527*, www. ristoranteanticoagnello.com. Charming rustic trattoria with emphasis on meat dishes (horse and donkey among them) and specialities from Piedmont. Closed Wed.

Villa Crespi €€€€ *Via G. Fava 18, Orta San Giulio, tel: 0322 911902*, www. villacrespi.it. An exclusive Moorish villa hotel (see page 141) with a Neapolitan chef who sources the finest ingredients: mozzarella from southern Italy, shrimps from San Remo, truffles from Alba, locally grown fresh fruit and vegetables. His creative dishes – many of which are Mediterranean – have earned the restaurant two Michelin stars. Feast on Sicilian scampi in Martini sauce, ravioli with clams and caviar, veal fillet with black truffle – washed down with wine from the 83-page wine list. For the ultimate gourmet sensation opt for the 10-course tasting menu. Closed Mon.

CITIES

Bergamo

Colleoni & dell'Angelo €€€€ *Piazza Vecchia 7, Città Alta, tel: 035 232596*, www.colleonidellangelo.com. Elegant palace setting with a much sought-after terrace on the stunning central square of the upper city. Exquisite pasta dishes on offer include Bergamo's *casoncelli*, ravioli with sage, butter and almonds parmesan, linguine with sea urchins, Beluga caviar, ravioli stuffed with pigeon breast and foie gras with pistaccio. These can be followed by sea bass or gilthead in a sea-salt crust or rack of lamb in a black truffle crust. Closed Mon and two weeks in August.

Da Mimmo €€€ *Via B. Colleoni 17, Città Alta, tel: 035 218535,* www.ristorantemimmo.com. In the same family for half a century, Da Mimmo sources the finest raw materials from Bergamo's market and serves strictly traditional regional fare: home-made Bergamasche pastas, outstanding fish dishes, rabbit and polenta, ageing *bagoss* cheese, bread cooked in wood ovens, delicious pizzas and home-made desserts. You can dine within the 14th-century *palazzo* or in the garden on summer evenings. It's a favourite haunt of locals so reservations (which can be done online) are advisable. Closed Tue lunch.

Elav Kitchen and Beer €€ *Via Solata 8, tel: 035 017 2871.* Run by an independent brewery, this restaurant-bar with modern furnishings is hidden on a back street of Bergamo's Citta Altà. Set menus present four courses, each with a beer pairing. The food is fresh and local, with risotto and pancetta pasta making regular appearances. Tue–Sun, dinner only.

Trattoria 3 Torri €€ *Piazza Mercato del Fieno 7, tel: 035 244474.* A cosy, characterful eatery with bare-brick walls and arched roof, serving a good polenta del Bergamì, among other local pasta dishes. The menu is small but has a good range of meat and vegetarian options. Closed Wed.

Vineria Cozzi €€ *Via B. Colleoni 22a, tel: 035 238836,* www.vineriacozzi. it. Inviting *bottega* popular for its huge choice of Italian wines and varied menu offering *antipasti*, vegetarian dishes such as polenta and *porcini* mushrooms, a selection of cold meats or cheeses and some delicious pastas. The *menu degustazione*, comprising four courses, has an excellent choice of house specialities with wines to go with them.

Brescia and Province

Caffè Floriam €€ *Via Gasparo da Salò 3, Brescia, tel: 030 41314,* www. caffefloriamrestaurant.it. In the heart of the historic centre near Piazza della Loggia, this is a long-established, welcoming café-restaurant serving traditional home-cooked dishes, including 11 different risottos.

Varese

Ristorante Bologna €€ *Albergo Bologna, Via Broggi 7, tel: 0332 234362,* www.albergobologna.it. A central, family-run hotel restaurant offering good-value set menus, featuring fresh pasta such as *tagliolini alla crema di asparagi* (with cream of asparagus), *gnocchi con salsa gialla di noce e zafferano* (with yellow walnut and saffron sauce), followed by meat or fish, and one of the creamy, calorific home-made desserts. Wine, coffee and a *digestivo* are thrown in too. Closed Sat and third Sun of the month.

Vecchia Riva €€€ *Via G. Macchi 146, Schiranna, Lago di Varese, tel: 0332 329300,* www.vecchiariva.com. Set on the banks of the unspoilt Lake Varese, Vecchia Riva has a sheltered garden and serves a large spread of regional *antipasti*, good fish, risotto and pasta dishes. The restaurant is attached to a small three-star hotel that offers functional modern rooms.

Verona

12 Apostoli €€€€ *Vicolo Corticella San Marco 3, tel: 045 596999,* www.12apostoli.it. Charming, traditional restaurant in an 18th century palazzo, with frescoed vaulted ceilings and classic cuisine. It is named after 12 friends who used to do business here in the mid-18th century over a simple dish of pasta or beans and a glass of wine. Closed Mon, Sun dinner and 20 days in Aug.

Al Bersagliere €€ *Via Dietro Pallone 1, tel: 045 8004824,* www.trattoriaalbersagliere.it. Tuck into top-notch Veronese and Venetian fare: polenta with home-cured salami, pasta and *fagioli* beans, *bigoli* (spaghetti-like pasta) with duck ragù or simply-grilled steak and fish. The speciality of stewed horse meat with polenta follows a Veronese recipe of the 15th century. There are three rooms, a summer garden and a 12th century cellar with 200 labels. Closed Mon and Sun.

Casa Perbellini €€€€ *Piazza San Zeno 16, tel: 045 8780860,* www.casaperbellini.com. The concept restaurant of multiple-starred chef Giancarlo Perbellini in the heart of Verona's historic centre. Pricey but excellent Italian cuisine. Closed Sun and Mon, 10 days in Feb and 20 days in Aug.

A–Z TRAVEL TIPS

A SUMMARY OF PRACTICAL INFORMATION

A

ACCOMMODATION

Accommodation in the region is plentiful, with grandiose lakeside villa hotels, romantic retreats in the hills, farmhouses, simple bed and breakfasts, and self-catering villas and apartments. Prices vary according to the season, being at their highest in midsummer. Many of the hotels on the lakes close in winter.

The busiest times are Easter, July and August, but for some hotels high season is now from Easter all the way through to the end of September. It is advisable to book well ahead throughout the season, especially for lakeside hotels. During the summer some smaller establishments may require you to stay for a minimum of three nights, and those with restaurants may only offer half- or full-board rates. A deposit of at least one night's stay, payable by credit card, is usually requested. Failure to turn up or to inform the hotel in advance of cancellation will normally incur the loss of a night's deposit.

If you arrive on spec, local tourist offices will advise on available accommodation and may do the booking for you. If possible, check out the guest room before committing to a reservation. Rooms can vary hugely, both in size and outlook. Prices normally reflect the difference, and it's usually worth stretching the budget to secure the more desirable rooms. In lakeside resorts, hotels are often located across the main road from the lake, with noisy rooms at the front. Breakfast is generally included in the overnight room rate. Depending on the category of hotel this will vary from a dull crusty roll with packaged butter and jam to a great spread of cereals, cheeses, cold cuts, yoghurts, croissants, home-made pastries and fresh fruit. If breakfast is not included in the room rate it is usually better value to pop out for a cappuccino and croissant in the local café.

An appealing alternative to hotel accommodation is *agriturismi*, working farms and other rural properties which rent out rooms or self-contained apartments to tourists. These are an excellent choice for exploring peaceful rural regions and for active holidays such as walking, cycling, horse-riding, wine-tasting or milking the cows. Some agriturismi offer breakfast and an evening meal, which is based on home-grown produce. Meals are communal affairs, often around the kitchen table. However, not all *agriturismi* conform to the picturesque farmhouse image – many are modern properties in unremarkable settings. Details of *agriturismi* are supplied by local tourist offices – or visit www.agriturist.com or www.agriturismo.net.

In recent years the region has seen a huge increase in the number of Bed and Breakfasts in private homes. These usually offer better value than hotels as well as the opportunity to get to know the owners and speak some Italian. For information, visit www.bbitalia.it.

AIRPORTS

The lakes region has no less than five airports, including the three that serve Milan. For the lakes in the west of the region (Orta, Maggiore and Como), the most convenient arrival points are Milan's Malpensa airport, 50km (31 miles) northwest of Milan (www.airportmalpensa.com) or Orio al Serio airport at Bergamo, 48km (30 miles) northeast of Milan (www.sacbo.it). This is also the ideal arrival point if you are heading to Lake Iseo. For Milan, Linate airport (www.milanolinate.eu), 10km (6 miles) to the east, is by far the closest airport to the city.

For Lake Garda's western shore, the quickest gateway is Brescia's airport (www.aeroportobrescia.it), 20km (12.5 miles) southeast of Brescia, which confusingly has three different names: 'Gabriele d'Annunzio', 'Brescia-Montichiari' and 'Verona (Brescia)'. If you are hiring a car the airport is also worth considering for access to Verona (52km/32 miles), Cremona (47km/29 miles) and Bergamo (65km/40 miles). Another useful gateway for Lake Garda, particularly the eastern shore, is Valerio Catullo Airport, also called Verona-Villafranca (www. aeroportoverona.it), which is only 15km (9.5 miles) from Verona. For the east shores of Lake Garda you could also consider the Venice airports of Marco Polo and Treviso which are less than an hour away.

Bergamo's Orio al Serio airport, used by Ryanair and other low-cost airlines, is linked by a half-hourly shuttle bus service to both Bergamo, 5km (3 miles) away, and to Milan's Stazione Centrale (Central Station). Gabriele d'Annunzio airport is linked to Brescia by regular shuttle buses, but to Verona by a very limited service. From Verona's Valerio Catullo airport there are buses to the city's railway station every 20 minutes from 6.30am to 11.30pm.

B

BICYCLE HIRE
Bikes can be hired in all the towns and resorts, but prices are quite steep. Local tourist offices can supply details of local bike-hire outlets as well as trail guides in popular biking regions. Hills and mountains have signposted tracks of varying degrees of difficulty. A few hotels lend their guests bikes free of charge.

BUDGETING FOR YOUR TRIP
In high season you can expect to pay around €150–250 for a comfortable double room with bath, €90–150 in a simple hotel. A good three-course meal with wine in a restaurant will cost from €30–60, a light lunch €10–25. In general the best-value accommodation and restaurants are located away from the lakefronts. Coffee and soft drinks are €1.50–4, beer € 3–5, while an aperitif or cocktail with canapés is €3–10. It is worth bearing in mind that, as in the rest of Italy, coffee or drinks taken at the bar are far cheaper than those taken at a table with waiter service. Entrance charges to museums, archaeological sites and gardens vary from €2–12; entrance is free for EU citizens under 18 and over 65. Opera tickets in Verona cost from €20–200.

C

CAMPING
Campsites are dotted around all the main lakes and range from basic

sites to four-star affairs with swimming pools, restaurants, bungalows as well as tents and organised activities. Lake Garda has by far the widest choice, with sites all round the shores and a profusion in the south. Details are available at www.camping.it where you can book online. Campsites are normally open from April to September and are at their most crowded from mid-July to late August.

CAR HIRE

Hiring a car is essential if you're planning a touring holiday, though the traffic and tunnels along many of the lakeside roads don't lead to leisurely driving. You must be over 21 and you will need a full, valid driver's license, held for at least a year. Car-hire bookings made in advance on the internet work out cheaper than hiring on arrival. In high season a small economy car will cost from around €250 a week, including third-party liability and taxes, but excluding insurance excess. Make sure you check all extras when comparing quotes from different companies. The major car-hire companies have offices in the main cities and airports. There is a small additional charge for an extra driver. Credit-card imprints are taken as a deposit and are normally the only form of payment acceptable. 'Inclusive' prices do not normally include personal accident insurance or insurance against damage to windscreens, tyres and wheels.

CLIMATE

The holiday season for the lakes is Easter to October. The best time to go is spring, early summer or autumn, ideal times being May, June and September when it's warm and sunny but not as crowded, hot or muggy as midsummer. In July and August temperatures can soar to 30ºC, though the lakes, with a gentle breeze, are slightly cooler than the cities. The wettest months are October and November. Winters are foggy and cold with chilly winds from the Alps. Most places around the lakes close down for the season and ferry services are limited.

	J	F	M	A	M	J	J	A	S	O	N	D
°C	5	8	13	18	23	27	29	29	24	17	10	6
°F	40	46	56	65	74	80	84	85	75	63	51	43

CLOTHING

Bring light to medium-weight clothing and rainwear during spring and autumn, and pack a jacket for summer evenings. Remember that Italy's churches are places of worship as well as repositories of art and architecture, and you should dress respectably – shorts, miniskirts, bare shoulders and midriffs are frowned upon and may even mean that you are not allowed entry.

CRIME AND SAFETY

It is wise to take simple precautions against pickpockets, especially in the larger cities. Avoid carrying large amounts of cash around with you and leave important documents and valuables in the hotel safe. Keep a firm hold of handbags, especially when using public transport or shopping at markets. For insurance purposes, theft and loss must be reported straightaway to the police. In case of theft take photocopies of flight tickets, driving licence, passport and insurance documents.

D

DISABLED TRAVELLERS

Italy is not easy for disabled visitors, but is making slow progress in improving transport, accommodation and buildings.

New trains and buses are low-level, and more museums now have lifts, ramps and adapted toilets, and recent laws require restaurants, bars and hotels to provide spacious and specially adapted toilets. The new legislation does not, however, necessarily cover access to the facilities.

Access at Last is a 'one-stop-shop' for accessible accommodation and services with a worldwide database of places to stay: www.accessatlast.com.

DRIVING

If taking your own car from the UK, you should allow for tolls on French, Swiss, German and Italian motorways. To take your car into Italy, you will need an international driving licence or valid national one, car registration and insurance documents, a red warning triangle and reflective vest in case of breakdown, a national identity sticker for your car, and headlamp deflectors. Tolls are levied on the motorway but it's worth the relatively small expense to cover ground fast. Signposting on main and rural roads is quite good, but beware of reckless drivers and motorcyclists.

Rules of the road. Drive on the right, pass on the left. Speed limits in Italy are 50kmh (30mph) in towns and built-up areas, 90kmh (55mph) on main roads and 130kmh (80mph) on motorways. At roundabouts the traffic from the right has the right of way. Seat belts are compulsory in the front and back, and children should be properly restrained. The use of hand-held mobile telephones while driving is prohibited. The blood alcohol limit is 0.08 percent and police occasionally take random breath tests.

Breakdowns. In case of general emergencies call 113, or for breakdown assistance call the Automobile Club of Italy on 116. The club has an efficient 24-hour service which is available to foreigners.

Petrol. Petrol is readily available, though many service stations close for three hours over the lunch period. On main roads there are plenty of 24-hour stations with self-service dispensers accepting euro notes and major credit cards but instructions are normally in Italian only. The majority of service stations accept credit cards.

Parking. Parking is not expensive but it can be difficult finding spaces in the centre of towns and lakeside resorts at busy times of the year. Parking in towns is controlled by meters or scratch cards, available from tobacconists and bars. The larger towns have multi-storey car parks. Some free parking is controlled by parking discs (if you have hired a car a disc will be provided). Parking in Milan is notoriously difficult and to be discouraged.

E

ELECTRICITY

220V/50Hz AC is standard. Sockets take two-pin, round-pronged plugs. UK appliances will require an adaptor, American 11V appliances a transformer.

EMBASSIES AND CONSULATES

If you lose your passport or need other help, contact your nearest national embassy or consulate.

Australia: Australian Consulate, Via Borgogna 2, 3rd floor, 20122 Milan, tel: 02 7767 4200, www.italy.embassy.gov.au

Canada: Canadian Consulate, Piazza Cavour 3, 6th floor, 20121 Milan, tel: 02 6269 4238, www.international.gc.ca

Ireland: Irish Honorary Consulate, Piazza S. Pietro in Gessate 2, 20122 Milan, tel: 02 5518 7569, www.dfa.ie/irish-embassy/italy

New Zealand: New Zealand Consulate, Via Terraggio 17, 20123 Milan, tel: 02 7217 0001, www.nzembassy.com/italy

South Africa: South African Consulate, Vicolo San Giovanni, Sul Moro 4, 20121 Milan, tel: 02 885 8581, www.sudafrica.it

UK: British Consulate, Via San Paolo 7, 20121 Milan, tel: 02 723 001, http://ukinitaly.fco.gov.uk

US: US Consulate, Via Principe Amedeo 2/10, 20121 Milan, tel: 02 290 351, https://it.usembassy.gov

EMERGENCIES

Police 112
General Emergency 113
Fire 115
Ambulance 118

G

GETTING THERE

By air. Ryanair, www.ryanair.com, currently flies from four UK airports to 'Milan-Bergamo' (Bergamo's Orio al Serio airport); and also from Stansted and Birmingham to Verona (Brescia). EasyJet, www.easyjet.com, flies from Gatwick to Milan's Linate and Malpensa, from Luton to Malpensa and from Gatwick to Verona. British Airways, www.ba.com and the Italian national airline Alitalia, www.alitalia.com, have regular flights from Heathrow to both Linate and Malpensa; BA also flies from Manchester to Malpensa, and from Gatwick to Valerio Catullo (Verona).

By car. The quickest route to Milan from the UK channel ports takes a minimum of 12 hours, over a distance of 1,040km (650 miles). For route planning and details on the cost of petrol, road tolls (levied on French and Italian motorways) and the Swiss motorway road tax, visit www.viamichelin.com.

By rail. You can get to Milan in 12 hours from London St Pancras via Paris on Eurostar (full details on www.seat61.com). From Milan there are fast train services to all the main lakes. For information on tickets, rail passes and to book online, contact the Italian train operator Trenitalia (www.trenitalia.com).

GUIDES AND TOURS

Local tourist offices, travel agencies and hotels can provide details of guides and tours. There is no shortage of choice whether it's a guided city tour, a ferry cruise, a Romeo and Juliet tour in Verona or an excursion to the cellars and vineyards in the wine-producing regions.

H

HEALTH AND MEDICAL CARE

All EU countries have reciprocal arrangements for reclaiming the costs of medical services, and residents should obtain the European Health Insurance Card (available in the UK from post offices or online at www.ehic.org.

uk). This only covers you for medical care, not for emergency repatriation costs or additional expenses such as accommodation and flights for anyone travelling with you. To cover all eventualities a travel insurance policy is advisable, and for non-EU residents, essential. For insurance claims keep all receipts for medical treatment and any medicines prescribed. Vaccinations are not needed for Italy, but take with you sunscreen and mosquito repellent in the summer. Tap water is safe to drink unless you see the sign *acqua non potabile*. A pharmacy (*farmacia*) is identified by a green cross. All main towns offer a 24-hour pharmacy service, with a night-time and Sunday rota. After-hour locations are listed in local papers and posted on all pharmacy doors. Italian pharmacists are well-trained to deal with minor ailments and although they do not stock quantities of foreign medicines they can usually supply the local equivalent. If you need a doctor (*medico*) ask at the pharmacy or at your hotel. For serious cases or emergencies, dial 118 for an ambulance or head for the *Pronto Soccorso* (Accident and Emergency) of the local hospital. This will also deal with emergency dental treatment.

L

LANGUAGE

Staff in hotels and shops in the main resorts speak English, but a smattering of Italian will come in useful if you're off-the-beaten-track. On the Swiss side of the lakes less English is spoken than German.

What time does the train/bus leave for the city centre? **A che ora parte il treno/pullman per in centro?**
Is there a campsite near here? **C'è un campeggio qui vicino?**
I would like to hire a car **Vorrei noleggiare una macchina**
for one day **per un giorno**
for one week **per una settimana**

I want full insurance. **Voglio l'assicurazione completa.**
I want to report a theft. **Vorrei denunciare un furto.**
My wallet/passport/ticket has been stolen **Mi hanno rubato il portafoglio/il passaporto/il biglietto**
I've had a breakdown **Ho avuto un guasto**
There's been an accident **C'è stato un incidente**
Fill it up please **Faccia il pieno per favore**
Super/normal **super/normale**
Lead-free/diesel **senza piombo/ gasolio**
Where's the nearest car park? **Dov'è il parcheggio più vicino?**
Can I park here? **Posso parcheggiare qui?**
Are we on the right road for...? **Siamo sulla strada giusta per...?**
I need a doctor/dentist **Ho bisogno di un medico/dentista**
Where is the nearest chemist? **Dov'è la farmacia più vicina?**
I want to change some pounds/dollars **Desidero cambiare delle sterline/dei dollari**
Do you accept traveller's cheques? **Accetta traveller's cheques?**
Can I pay with a credit card? **Posso pagare con la carta di credito?**
Where is the bank? **Dov'è la banca?**
Where's the nearest police station? **Dov'è il posto di polizia più vicino?**
Where's the nearest post office? **Dov'è l'ufficio postale più vicino?**
I'd like a stamp. **Desidero un francobollo.**
When's the next bus/train to ...? **Quando parte il prossimo autobus/treno per....?**
Where can I buy a ticket? **Dov'è posso comprare un biglietto?**
single (one-way) **andata**

return **andata e ritorno**
Thank you, this is for you. **Grazie, questo è per lei.**
Keep the change. **Tenga il resto.**
Where are the toilets? **Dove sono i gabinetti?**
Where is the tourist office? **Dov'è l'ufficio turistico?**

LGBTQ TRAVELLERS

Milan, along with Bologna, is the most gay-friendly city in Italy. The lakes region, however, is more conservative and, although not necessarily averse to gay couples travelling together, the locals do not always tolerate overt displays of affection. Larger towns like Brescia have gay bars and clubs. ArciGay, Via Bezzecca 3, Milan, tel: 02 54122225, www.arcigay.it, the Italian gay organisation, has centres in Verona, Brescia, Cremona and Mantua as well as Milan. For an excellent guide to gay life and tourism in Italy, visit the website www.gayfriendlyitaly.com.

M

MAPS

Touring Club Italiano (TCI) produces the detailed, easy-to-read 1:200,000 map of Lombardy which covers all the main lakes apart from Garda. Local tourist offices can normally provide you with free town and area maps.

MEDIA

Newspapers. English-language newspapers can be found in main towns and resorts, usually on the day of publication. National newspapers include the Milan-based centre-right daily *Corriere della Sera* (www.corriere.it) and its centre-left rival, *La Repubblica* (www.repubblica.it).

Television and radio. Most hotels provide satellite TV, which broadcasts 24-hour English-language news channels. The Italian state TV network, RAI (Radio Televisione Italiana), broadcasts three TV channels, RAI 1, 2 and 3, which compete with many private channels pouring out soaps, films, quiz shows and nonstop ads. The state-run radio stations, RAI 1, 2 and 3, mainly broadcast news, chat and music.

MONEY

Currency. The unit of currency in Italy is the euro (€) divided into 100 cents. Euro notes come in denominations of 500, 200, 100, 50, 20, 10 and 5; coins come in denominations of 2 and 1 euros, then 50, 20, 10, 5, 2 and 1 cents. In Switzerland the currency is the Swiss franc. In Swiss resorts you can usually pay with euros but your change will be in Swiss francs, and normally at a poor exchange rate.

Exchange facilities. Banks and post offices tend to offer the best rates, followed by exchange offices and hotels.

Credit cards and ATMs. The major international credit cards are accepted in the majority of hotels and restaurants, stores and supermarkets, but some smaller places only accept cash. ATMs (Bancomats) are widespread, but banks take a hefty commission – it is usually better value to use cash only when essential and pay off larger amounts such as restaurant bills and pricier items in shops by credit card.

Traveller's cheques and Cash Passports. Traveller's cheques are not as widely accepted as they used to be in Italy and are less convenient than Cash Passports (prepaid travel money cards). These offer the same security as traveller's cheques and if lost or stolen can be quickly replaced and the full amount refunded. The card can be used to withdraw cash at ATMs or pay hotels, restaurants and shops.

O

OPENING HOURS

Banks generally open Mon–Fri 8am–1.30pm and 3–4pm (afternoon opening times may vary). Banks at airports and main stations usually have longer opening hours and are open at weekends.

Museums have varying opening hours; the main ones open all day every day, but some small museums close for 2–3 hours over the lunch period and all day on Monday.

Villas/Gardens usually open all day every day in season.

Churches normally close at lunch time (noon–3pm or later). Sightseeing on Sunday morning, when services take place, is discouraged.

Shops are normally open Mon–Sat 9am–1pm and 3.30/4pm– 7.30/8pm. In main cities many shops open all day, and on Sundays too.

POLICE

The city police or *polizia urbana* regulate traffic and enforce laws, while the *carabinieri* are the armed military police who handle law and order. The *polizia stradale* patrol the highways and other roads. In an emergency the *carabinieri* can be reached on 112 – or you can ring the general emergency number, 113.

POST OFFICES

Post offices normally open Mon–Fri 8.15am–2pm, Sat 8.15am– noon or 2pm. Stamps *(francobolli)* can also be bought from tobacconists.

PUBLIC HOLIDAYS

Shops, banks, museums and galleries usually close on the days listed below. When a national holiday falls on a Friday or a Monday, Italians may make a *ponte* (bridge) or long weekend.

January 1 *Capodanno* New Year's Day

January 6 *Epifania* Epiphany

March/April *Pasqua* Easter

March/April *Lunedì di Pasqua* Easter Monday

25 April *Festa della Liberazione* Liberation Day

1 May *Festa del Lavoro* Labour Day

2 June *Festa della Repubblica* Republic Day

15 August *Ferragosto* Assumption Day

1 November *Ognissanti* All Saints' Day
8 December *L'Immacolata Concezione* Feast of the Immaculate Conception
25 December *Natale* Christmas Day
26 December *Santo Stefano* St Stephen's Day

R

RELIGION

Like the rest of Italy the region is primarily Roman Catholic. The church still plays a major role in the community though numbers of regular worshippers have been in decline for some years. Local patron saints' days are celebrated, such as San Giovanni Battista on Lake Como, but religious festivals are not as commonplace as in southern Italy. Milan has congregations of all the main religions (for details consult www.hellomilano.it under the 'Worship' section in Useful Information).

S

SMOKING

Smoking in Italy is prohibited in all public places including restaurants, bars and cafés.

T

TELEPHONES

Telecom Italia public telephones are widespread and have instructions in English. Calls are made with a pre-paid phone card (*scheda* or *carta telefónica*) available in denominations of €5, €10 and €20 from Telecom offices, tobacconists, newsstands and vending machines. Many phones also accept payment by credit card.

Pre-paid international telephone cards (from €5), available at post offices, travel agents and other outlets are far better value if you are phoning abroad. With these you call a free phone number, dial the PIN code on your card and then the number (clear instructions are given in English). Calls can also be made with a charge card bought from your telephone company prior to travel. This is useful for telephoning from hotels which levy hefty surcharges on long-distance calls.

When phoning abroad, dial the international code, followed by the city or area code and then the number. Off-peak rate for international calls in Italy is Mon–Sat 10pm–8am, Sun 1pm–Mon 8am. For an English-speaking operator and international reverse charge calls, dial 170 and for international directory enquiries dial 176. Numbers beginning 800 are free. To call Italy from abroad dial the country code, followed by the area code and then the number. Italian area codes have all been incorporated into the numbers, so even if you are calling from the same town that you are telephoning, the code must be included.

Mobile phones (cellphones). In order to function within Italy some mobiles need to be activated with a roaming facility or need to be 'unblocked' for use abroad. Check with your mobile company before leaving. Charges for using a UK- or EU-based mobile to make and receive calls and texts, and browse the internet elsewhere in the EU were scrapped in 2017. It was unclear at the time of writing whether UK-based companies will continue to uphold this after the UK leaves the European Union. For phones from outside the EU charges may still be high for all services. You can set your mobile to the cheapest network on arrival. You can also bar incoming calls, or on some mobiles limit them to specified numbers. If you are in Italy for some time it's worth purchasing an Italian SIM 'pay as you go' *(scheda pre-pagata)* with a new mobile number for the length of your stay. To do so you will need your passport or ID card. The SIM card can be bought from any mobile shop in Italy. UK customers can purchase a card before you go via www.uk2abroad.com and keep your mobile number.

Country codes. Australia +61; Ireland +353; New Zealand +64; South Africa +27, UK +44; US and Canada +1.

TIME ZONES

Italy is one hour ahead of Greenwich Mean Time (GMT). From the last

Sunday in March to the last Sunday in October, clocks are put forward one hour.

TIPPING

In restaurants a *coperto* or cover charge of €1.50–5 is often charged for service and bread. Tipping is not customary in Italy, though a bit extra will be appreciated. For quick service in bars, leave a coin or two with your till receipt when ordering. Taxi drivers do not expect a tip but will appreciate it if you round up the fare to the next euro.

TOILETS

Public toilets are rare. If you use the facilities of cafés and bars, it will be appreciated if you buy a drink.

TOURIST INFORMATION

Italian tourist offices abroad

The website for the UK, North America and Canada Italian tourist offices is www.enit.it.

Canada: 365 Bay Street, Suite 503, Toronto, Ontario, M5H 2V1 tel: 416-925 4882.

UK: 1 Princes Street, London W1B 2AY, tel: 020 7408 1254

US: 686 Park Avenue, New York, NY 10065, tel: 212-245 5618; 401 North Michigan Avenue, Suite 172, Chicago, Illinois 60611, tel: 312-644 9335; 10850 Wilshire Boulevard, Suite 575, Los Angeles, CA 90024, tel: 310-820 1898,

Regional tourist offices

Stresa: Piazza Marconi 16, tel: 0323 30150, www.visitstresa.com.

Como: Piazza Cavour 17, tel: 031 269712, www.lakecomo.org.

Sirmione: Viale Marconi 2, tel: 030 916114, www.sirmionebs.it.

Bergamo: Viale Papa Giovanni XXIII 57, c/o Urban Center, Città Bassa, tel: 035 210204; Via Gombito 13, Città Alta, tel: 035 242226; there is also a very helpful tourist office at Bergamo's Orio al Serio airport, www.visitbergamo.net/en.

Verona: Via degli Alpini 9 (Piazza Brà), tel: 045 8068680, www.tourism.verona.it.

Milan: Piazza Castello 1, tel: 02 80580614, www.turismo.milano.it.

TRANSPORT

By boat. Ferries, hydrofoils and excursion cruisers operate services on all the main lakes. Hydrofoils *(aliscafi)* and catamarans *(catamarani)* are faster than ferries *(battelli)* but are more expensive and have inside seating only. Useful car ferries *(traghetti)* link Intra and Laveno on Lake Maggiore; Menaggio, Varenna, Cadenabbia and Bellagio on Lake Como; and Maderno to Torri del Benaco and Limone to Malcesine on Lake Garda.

Timetables are available from ticket offices, tourist information offices and other outlets, or online at www.navlaghi.it (lakes Maggiore, Como and Garda) or www.navigazionelagoiseo.it (Lake Iseo). Tickets can normally be bought at the point of departure; if bought on board they are a bit more expensive. Ferries normally run from 7am to about 7pm, though in mid-summer the main lakes also offer occasional evening ferry trips with dinner on board.

The ferry companies offer a complex variety of tickets and deals for the major lakes. These include all-day tickets for all or part of a lake, single or return ferry or hydrofoil tickets and ferry tickets which include entry to (or a price reduction at) major attractions. Generally, children under the age of 4 travel free, 4–12s are just over half price, and over 65s from the EU are entitled to a 20 percent reduction on weekdays on the normal ferries *(batelli)*.

By bus. Reasonably priced and fairly regular buses link towns and villages along the lakeshores. Tickets can usually be bought on board for local services, but for urban routes you will need to purchase tickets in advance. These are available from tobacconists and newsstands or at bus stations and must be stamped when you board the bus.

By rail. For mainline train information visit Trenitalia on www.trenitalia.com. Milan is a major rail junction with excellent, reasonably priced services to the main lakes and towns across the region. The lakes themselves, however, are better served by ferries and buses. The cost of rail travel is cheap in comparison to other European countries. The price of a journey depends on the type of train. You can either take the slower services which stop at all the towns or the fast Intercity or Italia Eurostar (ES) trains which levy a supplement of at least 30 percent and require seat reservations. It is advisable to make a reservation well in advance. Many stations now have automatic machines to issue tickets (with instructions in English). Return tickets offer no saving on two singles. Tickets must be stamped in the yellow machines at the near end of the platforms before boarding the train. Tickets bought on the train incur a very hefty supplement.

Taxis. Taxis can be found in main squares in the larger towns. Beware of touts without meters – especially near airports and main train stations. Taxi fares are quite high and there are additional charges, posted in the taxis, for luggage, trips at night and on Sundays and holidays.

V

VISA AND ENTRY REQUIREMENTS

For citizens of EU countries a valid passport or identity card is all that is needed to enter Italy for stays of up to 90 days. Citizens of the US, Canada, Australia and New Zealand require only a valid passport.

Visas *(permesso di soggiorno)*. For stays of more than 90 days a visa is required. Contact your country's Italian Embassy.

Customs. Free exchange of non duty-free goods for personal use is allowed between EU countries. Those from non-EU countries should refer to their home country's regulating organisation for a current complete list of import restrictions.

Currency restrictions. Tourists may bring an unlimited amount of Italian or foreign currency into the country. On departure you must declare any currency beyond the equivalent of €10,000, so it's wise to declare sums exceeding this amount when you arrive.

W

WEBSITES AND INTERNET ACCESS

The official Italian Government Tourist Board site is www.enit.it which has links for the different regions covered by the lakes.

The following are official tourist board sites for the lakes:

www.distrettolaghi.it – Lake Orta and the west of Lake Maggiore.

www.lakecomo.com – Lake Como.

www.visitgarda.com – Lake Garda.

www.visittrentino.it – Trentino.

www.visitbergamo.net – Bergamo.

www.tourism.verona.it – Verona province including the east side of Lake Garda.

www.navlaghi.it – excellent ferry website for the major lakes with time-tables and descriptions of destinations.

www.agriturismo.com – details of farm holidays and B&Bs.

For websites of tourist offices in the main towns, see page 130.

Most hotels offer internet access, and an increasing number have Wi-Fi. Charges sometimes apply though in many hotels Wi-Fi is free in public areas and increasingly, in the rooms. Cafés and centres with Wi-Fi services can be hard to come by outside the larger towns. There is usually a nominal fee and if you are using an internet point you will normally be required to produce your passport or ID.

Y

YOUTH HOSTELS

The lakes region only has a dozen or so youth hostels and reservations are essential in summer. An HI (Hostelling International) card is normally required but temporary membership is available at hostels for a small fee. Italian youth hostels are run by the Associazione Italiana Alberghi per la Gioventù (AIG), www.aighostels.com; information is also available through Hostelling International (www.hihostels.com).

RECOMMENDED HOTELS

In high season, hotels with their own restaurant may insist on half board, with stays of no less than three days. Lakeside hotels usually charge a supplement for lake views and it is usually worth paying the extra. Many of the hotels in the lakes close for winter, but those in the cities stay open all year. Booking ahead is recommended in high season.

The symbols below are a rough indication of what you can expect to pay in high season for a twin room with bathroom, including breakfast, taxes and service.

€€€€	over 350 euros
€€€	200–350 euros
€€	130–200 euros
€	below 130 euros

LAKE MAGGIORE

Borromeo Islands

Hotel Ristorante Verbano €€ *Isola dei Pescatori, tel: 0323 30408*, www.hotelverbano.it. A delightful alternative to the grand old hotels of Stresa, the Verbano is a 5-minute ferry ride away on the tiny Isola dei Pescatori. The simple pink villa and its restaurant terraces enjoy romantic views of the lake and Isola Bella. The 12 guest rooms, all named after flowers, have parquet floors, handsome antiques and large bathrooms. The island is busy with tourists by day, but delightfully peaceful at night. The hotel provides a free private boat service to Stresa and Baveno at night when the ferry service ends.

Cannero Riviera

Cannero €€ *Piazza Umberto 12, tel: 0323 788046*, www.hotelcannero.com. In a fine lake setting, this is a traditional hotel in what was formerly a monastery and an adjacent private mansion. Family-run and friendly, it provides first-class service and delightful lake and mountain-view guest rooms. Facilities include a sitting room with foreign-language books, an open-air pool, tennis court and restaurant with lakeside terrace.

Cannobio

Cannobio €€ *Piazza Vittorio Emanuele III 6, tel: 0323 739639*, www.hotelcannobio.com. A long-established hotel with a romantic setting on the lakefront by the old harbour. The décor successfully combines the original features of the historic building with contemporary colours and designs. At the Porto Vecchio restaurant (attached to the hotel but under different management), the ravishing lakeside terrace more than compensates for run-of-the-mill cuisine.

Pironi €€ *Via Marconi 35, tel: 0323 70624*, www.pironihotel.it. Twelve comfortable rooms in a beautifully converted medieval Franciscan monastery in the picturesque centre of Cannobio. The three-star hotel is furnished with antiques and retains wonderful original features such as frescoes, vaulted ceilings and old stone columns. The old cellars have been converted into a chic wine bar.

Luino

Camin Hotel Colmegna €€ *Via A. Palazzi 1, Colmegna (3km/2 miles north of Luino), tel: 0332 510855*, www.caminhotel.com. The villa was built on the lake in the early 18th century as part of a hunting estate and retains a large park with romantic trails and a waterfall. Facilities include a private beach, a small stone harbour where motorboats can be rented and lake-side terraces for summer meals. Three apartments are also available.

Stresa

Grand Hotel des Iles Borromées €€€€ *Corso Umberto I, 67, tel: 0323 938938*, www.borromees.it. The grandest hotel on Lake Maggiore, where literary luminaries such as Ernest Hemingway, George Bernard Shaw and John Steinbeck, as well as numerous European royals, have stayed (you can stay in Hemingway's room for €3,000 a night). Sumptuous public rooms are decorated with Murano chandeliers, stucco and antiques; many of the luxurious guest rooms have fabulous views of the Borromeo islands and the Alps. Facilities include one indoor and two outdoor swimming pools, spa club, tennis court, private heliport and landing for private boats.

LAKE COMO

Argegno

Villa Belvedere €€–€€€ *Via Milano 8, tel: 031 821116,* https://villabel vedererelais.com. An alluring villa hotel right on the lake, with glorious views from the terrace where meals are served in summer. Run by the Cappelletti family for 60 years the villa has 20 simply furnished rooms – it's worth paying extra for the ones with lake views. Argegno is a small village with a landing stage close to the hotel for ferry trips of Lake Como.

Bellagio

Florence €€ *Piazza Mazzini 46, tel: 031 950342,* www.hotelflorencebel lagio.it. An 18th-century villa (with a later extension) which has been in the same family for over 100 years. The beamed and vaulted foyer combines traditional furnishings with modern colours and innovative works of art. The shady lakeside terrace is an idyllic spot for a drink or summer dining. Comfortable bedrooms in classical style are priced according to views – most look out on to the lake. The spa offers massage, aromatherapy, sauna and jacuzzi.

Grand Hotel Villa Serbelloni €€€€ *Via Roma 1, tel: 031 950216,* www.villaserbelloni.com. Built as a luxury villa on the banks of the lake for an aristocratic Milanese family the villa was converted to a hotel in 1873. Since then it has been hosting royalty, famous politicians and film stars. Grand and opulent public rooms boast crystal chandeliers, stuccowork, marble, gilding and antiques. Guests can take advantage of the spa, tennis courts, swimming pool – and Ettore Bácchia's artfully presented molecular cuisine in the Michelin-starred lakeside restaurant.

Cadenabbia di Griante

Alberghetto della Marianna € *Via Regina 57, tel: 0344 43095,* www.la-marianna.com. A home-from-home bed and breakfast with eight simply-furnished rooms overlooking the lake. Small and friendly, it is run by Paola, who is very hospitable and will help you arrange the day's itinerary. Guests receive a 15 percent discount at La Cucina della Marianna restaurant on the same premises, which offers excellent regional cuisine created by Paola's husband, Ty Valentini.

Cernobbio

Villa d'Este €€€€ *Via Regina 40, tel: 031 3481,* www.villadeste.com. This famous and palatial 16th-century villa in luxuriant gardens on the shores of Lake Como ranks among the best hotels in the world. It was once home to the estranged wife of George IV, and since becoming a hotel the roll call of famous guests has included J.F. Kennedy, Alfred Hitchcock and Madonna. Expect exquisite decor, with antiques and Como silks, and ample facilities including watersports, eight tennis courts, fitness centre, beauty centre, an indoor and a lake-floating swimming pool, and a helipad.

San Fedele D'Intelvi

Villa Simplicitas €€ *San Fedele d'Intelvi (15 mins' drive from Lake Como), tel: 031 831132,* www.villasimplicitas.it. Between lakes Como and Lugano, this 19th-century country house enjoys a peaceful rural setting. Downstairs there's a large open fireplace, an antique billiards table, and a conservatory and terrace for meals. Ten characterful guest rooms are decorated with antiques, curios and wrought-iron and brass beds.

Sotto il Monte

Agriturismo Casa Clelia € *Via Corna 1/3, Sotto il Monte, tel: 035 799133,* www.agriturismocasaclelia.it. This wonderfully peaceful retreat, 20km (12 miles) west of Bergamo, dates back to the 11th century in the days when it was a convent. Thanks to a creative and ecological restoration, it is now a working farm with surrounding woodlands, gardens and farm animals. The ten spacious and stylish guest rooms have wooden floors, beamed ceilings and polished antiques. The stonewalled rustic dining room with log fire or the wisteria and jasmine clad arbour in summer are the setting for excellent and affordable cuisine, with many ingredients straight from the farm.

Varenna

Albergo Milano €€ *Via XX Settembre 35, tel: 0341 830298,* www.varenna. net. A gem of a hotel in the centre of picturesque Varenna. There are only 12 rooms (book well in advance), all individually furnished, with balconies and lake views. There are also a couple of apartments with a kitchenette in the new annexes. The inviting La Vista restaurant has a terrace with gorgeous lake views.

Albergo Olivedo €€ *Piazza Martiri della Libertà 14, tel: 0341 830115,* www. olivedo.it. This Art Nouveau villa lies across from the ferry dock at Varenna so while it's not as peaceful as some lakeside hotels it's ideal for hops across to Bellagio or Menaggio. Most of the guest rooms (and all five in neighbouring Villa Torretta, under the same ownership) have wonderful views of the lake. The Olivedo restaurant, with reasonable prices and top-notch home-made ravioli, is a great spot for watching the world go by.

LAKE GARDA
Gardone Riviera

Grand Hotel Fasano €€€ *Corso Zanardelli 190, tel: 0365 290220,* www. ghf.it. A converted 19th-century hunting lodge, this 5-star hotel has extensive gardens, new luxury spa and a variety of rooms and views, priced accordingly. The separate Villa Principe on the lake offers water sports, a tennis court, golf and a lakeside restaurant.

Villa Fiordaliso €€€€ *Corso Zanardelli 150, tel: 0365 20158,* www.vil lafiordaliso.it. Exclusive Art Nouveau villa where Mussolini and Clara

Petacci stayed before they were caught and executed in 1945 (see page 23). The hotel is on a busy road but there are gardens leading down to the lake and the Michelin-starred restaurant (one of the best on Lake Garda) has a romantic lakeside setting. There are just seven rooms: six doubles and the pricey Clara Petacci suite.

Gargnano

Gardenia al Lago €€€ *Via Colletta 53, Villa di Gargnano, tel: 0365 71195, www.hotel-gardenia.it.* Enchanting villa hotel with gardens down to the lake. The welcoming Arosio family have run the hotel for over half a century; guest rooms are traditional with antiques and tiled floors, each with terrace or balcony. Weather permitting, you can breakfast by the water's edge, in the shade of olive and bay trees.

Hotel du Lac €€ *Via Colletta 21, Villa di Gargnano, tel: 0365 71107, www.hotel-dulac.it.* Sister hotel of the Gardenia, the Hotel du Lac has a heavenly setting, with the same lovely views and family-run atmosphere. Charmingly old fashioned, with handsome antiques in the bedrooms; the restaurant, with summer terrace, overhangs the lake.

Riva del Garda

Locanda Restel de Fer € *Via Restel de Fer 10, tel: 0464 553481, www.resteldefer.com.* The Meneghelli family, who have been here since 1400, run a highly regarded restaurant (see page 110) and offer five simple guest rooms, and more modern apartments in a new building which can accommodate 2–4 guests. Three nights minimum stay.

Sirmione

Meublé Grifone € *Via Gaetano Bocchio 4, tel: 030 916014, www.sirmionehotelgrifone.it.* One of the few cheaper options in Sirmione, and romantically located right by the castle, the Grifone books up fast. It is a very simple hotel with 16 basic rooms, the best of which have balconies over the lake.

Villa Cortine €€€€ *Viale C. Gennari 2, tel: 030 9905890,* www.palace hotelvillacortine.com. Opulent and exclusive villa, built in 1870, with a 20th-century wing added to convert it into a hotel. Away from the bustling centre of Sirmione, the hotel enjoys an enticing setting within 4.8 hectares (12 acres) of parkland leading down to the lake-shore. Half board is compulsory in season. Facilities include a jetty with boats to hire, heated and outdoor swimming pool and tennis courts; water sports can be arranged.

Torri del Benaco

Gardesana €€ *Piazza Calderini 5, tel: 045 7225411,* www.hotel-garde sana.com. Historic hotel with a very congenial atmosphere, a nice restaurant (see page 110) and comfortable, reasonably priced rooms overlooking the harbour and castle. Royalty, politicians and film stars have stayed here, among them Churchill, Vivien Leigh, Lawrence Olivier and Maria Callas.

LAKE ISEO

I Due Roccoli €€€ *Colline di Iseo, tel: 030 9822977,* www.idueroc coli.com. Charming villa hotel in the hills above the town of Iseo. Half board is to be recommended given the quality of the cuisine, the local Franciacorta wines and the fabulous lake views from the candlelit courtyard. The seductive setting appeals to honeymooners looking for a peaceful retreat away from the busy lake resorts. Facilities include an outdoor pool and tennis court.

LAKE ORTA

Orta San Giulio

Aracoeli €€ *Piazza Motta 34, tel: 0322 905173,* www.ortainfo.com. A hotel with an enchanting location on the main square, with romantic views of the lake and island. The décor is a mix of wood-beamed ceilings and stone walls and contemporary design. However, it has seen better years.

Villa Crespi €€€€ *Via Fava 18, tel: 0322 911902,* www.villacrespi.it. Opulent Moorish villa dominated by a lofty minaret within parkland near the lake. Charmed by his visit to Baghdad, Cristoforo Benigno Crespi built the villa in 1879. It is now a 4-star hotel, run by a Neapolitan and his wife, offering luxury guest rooms with marble bathrooms (six doubles, eight suites), fitness room, shiatsu and a gourmet restaurant with two Michelin stars (see page 111).

Pettenasco

L'Approdo €€ *Corso Roma 80, Pettenasco, tel: 0323 89345,* www.lagodorta hotels.com. On the lakeshore at the small village of Pettenasco, just north of Orta San Giulio, this modern hotel would suit any sports enthusiast. You can windsurf, water-ski, canoe, rent boats, play tennis, swim from the beach or do leisurely lengths in the 25-metre heated outdoor pool. Most of the 72 balconied guest rooms overlook the lake; others look out on to the garden.

CITY HOTELS
Bergamo

B&B Bergamo Alta € *Via San Lorenzo 24, tel: 334 1099335,* www.ber gamoaltabb.it. Located in a centuries old building in the historical centre of the Città Alta (the upper town), this is a pleasant family-run spot with a good breakfast. There are views from the property over the surrounding countryside. Many of the city's main sights are minutes away on foot.

Gombit Hotel €€ *Via Mario Lupo 6, tel: 035 247009;* www.gombithotel. it. Opened in 2010 next to the 13th century Torre del Gombito, this was the first designer hotel in the Città Alta. Modern and stylish, the 13 guest rooms are individually decorated, typically with exposed brick stonework or timbers, warm wood floors, pastel-coloured furnishings and chic modern bathrooms. There is no restaurant but Bergamo is full of gastronomic delights and there are excellent places to eat within a stone's throw.

Verona

Due Torri Hotel Baglioni €€€€ *Piazza Sant'Anastasia 4, tel: 045 595044,* https://hotelduetorri.duetorrihotels.com. Luxury hotel in imposing 14th-century villa, beside the church of Sant'Anastasia. Public rooms are grandiose, with antiques, vaulted ceilings and frescoes. Guest rooms are old-fashioned in style but well-equipped. This is a favourite location of opera stars.

Torcolo €€ *Vicolo Listone 3, tel: 045 8007512,* www.hoteltorcolo.it. Small, homely and appealing 2-star hotel very close to the Arena and popular with opera fans who book their favourite room months in advance of the season. Comfortable guest rooms are individually furnished, all in an attractive traditional style. Out of the opera season breakfasts are not included in the room rate, so you may choose instead to have coffee and croissants on Piazza Brà overlooking the Arena.

INDEX

INSIGHT ⊙ GUIDES POCKET GUIDE

ITALIAN LAKES

Second Edition 2019

Editor: Sian Marsh
Author: Susie Boulton
Head of DTP and Pre-Press: Rebeka Davies
Picture Editor: Tom Smyth
Cartography Update: Carte
Update by: Paul Stafford
Photography Credits: Alamy 88; Britta
Jaschinski/Apa Publications 92; Fotolia 32,
34, 38, 76, 78; Getty Images 1, 4ML, 17; Greg
Gladman/Apa Publications 6L; iStock 4TC,
4TL, 5T, 5M, 5MC, 13, 26, 46, 50, 52, 60, 62, 64,
75, 98, 102; Mary Evans Picture Library 15, 22;
Neil Buchan-Grant/Apa Publications 7R, 11,
18, 42, 44, 48, 54, 56, 58, 66, 82, 85, 90, 101;
Shutterstock 4MC, 5TC, 5MC, 5M, 6R, 7, 21,
29, 31, 37, 69, 70, 72, 81, 86, 94, 97; Switzerland
Tourism 40
Cover Picture: Shutterstock

Distribution

UK, Ireland and Europe: Apa Publications
(UK) Ltd; sales@insightguides.com
United States and Canada: Ingram
Publisher Services; ips@ingramcontent.com
Australia and New Zealand: Woodslane;
info@woodslane.com.au
Southeast Asia: Apa Publications (SN) Pte;
singaporeoffice@insightguides.com
Worldwide: Apa Publications (UK) Ltd;
sales@insightguides.com

**Special Sales, Content Licensing
and CoPublishing**
Insight Guides can be purchased in bulk
quantities at discounted prices. We can
create special editions, personalised jackets
and corporate imprints tailored to your
needs. sales@insightguides.com;
www.insightguides.biz

Contact us
Every effort has been made to provide
accurate information in this publication,
but changes are inevitable. The publisher
cannot be responsible for any resulting loss,
inconvenience or injury. We would appreciate
it if readers would call our attention to any
errors or outdated information. We also
welcome your suggestions; please contact
us at: hello@insightguides.com
www.insightguides.com